Praise for Revolution!

If every young person in this nation would read this book
and take it to heart, REVOLUTION! would be the catalyst
for igniting a new Jesus Movement!

CHÉ AHN
PRESIDENT, THE CALLDC
AUTHOR OF INTO THE FIRE

REVOLUTION! has the answers to change the world.

JIM BURNS
PRESIDENT, NATIONAL INSTITUTE OF YOUTH MINISTRY

Michael Brown's teachings have had a profound impact on the men of
Sonicflood. I pray the Holy Spirit will work through REVOLUTION! to
stir up the lost passion and power of God's people.

JASON HALBERT
KEYBOARDIST, SONICFLOOd

A clarion call from a man who knows the One who calls the
signals and shapes our ultimate destiny.

WINKIE PRATNEY
AUTHOR OF FIRE ON THE HORIZON

Michael Brown's REVOLUTION! is the prophetic road map for what
will be the greatest youth awakening the West has ever seen.

BOB WEINER
WEINER MINISTRIES INTERNATIONAL

Revolution!
The Call to Holy War

Michael L. Brown

Renew
FROM REGAL

A Division of Gospel Light
Ventura, California, U.S.A.

Published by Regal Books
A Division of Gospel Light
Ventura, California, U.S.A.
Printed in the U.S.A.

Regal Books is a ministry of Gospel Light, an evangelical Christian publisher
dedicated to serving the local church. We believe God's vision for Gospel Light
is to provide church leaders with biblical, user-friendly materials that will help
them evangelize, disciple and minister to children, youth and families.

It is our prayer that this Regal book will help you discover biblical truth for your
own life and help you meet the needs of others. May God richly bless you.

For a free catalog of resources from Regal Books/Gospel Light, please call your Christian supplier
or contact us at 1-800-4-GOSPEL or www.regalbooks.com.

Cover Design by Larry Smith and Associates
Interior Design by Robert Williams
Edited by Deena Davis

Library of Congress Cataloging-in-Publication Data
Brown, Michael L., 1955-
        Revolution! / Michael L. Brown.
        p. cm.
        Includes bibliographical references.
        ISBN 0-8307-2640-3 (trade paper)
            1. Evangelistic work—United States. 2. Revivals—United States
3. Revolution—Religious aspects—Christianity. I. Title.

        BV3793.B695 2000
        269'.2—dc21   00-034157

1 2 3 4 5 6 7 8 9 10 11 12 13 14 15 / 09 08 07 06 05 04 03 02 01 00

Rights for publishing this book in other languages are contracted by Gospel Literature
International (GLINT). GLINT also provides technical help for the adaptation, transla-
tion and publishing of Bible study resources and books in scores of languages worldwide. For further information, contact GLINT, P.O. Box 4060, Ontario, CA 91761-1003,
U.S.A. You may also send e-mail to Glintint@aol.com, or visit their website at
www.glint.org.

Dedication

To the students and graduates of the

Brownsville Revival School of Ministry,

fellow servants and fellow soldiers,

devoted to Jesus by life or by death.

On with the revolution!

—1 THESSALONIANS 3:8-9

Contents

Preface

Sometime in the first half of 1999, something snapped. Perhaps it was the Columbine killings; perhaps it was the accumulated frustration mounting from years of political corruption and moral decline in America; perhaps it was the realization that the American Church had gone as far it could with its present mind-set and methods. Whatever the exact factors were, I am sure of this: Believers across the land began to say, "Enough is enough. We need a revolution!" This book, written almost entirely during an intense six-week period (from the last week of December 1999 to the first week of February 2000), is a clear and definite call to get the revolution under way.

But language like this can easily be misunderstood, so let me make some things perfectly clear: This book is *not* a call to the violent overthrow of the government, nor is it a call to take up arms or to use intimidation tactics against those with whom we differ. It is not a call to political activism in and of itself. It is a call to something far more extreme: a call to live out the gospel with all its radical claims, a call for the people of God to impact this generation with the prophetic message of repentance, a call to spark the most sweeping counterculture movement in our nation's history, a call to take back the moral ground that has been stolen from under our feet, a call to follow Jesus by life or by death. In that sense, it is a call to start a revolution—now.

When the theme of revolution began to dominate my mind in 1999 (although the seeds had been planted within me for years), I bought some books on the counterculture revolution of the 1960s. I was a product of those days. Heavily influenced by the power of rock music, I began smoking pot and using LSD in 1969 (at the age of 14), turning also to speed and heroin the next year before meeting the Lord at the end of 1971. I knew how decadent that decade was—being primarily associated in my mind with drugs, rock music, rebellion, and immorality—and I knew how much our society changed in that decade. But I had forgotten just how much the 1960s was fueled by *counterculture* impulses, not merely *carnal* impulses. From the antiwar movement to Civil Rights, from the rise of feminism and homosexual activism to the hippie movement, the status quo was attacked. Most of the attack left a tragic mark on America (and even the world).

Author David G. Myers gives us a clear picture:

Had you fallen asleep in 1960 and awakened today (even after the recent uptick in several indicators of societal health) would you feel pleased at the cultural shift? You would be awakening to a:

- doubled divorce rate.

- tripled teen suicide rate

- quadrupled rate of reported violent crime

- quintupled prison population

- sextupled (no pun intended) percent of babies born to unmarried parents

- sevenfold increase in cohabitation (a predictor of future divorce)

- soaring rate of depression—to ten times the pre-World War II level, by one estimate.[1]

We have yet to recover from the 1960s! In fact, it has been observed that "a set of counterculture values embraced by an entire generation of young Americans in the '60s and '70s has now become, in effect, the establishment culture itself."[2] Yet in the midst of the darkness I see great hope: God is raising up an army, and most of it is young. Simply stated, *America can be changed.*

A graduate from the Brownsville Revival School of Ministry wrote this song in response to our emphasis on revolution. Its lyrics describe the mood of many today:

> Can you feel it coming?
> Can you feel it stirring?
> Can you feel it shaking everything?
> This is the hour—this is the generation.
>
> There's a people standing.
> There's a voice that's sounding.
> There's a banner being raised for righteousness.
> This is the hour—this is the generation.
>
> Revolution—we're taking ground.
> Revolution—we won't bow down.
> Revolution—let the trumpet sound.
> Revolution now!
>
> We will fight to the death.
> Worthless idols we detest.
> Let the army's anthem roar,
> Holiness to the Lord.[3]

Yes, enough is enough, this is the hour, and we won't back down.

I remember well the night of the tragic murders at Wedgwood Baptist Church in Fort Worth, Texas (September 15, 1999). We were holding our weekly service in Pensacola with more than 1,000 students from the school of ministry, along with hundreds of visitors and guests. I was scheduled to preach that night. My message, although convicting and challenging, was probably going to have a lot of humor in it as well. Early in the service I was given a handwritten note about the shootings, followed by a printed report from the Internet. I wondered, *Should I interrupt the service and make an announcement, calling for prayer, or should I wait until the end of the meeting?* Obviously, I couldn't simply go ahead with the planned message. But if I shared the terrible news, there was no telling how things would turn. I decided to stop the service and make the announcement. The effect was dramatic.

First, people began to weep, cry out, and intercede—grieving over the violence destroying our country, feeling pain for the victims and their families, and praying for God to make His help known. But then the atmosphere changed: It went from brokenhearted to militant. It was as if the believers—especially the students—were saying to the devil himself, "You think this is going to intimidate us? You think these kinds of acts will stop us from being a fearless witness? Well, you're wrong. Here we come! Bullets can't stop us; they only make us bolder. Satan, you've gone too far! All you've done is helped to wake up a sleeping Church. You lose!" Something swept through the sanctuary.

I changed my message and preached a short word on holy militancy—on scorning the power and works of the enemy (based on Isaiah 37:21-38). That same night, "coincidentally," there was a pastor visiting from India where he and his family had been severely beaten for preaching the gospel to their people. I called him forward to speak. "They killed Stephen," he said, "but the disciples kept preaching. James was killed, but they kept preaching. My wife doesn't have any real teeth, only plastic ones, because she was beaten for the gospel. They beat me and almost killed me. They almost killed my sons. But we keep preaching!" In other words, *on* with the revolution, by life or by death.

That same spirit is sweeping the land, and the theme of a holy revolution is on the lips of pastors, youth leaders, Christian educators, and believers of all ages—especially young people. Yes, the gospel is the ultimate revolutionary message. Following Jesus is the ultimate counterculture movement. Historians have even pointed to this. For example, *Christian History* magazine could refer to the Great Awakening as a revolution of sorts: *"Decades before the Revolution that gave birth to the United States, a different kind of revolution born of God's Spirit swept the land."*[4] Other scholars have freely associated Church history with the concept of revolution.[5] In the coming months and years, we have the opportunity to write our own revolutionary history. How will the story end?

When God moved on me to write, I ordered dozens of books—almost all of them describing violent revolutions, most of them representing ideologies that I completely reject. Still, I wanted to understand why revolutions take place and how they succeed, comparing them with revolutionary movements within the Church (like the sixteenth-century Reformation or the eighteenth-century Methodist Revival) and with the commands of Jesus in the New Testament. My office staff began to wonder as they opened box after box of books and put on my desk new volumes of *The Communist Manifesto,* Chairman Mao's *Little Red Book,* Che Guevara on guerrilla warfare, Mahatma Gandhi on nonviolent resistance, several volumes on Islamic *jihad,* and more.[6] Needless to say, I do not accept the views of everyone I quote in the book you hold in your hands! But when we see the inspiration and dedication that fueled many a worldly—or even satanic—revolution, we can better understand what it will take for us to impact our generation. Are you still coming along?

Although I am used to a nonstop writing schedule, this one completely overwhelmed me, with pages pouring out at an unprecedented rate. (Two-thirds of the book was written in three weeks.) Why, I asked, is there *such* urgency? Little did I realize that, due to the speed with which the book was finished, the publisher would be able to schedule its release for September 1, 2000, exactly one day before The CallDC, allowing us to donate tens of thousands of copies to the young people who would gather there. I take this as God's plan, since the timing of all this never once entered my mind the entire time the book was being written. (To all teenagers reading this book: Don't be scared by the notes in the back! Use them if you like; ignore them if you choose—although there are lots of good quotes buried there.)

But this book is not only for the young. Before the final editing was completed, the manuscript found its way into the hands of several influential political leaders. They too are talking about a revolution. We will see what the future holds.

And then there are my fellow soldiers saved during the Jesus People Movement of the early to mid-1970s.[7] In a special way, this book is for you. So many of us were radical before we came to the Lord, but in the process of time we lost our radicality, even though many of us are now in leadership positions (quite respectable ones, at that!) in the Body. Yet deep down, we have always known there was more. Perhaps this is our time, our sacred hour to turn a generation back to God. Who knows? My heart is bursting with anticipation.

More than thirty years ago, Bob Dylan wrote these words in

his famous ballad "All Along the Watchtower": "There are many here among us who feel that life is but a joke. / But you and I, we've been through that, and this is not our fate, / So let us not talk falsely now, the hour is getting late." How late is the hour now? Surely it is time to act.

My thanks to Bill Greig III and Kyle Duncan of Gospel Light for believing totally in the message of this book, making more than 100,000 copies available at *printing cost* for The CallDC; to my faithful, tireless assistant, Scott Volk, for supplying me with some important quotes and tracking down others for me; to Bennie and Hazel Johnson, for reading each chapter as soon as it was written and providing me with great encouragement and valuable feedback; to Charles Moore of Plough Publishing, for introducing me to the writings of Eberhard Arnold and sending me some excellent source material; to Bob Gladstone, our academic dean, Ward Simpson, our executive director, and the incredible faculty and staff of the school for carrying the revolution theme forward; and to my extraordinary wife, Nancy, who does not know the meaning of the word "compromise" and who does not relate to the fear of man. I cannot imagine life without her.

I have dedicated this book (even now, with tears) to the students and graduates of the Brownsville Revival School of Ministry, the most wonderful group of people I have ever known and the joy of my life. When I look in their eyes, I know I'm not dreaming: We will see a revolution. On with it!

Chapter One

Why I Will Never Be a Sunday-Morning Christian

I believe we have come to a place where the thinking of [Christians]
must change, and it must change now or the church will become a
little cult in the corner. I am not interested in following a religion that
does not impact the world in which we live. . . .
Jesus was a rebel, and He has called us to join this rebel movement,
and change the world together.

NEVERS MUMBA
ZAMBIAN CHRISTIAN LEADER

As we turn to the evangelical leadership of this country in the last
decades, unhappily, we must come to the conclusion that often it has
not been much help. It has shown the mark of a platonic, overly
spiritualized Christianity all too often. Spirituality to the evangelical
leadership often has not included the Lordship of Christ over the
whole spectrum of life. Spirituality has often been shut up to a very
narrow area. And also very often, among many evangelicals, including
many evangelical leaders, it seems that the final end is to protect
their own projects. . . . I am again asking the question, why have
we let ourselves go so far down the road?

FRANCIS SCHAEFFER
A CHRISTIAN MANIFESTO

The attack by socialism and communism on the status quo is a call to
our consciences—those of us who consider ourselves Christians.
This call warns us more strongly than any sermon that our task is
to live in protest against everything that opposes God in this world.
So poorly have we Christians filled this role that the question must
be asked: Are we Christians at all?

EBERHARD ARNOLD
WRITING IN 1919

I was not raised in a Christian home, and my first exposure to real Christianity did not come until I was sixteen years old. At that time I was heavily into drugs and rock music, deeply influenced by the counterculture mentality of the late 1960s, fundamentally unconcerned about God, and completely uninterested in religion. Religion? It had no place in my life!

Brought up in a Conservative Jewish family, I thought I knew what religion was all about. It was dead, dry, and hypocritical! Most of the men who attended Sabbath services in my community would drive to the synagogue, park their cars about one block away, and then walk to the building. Why? Because Jewish law forbade driving on the Sabbath, so it was necessary to give the appearance of keeping the law—by walking up to the building—while driving the rest of the way. The rabbi, being the deeply religious spiritual leader of the community, would of course walk the whole way there and back. But that's what rabbis were supposed to do.

It was also expected of the men that they would not smoke on the Sabbath. This too, however, presented no problem for them. They would light up as usual, enjoying the post-service meal in a downstairs room, and as soon as they heard the rabbi's footsteps, they would quickly surrender their cigarettes to Walter, the Gentile custodian. How fascinating it must have been for the rabbi to discover good old Walter with several lit cigarettes between his fingers and between his lips. Yes, this was religion as I knew it.

The synagogue itself (or Temple, as it was called) was quite small, seating fewer than 200 people. Still, on some Saturday mornings, there were not even 10 men there. On such occasions, my father would receive an emergency call, asking if he could rush over to the Temple and join the service. (Jewish tradition requires 10 men for a formal religious gathering, so it presented quite a problem when only 9 were there.) Thankfully, Abe (my dad) would always come through and bail them out. Such was the level of spirituality in our community! Yet on the High Holidays (Passover, the Jewish New Year, the Day of Atonement, etc.), the synagogue was so packed that the members decided to build a special annex that would seat five times the capacity of the main sanctuary. And at those special times of the year it would be filled. What hypocrisy!

As a youngster, I would go with the family to those annual services, trying my best to occupy my mind while wishing that the hours would hurry up and speed by. I could not imagine a more boring way to spend my time, nor could I relate to anyone who would want to go to synagogue every week or, worse still, every day, like those fanatical Orthodox Jews in the next town who actually kept the dietary laws and said their prayers morning, noon, and night.

Still, when I started getting older—in preparation for my 13th birthday—I had to attend Hebrew School with my friends, meaning terribly dull classes two days a week followed by hours of work spent learning a passage from the Hebrew Bible to be recited at my Bar Mitzvah.[1] (Oddly enough, no one thought of telling me what the biblical passage was about. I did not discover the location of my Bar Mitzvah reading in the Scriptures until 1988, 20 years after the fact.)

The week before my Bar Mitzvah, I experienced something fascinating: I saw parts of the Sabbath service for the very first time! You see, when I had to go to Temple with my father, we always arrived about 30 minutes late. This time we had to be there from the very beginning. I didn't know *that* part of the service even existed!

Of course, none of this shallowness and hypocrisy was the fault of Judaism itself. Rather, it was the *form* of Judaism I was exposed to that was shallow. But I didn't know any better, since this Long Island, Conservative, wishy-washy version of Judaism was all I had ever experienced firsthand. How different it was with the gospel. My first real encounter with the message of Jesus was powerful and vibrant. The people in the church I visited really believed!

I had gone there to pull my two best friends out—they were starting to change, and I was concerned—and my reputation was so horrific that one of the young ladies wrote in her diary that night: "Antichrist comes to church." I really was a wretch!

I *loved* to shoot heroin into my veins, to do large doses of LSD and speed, to listen to sinful, satanic music, and to cut people down with my sharp, quick tongue. My whole identity was caught up in being a proud, drug-abusing, rock-drumming rebel. Yet the work of the Spirit in my life was so dynamic that on my second trip to this little church (smaller even than my synagogue) I asked Jesus to forgive my sins, and shortly after that, I was free from drugs and drink. Completely free!

FAITH THAT IS PRIMARILY EXPRESSED ON SUNDAY MORNINGS STRIKES ME AS A COMPLETE ABERRATION OF TRUE NEW TESTAMENT FAITH.

I began attending church on Tuesday and Friday nights, soon adding in prayer meetings on Monday nights with about 10 to 15 others. Jesus was becoming my all and all, and my life was being transformed every day. But I had not yet attended a Sunday morning service. After all, Sunday had no special meaning to me, nor did I have fond memories of "morning religion" in my past.

(What difference was there between Saturday and Sunday anyway?)

When I finally did attend church on Sunday, I was shocked. *Who are all these people?* I wondered. *I've never seen them before! And why are they all dressed so nicely?* It was then that I began to get my first hint—although I hardly grasped it at the time—that just as there was such a thing as "Saturday morning Judaism" there was such a thing as "Sunday morning Christianity."

That first Easter, about five months after I was born again, I was thrilled to see the little building totally packed. We served communion to more than 125 people—the highest total in the history of the church—and I was thoroughly impressed with these wonderfully spiritual believers who came to our service on that special day. One year later, I started to catch on, realizing that there were "High Holiday Christians" just as there were "High Holiday Jews." To this day, I cringe when I see church buildings that are normally half full completely packed on Easter—although this is an evangelist's dream—and I find no special significance in Sunday morning church. In other words, faith that is primarily expressed on Sunday mornings or limited to a few special occasions a year strikes me as a complete aberration of true New Testament faith. Do you think Jesus differs with this?

There is something else that contributes to my attitude toward traditional religion. By "traditional" I mean religion that is more the product of human tradition than the product of divine truth, religion that is stifled and suffocated by man-made customs and regulations as opposed to religion that is alive and vibrant in the reality and power of the Spirit. Simply stated,

I refuse to accept the status quo—be it in the society at large or in the Body in particular—if that status quo is contrary to the Word of God. It doesn't matter if public opinion embraces a certain concept or if the majority of believers accept a certain standard. If that concept or standard is contrary to the will of God, it must be questioned, challenged, or rejected.[2]

For example, it is very common for people in Scandinavia to live together out of wedlock, functioning almost as husband and wife without being legally married. Sadly, such couples are often welcomed as *believers* in the national evangelical churches, since their lifestyle—widely practiced as it is—isn't considered sinful by society; in the same churches, the people of God have become so much like the world that they too have lost their moral sense.

True believers cannot tolerate such compromise! We must reject the status quo when it stands in violation of the principles of God. I will have much more to say about this in subsequent chapters—in a sense, this whole book is about a holy and healthy rejection of the status quo—but I want to share a little more about my personal background in order to give you a broader understanding of where I'm coming from.

Let me take you back again to the late 1960s and early 1970s, the days of student riots and campus protests. Defiance was in the air. In our eyes, rebellion was right and the Establishment was wrong. Policemen, in their role as enforcers of the law, were "pigs"; parents, representing everything that was wrong with the older generation, were hopelessly outdated and out of touch. We, the young people, were going to change our world. The traditional American dream had little hold on us. We were going to do our own thing. In an age of war, we were going to stand for peace, even if it meant getting a little violent at times. Such was the attitude of that stormy era!

Of course, I was just a fun-loving, flesh-driven teenager at that time; but the counterculture message of rock music, coupled with the consciousness-altering, mind-expanding drugs I was using, led me to repudiate the values and standards of my society. And so it was that when unrest began to stir in my high school (located in West Hempstead on Long Island), I was in the thick of it. A number of students got fed up with some new restrictive rules and decided to organize a protest. Word was spread to the whole student body: "Tomorrow morning, gather in the main hallway. When the bell rings for class, don't move! We'll make our demands known to the school leaders and they will have to yield to us."

Well, that morning came and, to my shock, most of the student body was there. It was not just the radicals, but some of the nice, law-abiding students who filled the hallway too. This was great! Then the bell sounded for class and most of them began to scatter. I couldn't believe it! So much for protest. The assistant principal, Mr. S——, walked into the crowd, located the chief troublemakers, and called them by name into his office. The whole thing was about to come to a screeching halt almost before it got started. So I yelled out, "If they're going to Mr. S——'s office, we're all going!" Soon the office was completely packed, and more students were piling in. It worked! We were sent to the main auditorium, which meant that even more students decided to join, and we were asked to air our demands. (I know this sounds crazy, but it happened. I was there!)

There was one young lady in our midst, a white student who was going out with a member of the Black Panthers. (His father was black and his mother white, and he was probably in his early 20s.) She stood and spoke with emotion, ending her speech with her right fist thrust into the air, Black Panther style, militant to the core. I loved it! And of course I chimed in. Things in our school had to change!

The principal, being a wise man, used an interesting strategy. Within a day he brought together the entire student body for a special assembly, and we crowded into the gymnasium, sitting cross-legged on the hardwood floor. He told us that if we—meaning the radicals—could put our demands in writing and circulate them through the school within a day, he would comply. Of course, he knew that such a thing could not and would not happen, since there was no way we could come together, agree on our demands, print them up, and circulate them through the school in a matter of hours. He was wrong.

With the help of some sympathetic counselors and teachers in the psychology department, and with a few of us taking the lead, we made our list of demands and copied and distributed them schoolwide. Even more amazing was that with the help of a few faculty members—one of whom had some legal ammunition he held over the administration's head—the principal agreed to our demands. A few months later, at the beginning of the new school year (fall of 1971), S.A.F.E. school was born, consisting of about 60 to 65 students and four teachers. (The acronym stood for Student And Faculty Education, since this was to be a learning experience for everyone. The name proved to be entirely accurate!)

Think of it: While the rest of the student body was in school until three o'clock daily, we got out at noon. While the rest of the school building was kept neat and clean, the windows of our four rooms in the S.A.F.E. wing were covered with graffiti. While the rest of the students were required to attend classes—obviously!—we could choose whether or not to attend. (I kid you not. God is my witness to all this.) And while the rest of the students received number grades for their work, we could choose to be graded on a pass or fail system. It was wild and, in retrospect, totally absurd, especially in light of the fact that some of our *teachers* condoned our rebellious, drug-filled ways.

During the last two years of high school, the only formal class I had was band and orchestra. For all my other classes taught in S.A.F.E. school, I received all Ps for my passing efforts. Although some of the faculty members actually had us read textbooks (I can recall one or two), write papers (I distinctly remember writing at least a couple during those years), and take tests (I helped some students study for one, I'm sure!), other faculty members were more lenient. In fact, the most radical of the faculty members said this: "If your education is to go into the field and get high in the morning, and you would like to receive an A for it [this was even better than a mere P!], just tell me and I'll give you an A." I took him up on his offer (although I settled for a P) and got high with my friends each and every morning. What an education!

Less than three months into the semester, I was born again, and S.A.F.E. school became a mission field. You see, we already had an "anything goes" mentality. Among the classes taught were Existentialism, Witchcraft and the Occult, and Philosophy (not to mention Logic and American History), so it was very easy to share the gospel with my friends.

The first year, about 40 friends and two faculty members visited my little church. I even got permission to invite my pastor to the school. He addressed the entire S.A.F.E. student body and gave an altar call! Then one of the Jewish students got upset and invited her rabbi to the school, and he spoke, too. We also had various cult leaders and teachers of TM (transcendental meditation) visit the school and share their views.

Most of us were on a spiritual search, and some of us really met the Lord. Yes, S.A.F.E. school was quite a place! (In case you're wondering, the entire experimental program was closed down after a few years. For me, however, it served as a great place to talk about Jesus, and the abbreviated schedule gave me hours to read the Word, pray, and memorize Scripture.)

Now, I have related all this to you for two reasons. First, it proves that things *can* change, even in the most unlikely and unforeseeable ways. Who would have dreamed that such an extremist school could exist on Long Island in the early 1970s, *right in the midst* of a typical, traditional school?

Second, my experience in S.A.F.E. school shaped some of my thinking about the status quo. Of course, from a moral point of view, S.A.F.E. was a travesty, while from an academic point of view, it was a total disaster—a fact confirmed to me by old high school friends whom I saw for the first time in 25 years at a student reunion in 1998. Some of them were ill-prepared for college when they sailed from the surreal shores of S.A.F.E. school. Yet as I continued in my own studies, from college to grad school and a Ph.D., I realized that academic education in our society does not necessarily prepare us for life, nor does it advance us in our personhood or guarantee individual development and growth. You can be a Ph.D. and be totally ignorant, while someone else who is completely illiterate can be wise. The standards of this world are not always an indication of our real giftings and true worth.

Formal education does not always make us smarter, and in many ways it has become an idol in our culture, an icon to which we bow—we *must* get our degree—instead of a tool for the enhancement of God's purposes in our lives. It is one thing to set lofty goals and strive for excellence. It is another thing to bow down to the system of this world. We think we *need* to go to the best university and get the best grades and finish at the top of our class if we are to be truly successful. (Could there be at least a hint of pride here, either in the students who have this attitude or in the parents who drive their kids to academic excellence?) Far be it from us to send our brilliant young people to some unaccredited Bible college where they will be trained for missionary work. They must finish secular school first!

Of course, I would be the first to tell you that God Himself is calling many of His children to fine colleges, secular schools, and advanced academic degrees and that these things can be utilized to accomplish His purposes, just as my studies in Semitics have been used for His glory. But I am equally convinced that academics have become an idol in our lives, and there is something stirring in our culture today—just as it was stirring in the late '60s and early '70s—that is ready to repudiate the status quo, for good reason. I'll return to this theme in the "Smashing the Idols" chapter.

What I am saying is simply this: I have a certain perspective that has been shaped by my life experiences, a perspective that has been brought into sharper focus through ministering around the world. Some of my closest ministry friends and colleagues have suffered much for the gospel—they have been stoned, shot, or tortured, or they lost their colleagues to martyrdom—while others have forsaken everything for the sake of the Kingdom. In the spirit of John Wesley, they believe there is nothing to do but save souls. They are "holy radicals" in the truest sense of the words. In light of all this, I find it impossible to sell out to the world's ways and simply conform to what the Church and the society call normal.[3] It's time for change, and I mean *real* change, radical change, revolutionary change.

The whole reason I have written this book is because I am convinced that a countercultural revolution is ready to break out in our society, a revolution as far-reaching as the counterculture movement of more than 30 years ago, a revolution that will be marked by either violence and destruction or by repentance and reformation. This time, however, God's people will not be caught off guard. We will not be merely reactionary, nor will we be ignorant of what the Lord Himself is doing. (How perverse it is for the Body not to know what the Head is doing!)

During the Hippie movement of the '60s and '70s, the Spirit of God exploited the spiritual search many of us were on, saving countless thousands of people from drugs and immorality. But the churches were hardly ready, and the majority of those converted in those days subsequently fell away. (This remains a source of pain to me. My best friend at that time, the fellow band member who led me to Jesus, has been backslidden now for almost 25 years.)[4]

This time around, it will be different! Not only will we understand and recognize this cultural revolution before it happens—especially among the youth—but we will also lead the way. We will be the ones to repudiate the idols of this age. We will be the ones who will march to the beat of a different drummer. We will set the pace and show the way. It's time to change the world!

In 1989, I wrote my first book on revival, *The End of the American Gospel Enterprise*. I stated at that time,

> The final chapter has not yet been written. The verdict is not yet in. America stands in the balance. The judgments have already begun. Will we live or will we die?
>
> Hear the Word of the Lord:
>
>> "'Even now,' declares the Lord, 'return to Me with all your heart, with fasting and weeping and mourning.' Rend your heart and not your garments. Return to the Lord your God, for He is gracious and compassionate, slow to anger and abounding in love, and He relents from

sending calamity. Who knows? He may
turn and have pity and leave behind a
blessing—grain offerings and drink
offerings for the Lord your God" (Joel
2:12-14).

Who knows? The best could be yet to come.[5]

In the preface to that book, I wrote with deep conviction
that almighty God wants to send a flood of revival to America.
It was clear in the late 1980s that something was happening in
the land. The Church had been brought to her knees, and
national prayer for revival was ascending to heaven. Revival was
drawing near! Five years later, in 1994, I wrote a more extensive
book on the subject of revival, *From Holy Laughter to Holy Fire:
America on the Edge of Revival*.[6] I was sure we were in the early
stages of spiritual renewal in America, and if we avoided the twin
pitfalls of religious criticism on the one side and manifestation
mania on the other side, we could move from renewal to revival.
If holiness and harvest were our themes and if we sought God
earnestly with prayer and fasting, revival could erupt!

That book came out in March 1995, and within a few
months, revival fires were blazing in different parts of the
nation. Interestingly, as I reviewed the sermons I preached in
churches in America and abroad in 1993 and 1994, a recurring
theme was "It's time! Revival is at the door! This is the hour for
visitation!" And then it happened: the fire fell, and revival—in its
wonderful, initial stages—was upon us.

Yes, renewal had already touched many, but to fully run its
course it had to lead to revival, where sin would be confronted
and the root problems of the Church would be exposed and
eradicated. And that has been happening! Now, if revival is to

fully run its course, it must lead to awakening on a national scale. It must lead to revolution! I tell you with an overflowing heart: It's time! A holy revolution is ready to explode! This is the hour to change an entire generation!

Will you come along for this adventure of a lifetime? Will you enlist yourself in the service of the Lord, regardless of the consequences or cost? Will you give your life for the Master's cause—to make disciples of your nation and the nations of the world, to shine the light in dark places, to glorify Jesus as Savior and Deliverer and Redeemer and Lord? Will you be a revolutionary?

This is the moment we've been waiting for. History makers, arise! The time is short, the hour is late, and the battle for the soul of our nation is intense. But victory is ours. Our Savior lives! All authority in heaven and on earth belongs to Him, and there is no power or force that can withstand His mighty name. Therefore, we must *go*.

Fellow soldiers, holy servants of the risen Lord, blood-bought disciples of the Master, heed the call. It's now or never; it's time to put up or shut up. Either we take a stand once and for all, or forever we hang our heads in shame. History is awaiting our move. So on with it! Let's start a revolution!

Chapter Two

From Revival
to
Revolution:
The Time is
Now!

January 14, Salt Lake City, Utah (1 dead, 1 wounded)
March 18, Johnson City, Tennessee (2 dead)
April 15, Salt Lake City, Utah (3 dead, 4 wounded)
April 20, Littleton, Colorado (15 dead, 23 wounded)
May 20, Conyers, Georgia (6 wounded)
June 3, Las Vegas, Nevada (4 dead)
June 11, Southfield, Michigan (3 dead, 4 wounded)
July 8, Sidney, Ohio (4 dead, 1 wounded)
July 12, Atlanta, Georgia (7 dead)
July 29, Atlanta, Georgia (10 dead, 13 wounded)
August 5, Pelham, Alabama (3 dead)
August 10, Los Angeles, California (1 dead, 5 wounded)
September 15, Fort Worth, Texas (7 dead, 8 wounded)
November 2, Honolulu, Hawaii (7 dead)
November 3, Seattle, Washington (2 dead, 2 wounded)
December 6, Fort Gibson, Oklahoma (4 wounded)
December 30, Tampa, Florida (5 dead, 3 wounded)

MULTIPLE SHOOTINGS IN AMERICA, 1999

The state of our union is the strongest it has ever been.

PRESIDENT BILL CLINTON
IN HIS FINAL STATE OF THE UNION ADDRESS
JANUARY 27, 2000

I don't want to be an alarmist, a sensationalist, or an end-times extremist. I don't want to say the sky is falling unless the sky really is falling. If you're like me, you've had it with ominous predictions that never come to pass, urgent warnings that seem to vanish into thin air, and fruitless speculation that never seems to produce anything constructive. I hate foolishness, and I assume you hate it, too. We have better things to do than endlessly air our own opinions and excitedly exchange our latest "revelations." Where is the reality in any of this?

Allow me to put this in perspective for you. I began preaching at the age of 18, in August 1973. My 13th message, preached a number of months later, was the only one of those early messages that was recorded. A few years ago, I listened to it with considerable interest. The New York accent was heavy (what has become of it?). The tone was a little harsh (I was only a kid!). But the message was just about the same as it has been for almost 30 years: "America is in a mess! Look at the state of our society: It doesn't take a prophet to know that we're living in perilous times. Let's wake up and go for it! Let's make a difference for Jesus!"

Now, putting youthful enthusiasm aside and discounting the old New York accent, I was intrigued by that old message and I asked myself a few obvious questions: Was this just my own narrow perspective? Was I exaggerating things then, and am I exaggerating them now? Or were things back then really that bad, becoming increasingly worse ever since?

It's true that almost every generation tends to get nostalgic and look back to "the good old days" when, in fact, those days are sometimes the figments of our own imaginations. It is also true that almost every generation tends to regard the younger, upcoming generation as rebellious, disrespectful, and out of control. We think, *I wasn't like that as a kid! I would never have treated my parents like that. Boy! Things have gotten really bad.*

But that perspective is not always accurate. Even considering where we stand today, we have to admit that in many ways much progress has taken place during the past 30 years—at least among God's people: Churches are experiencing more and more gracious seasons of visitation; desperate spiritual hunger is on the rise; New Testament patterns are being recovered (in worship, in leadership structure, in discipleship, in mission, in sacrifice, in prayer); and restrictive denominational walls are coming down. (This is not to say that all denominations are bad but only that restrictive walls are falling.)

Among the youth in particular, standards that were all but forgotten are being recovered. For example, courtship has replaced dating for countless thousands. (How many of us as teens thought of asking for parental permission and blessing before pursuing a relationship, and how many of us pursued a relationship only if we thought it could lead to marriage?) Sexual abstinence before marriage is becoming more prevalent once again; holy militancy is on the increase; more and more young people are heeding the call to foreign missions.

Yes, the list of positive things happening in the church today, even here in North America, is substantial, which leads me back to my questions: What about that message I preached many years ago? Was it symptomatic of the "Old Testament prophet in New Testament garb" syndrome? In other words, was it evidence of a gloom-and-doom mentality that always sees the satanic side of things and ignores the divine side of things? More to the point, does the recurring refrain, "Look at how bad things are!" mean that believers like me, who claim that our society is in grave danger, should simply be dismissed as spiritual hypochondriacs? Does it indicate that the sense of urgency we feel is really a projection of our own personal struggles?

In the summer of 1999, after speaking briefly at a major Christian rally attended by thousands, I returned to my hotel room and watched a riveting documentary on the worldwide rise of religious fundamentalism, beginning in 1979. (Generally, I don't watch TV at all when I'm on the road, but this documentary caught my interest.) During the program, a respected national evangelist was seen addressing a 1979 Christian rally that ultimately centered on a presidential candidate named Ronald Reagan. To my shock, I realized that his words were virtually identical to the words I had spoken earlier that night at the rally. Both of us had basically said, "Homosexuals [and others] have come out of the closet. It's time that Christians come out of the closet!" Yet he delivered his message 20 years before I delivered mine!

Of course, the thrust of our messages was quite different. His was more of a call for Christian involvement in politics; mine was a call to take the gospel to the streets at any cost. Still, the similarities in language were striking, causing me to ask myself, *What's going on? What are we doing? Are we merely repeating the rhetoric of the previous decades? Are we making a lot of noise but only a little progress? Or, of even more concern, are we getting worked up about nothing?*

Let's face it: There were problems in Jesus' day; there were problems in Luther's day; there were problems in Wesley's day; there are problems today. So why all the fuss? Given a certain perspective, things can always look pretty bad, and someone can always make a case that serious judgment is near and great collapse is coming.[1] But, as the argument goes, those who are mature will have a more balanced outlook. They won't panic all the time and they won't cause everyone else to panic needlessly. They will go about their business, preaching the gospel and helping those in need, and they will do it with balance. They will be stable and steady, not easily moved by the latest prophetic fad.

Who then is right? Where do we stand today? What is the biblical (realistic!) point of view as opposed to the hopeless (overly pessimistic!) point of view or the foolish (too optimistic!) point of view? What is the truth? What are the facts? What is God's perspective on the state of our nation?

Since the 1980s, I have believed that revival was the only hope for America, believing at the same time that revival was a very *real* hope for America. I have never accepted the mentality that it was too late for our nation, nor have I held to an end-time theology of total defeat.[2] No! The Church of the Lord Jesus will not end this age with a demonstration of the failure of the Spirit, nor has God completely cast America behind His back. Instead, in His mercy and grace, He has been pouring out His Spirit, beginning especially in the mid-1990s. Now, after several years of revival—not nationwide, to be sure, but certainly in pockets throughout the nation—the hour is more urgent than ever.

You see, while it is very true that God is moving in our midst, Satan is also moving, and all too many believers—actually, most believers—remain asleep in the light. The present revival must become a revolution! The current outpouring must become an awakening! If it doesn't happen soon, it may not happen at all.

What gives me the right to say this? What facts support these statements? Isn't it true, you ask, that there have been many signs of positive, moral change in our midst? Yes, there have, and for this we thank God. As William Bennett noted in his important 1999 study that documents the leading cultural indicators of America,

> The decade of the nineties has seen progress in some key social indicators: reductions in welfare, violent crime, abortion, AIDS, divorce, and suicide. . . . Since 1994, for example, there has been a 46.5 percent decrease in welfare rolls. The murder rate is at its lowest point since 1967. Alcohol-related traffic fatalities are at their lowest level since the government began keeping such statistics. Since 1993, the number of AIDS cases has decreased by more than 50 percent. Near the end of the decade, there are 243,000 fewer abortions per year than at the beginning.[3]

There have been many positive developments in recent years, and this is certainly cause for great thanksgiving! But at the same time, many other things are worse than they have ever been in our land (I'll come back to this in a moment), while many other things sit like simmering volcanoes, ready to erupt at any time.

We have not yet paid the full penalty for the abortion holocaust in our land (we knew better than other nations, and to whom much is given, much is required [see Luke 12:48]). We have only seen the tip of the iceberg regarding the impact of rampant divorce on our society (the vast majority of criminals come from broken homes). We have not yet seen the unbridled aggression of the homosexual movement (when it is challenged, it will become violently aggressive). We have not yet reaped what we have sown.

The majority of sexual and violent crimes are committed by people who were raised without a father. According to Bennett's study, "Seventy-two percent of America's adolescent murderers, 70 percent of long-term prison inmates, and 60 percent of rapists come from fatherless homes."[4] Yet, the generation birthed in the 1990s will be the most fatherless generation in our history, and only half of those raised in the first decade of the twenty-first century "will spend their entire childhood in an intact family."[5] What does this mean for our future?

THE DEVIL IS TURNING UP THE HEAT OF SIN AND POLLUTION IN OUR SOCIETY, AND WE, LIKE THE PROVERBIAL FROG IN SLOW-BOILING WATER, HARDLY REALIZE THE TEMPERATURE IS RISING.

The devil is turning up the heat of sin and pollution in our society, and we, like the proverbial frog in slow-boiling water, hardly realize that the temperature is rising. While we should rejoice over everything the Lord is doing in our land, we must not deceive ourselves. The percentage of church-attending Americans has actually *decreased* from 1965 until today, rising only slightly even within the 1990s themselves.[6]

Even more sobering, "in 1997, Gallup replicated a survey it originally conducted in 1947. It found that the same percentage of Americans pray (90 percent), believe in God (96 percent) and attend church once a week."[7] This means that we are just as religious today as we were more than 50 years ago, but we are far less moral! The frog is now boiling but somehow thinks it's bathing. It is simmering and stewing but somehow thinks it's sunbathing and swimming. How pathetic.

Let me put all this in perspective for you. Please step back and consider the facts. In 1961, the beginning of one of the most turbulent decades in our history, things seemed relatively peaceful. Speaking of the day of JFK's inauguration, Irwin and Debbie Unger wrote:

> America, on that blustery inauguration day in January 1961, was still deep in the throes of postwar conformity. Skirts were worn below the knee, dresses were tailored, and women's shoes had high heels and pointy toes. On prime-time TV, the favorite programs were *The Flintstones*, *Ozzie and Harriet*, *One Happy Family*, and *The Bob Hope Show*. In film, the 1961 Academy Award for best picture went to a musical fable about feuding new York gangs, but *West Side Story* was monumentally innocent despite its subject matter. On Broadway, *My Fair Lady* was still drawing crowds after 2,300 performances. Elvis had already stirred the rage of parents and moralists with his swiveling hips and suggestive phrasing, but the most popular recording artist in 1961 was Eddie Fisher, the quintessential boy next door. Sexual mores were strict. Illegitimacy was rare in the middle class, and most Americans considered homosexuality a sin, and drove its practitioners deep into the closet. . . . On college campuses, except for a sprinkling of the most "progressive" and cosmopolitan ones, fraternities and sororities, pledge week, pep rallies, dances, and "sandbox" politics were the dominant extracurricular activities.[8]

Of course, by the end of the decade, things had changed radically:

> The Pill, announced with little fanfare in 1960, had ended fear of pregnancy; penicillin had diminished fear of disease. Sex, in any position, in any form, was consid-

ered good; denial was bad. The new sexual liberation movement soon spread beyond youthful flower-child dropouts. All through middle-class and working-class America ran a new current of permissiveness.[9]

By 1970, Woodstock was history, along with Stonewall (the watershed event in the homosexual movement).[10] The feminist movement had been birthed, and campus riots had drawn national attention. (Was any of this connected at all to the 1962 Supreme Court decision—hardly resisted by the Church—that removed organized public prayer from our schools?)

The 1960s really did mark a turning point in our culture, sending us into a moral free fall. Promiscuity increased during that decade. Drug and alcohol use increased. Divorce increased. Juvenile crime skyrocketed. Yet the legalization of abortion on demand did not occur until 1973 (since which time we have *legally* snuffed out more than 40 million innocent lives), while the incidence of teen sex, teen violence, and teen substance abuse was much lower in the late 1960s than in the late 1980s or early-to mid-1990s.

Despite some significant gains, the moral climate continues to degenerate in our land—something that becomes clear when we look at the larger context. While violent crimes, for example, decreased by 17 percent between 1990 and 1997, the comparison from 1960 to 1997 is very negative: Violent crimes actually *increased* by 280 percent over those years.[11] At the same time, our nation's prison population has increased dramatically, growing from 196,429 prisoners in 1970 (representing 96 people for every 100,000 Americans) to 1,197,590 prisoners in 1997 (445 out of every 100,000). In fact, that number has risen most dramatically in the 1990s (from 297 out of 100,000 in 1990, to 445 out of every 100,000 in 1997).[12]

Let's take a closer look at America in 1961 as compared with America in the 1990s: There were popular, animated TV shows then and now. In 1961, *The Flintstones* ruled; today it is *The Simpsons*. What a shocking contrast! In 1961, *West Side Story* was considered to be a violent flick; today it's *Natural Born Killers*. Americans then were entertained by *Ozzie and Harriet* and *One Happy Family*; today they are enthralled with Jerry Springer and Jenny Jones. I wish it were not so! Even 10 years ago, most Americans would not have tolerated such vulgar trash on major network TV. Yet it abounds today. Just stop and look around. The devil is putting his cards on the table.[13]

Every afternoon in homes across America—in broad daylight—TV screens glow with lively discussions about such topics as sex-change operations, transvestitism, flagrant cheating on spouses (often with same-sex affairs), and prostitution, to name just a few topics. How can this be? (Of course, to brighten things up you can always turn to the soap operas!) Profanity is also making inroads on the airwaves as standards drop year by year.[14] And all this takes place on major network TV.

What about shows and movies aired on cable and satellite TV? What about the availability of pornography or the increase in movie violence? What about the fact that the average 10-year-old child today sees and hears things that the average 30-year-old adult rarely saw or heard one generation ago? (And I haven't even mentioned the Internet!)

As noted in a 1998 *Time* magazine report on teen sex:

> Even if kids don't watch certain television shows, they
> know the programs exist and are bedazzled by the for-

bidden. From schoolyard word of mouth, eight-year-old Jeff in Chicago has heard all about the foul-mouthed kids in the raunchily plotted *South Park*, and even though he has never seen the show, he can describe certain episodes in detail. (He is also familiar with the AIDS theme of the musical *Rent* because he's heard the CD over and over.) Argentina, 16, in Detroit, says, "TV makes sex look like this big game." Her friend Michael, 17, adds, "They make sex look like Monopoly or something. You have to do it in order to get to the next level."[15]

As to the impact that TV and movie violence has had on our society, even a secular Hollywood source had this to say: "It is not that violent pictures create more violence, but the constant litany of gratuitous violence is destructive to the fabric of the culture because it lowers our threshold for sensitivity to the issue."[16] How our threshold for sensitivity has been lowered! A recent crime report provided the following shocking statistic: "In 1995, handguns were used to kill 2 people in New Zealand, 15 in Japan, 30 in Great Britain, 106 in Canada, 213 in Germany, and 9,390 in the United States."[17] What do we say to facts such as these?

Have you seen how with each new act of violence and each new atrocity we become less shocked and more insensitive, less outraged and more uncaring, less grieved and more hard-hearted? As the year 1999 wore on, Americans reacted with increasing indifference to the mounting wave of multiple shootings in our land. January started slowly: 1 dead and 1 wounded; by the end of March, we reached 3 dead and 1 wounded; and by the end of April, we were up to 21 dead and 28 wounded. By the end of June, the numbers were 28 dead and 38 wounded. By the end of July we reached 49 dead and 52 wounded, and by the end of September we were at 60 dead and 65 wounded. At the year's end, we reached 74 dead and 74 wounded—all in multiple shootings.[18] Some of these tragedies didn't even hold our attention for a full day. Some of them—including the unprecedented shootings at the Wedgewood Baptist Church in Fort Worth—didn't even make the top headline in some national newspapers.

Men of God have warned us for years, urging us to wake up from our stupor, yet still we slumber on. We are becoming so accustomed to filth that we hardly notice its stench. We have become so inoculated to evil that we are numb to its stinging bite. Do you hear the alarm? In the mid-1990s, when a major TV show introduced an openly lesbian character, there was an uproar. By 1999, *more than 30* characters on network TV were playing homosexual roles. What is happening?

WE HAVE BECOME SO INOCULATED TO EVIL THAT WE ARE NUMB TO ITS STINGING BITE. DO YOU HEAR THE ALARM?

More than 300 years ago, Thomas Manton observed, "First we practice sin, then defend it, then boast of it." We see this happening before our eyes with the homosexual movement. First, the sin was practiced in secret; then it was defended as a healthy, acceptable lifestyle; and now anyone who objects to it is homophobic. There is something wrong with *us* if we reject the practice as ungodly! And things have only heated up with the beginning of the new millennium: Homosexual activists are fighting for government recognition of same-sex marriages, and in some parts of our nation, they are rapidly gaining ground. (On April 25, 2000, the state of Vermont passed laws to grant marital rights to same-sex unions.) Don't we see the handwriting on the wall?

Even Satanism is becoming more blatant and overt. Why should the devil hide in the shadows when he can freely operate in the open? Of course, I'm aware that we have had our horror pictures for years, like *Dracula* and *Frankenstein* of old and *The Exorcist* and *Rosemary's Baby* of more recent decades. But the increased interest in these ever-more-explicit themes is striking. In 1999 alone, at least six hit movies had strongly occultic themes, including *The Blair Witch Project* and *The Sixth Sense*.

Yes, the battle lines have been drawn, the enemy is taking ground, and many of us hardly realize that the war is on. The devil is moving forward with energy and aggression. What in the world are *we* doing?

In 1961, women and girls commonly wore skirts or dresses (rather than pants), always wearing them to school, and those skirts or dresses were worn below the knee. Today, even women tennis players—I'm talking about athletes, not strippers or nightclub dancers—are often known for their skin-hugging, highly revealing, sensual outfits. Do trends like this mean nothing? Or consider the look of magazine covers over the past 40 years. Pictures of not-quite-nude women that were not seen as recently as 10 years ago—I'm talking about on the covers of weight-lifting magazines, not porno magazines—now "grace" many a magazine cover. What's next?

Yes, the world pursues its agenda with very little spiritual or moral resistance from the people of God. And even in those moral areas where we have seen some progress—for example, in the recent decline in the abortion rate—there is bad news, because one major reason for the decline in abortions is the increased use of condoms among unmarried, sexually active young people.[19]

We live in a society today where students can wear satanistic T-shirts to school but cannot pray in the name of Jesus at their graduation ceremonies, where teens can get abortions without parental permission but where teachers cannot read the Scriptures to those same teenagers without fear of parental prosecution. We live in a society where 11-year-olds and 13-year-olds can be skillful, purposeful murderers—using schoolmates for target practice—and where favorite video games include *Doom* and *Mortal Kombat* and favorite cartoon movies include the *South Park* series.[20] Gone are the days when the gyrations of Elvis stirred moral outrage. MTV has long since made its antimoral mark, and "gangsta rap" is here to stay—unless we have a moral and spiritual revolution.[21]

So what are we waiting for? What else needs to happen? How many more massacres in our schools and massacres in our workplaces and massacres in our houses of worship do we need? At what point will we realize that *now* is the time to act? The hour really is later than we know!

When Congress must debate issues like whether it's ethical to harvest and sell aborted baby parts—spinal cords and skin and brains and limbs—what have we come to as a nation? Yet in November 1999, such a debate took place:

> On Tuesday, November 9, 1999, by voice vote, the House of Representatives passed a nonbinding resolution calling for congressional hearings to investigate trafficking in tissues, organs and whole bodies of aborted babies.

Representatives Joseph Pitts (R-PA), Tom Tancredo (R-CO) and Christopher Smith (R-NJ) introduced the resolution (H.R. 350). In the midst of debate concerning H.R. 350, Pitts said, "I wish this gruesome price list [of baby body parts] was a cruel Halloween hoax, but it is not. It's the price list for human body parts from aborted babies. It's almost like the bureaucratization of the Nazis' final solution hammered out in conferences and committed to legal documents. Except now it's in the form of a capitalistic price list, organized for commerce, sanitized for the grim reality, which it is."

Pro-abortion House members believe those in favor of the resolution are "attempting to corrupt medical research with the politics of abortion." They also challenged the evidence and stated that "no one is going out selling baby parts, arms or legs for any purpose." Two weeks earlier, during Senate debate over the Partial-Birth Abortion Ban (PBAB), Sen. Robert Smith (R-NH) detailed carefully documented information concerning the harvesting of baby parts. Smith reasoned this was one of the terrible secrets behind the push to keep partial-birth abortions available to abortionists and offered a sensible amendment to the PBAB, providing for immediate regulation of the fetal tissue industry, but it was rejected by the Senate, 46-51.[22]

Do you realize what you just read? It is unspeakably tragic that the Clinton administration vetoed the Partial-Birth Abortion Ban three times, helping to pave the way for the gruesome horrors just described. Such are the times in which we live!

With our president leading the way, we have learned that oral sex is not sex, that you can go to church on Sunday and lie to the nation on Monday, that you can be a very good leader and a very bad person—simultaneously!—and that homosexuality is acceptable while rejection of homosexuality is not. No wonder so many young people are so confused. And no wonder we adults don't seem much more clearheaded. In fact, we have our own foolish obsessions.

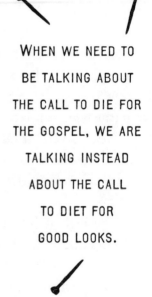

WHEN WE NEED TO BE TALKING ABOUT THE CALL TO DIE FOR THE GOSPEL, WE ARE TALKING INSTEAD ABOUT THE CALL TO DIET FOR GOOD LOOKS.

Just think: We live in a time of moral madness and social uncertainty, a time when talk of a moral revolution should be everywhere. Instead, the best-selling "revolutionary" books are books about new diets![23] What does this say for us as a people? When we need to be talking about the call to die for the gospel, we are talking instead about the call to diet for good looks. What a sad indictment! And what does it say of our self-deception and lack of discipline when we are at one and the same time the world's best-read nation on diet and nutrition and the world's most obese? Even our pets are overweight.[24] We need a revolution!

To quote William Bennett once again, relating to our present moral stupor:

The percentage of births to unwed mothers—already at the alarmingly high level of 28 percent at the beginning of the decade [meaning the 1990s]—is even higher today, at 32.4 percent. . . . Among men and women between their mid-twenties and mid-thirties, living together before marriage is far more common than not. . . . In 1998, 5.6 percent of high school seniors reported using marijuana on a daily basis—a 180 percent increase since 1991. In math achievement, American twelfth graders rank nineteenth out of twenty-one nations.[25]

The United States boasts the highest percentage of professing evangelicals in the industrialized world. In fact, according to polls, 36 percent of Americans consider themselves to be born-again (the highest percentage is in the black American community, where 51 percent make that same claim). That means one in three Americans—more than 90 million people!—claim to be born-again.[26] Yet, America has

- The highest percentage of single-parent families in the industrialized world[27]

- The highest abortion rate in the industrialized world[28]

- The highest rate of sexually transmitted diseases in the industrialized world (the rates of syphilis and gonorrhea transmission are almost 500 percent higher than the highest rates in the other industrialized nations)[29]

- The highest teenage birth rate in the industrialized world (by far!)[30]

- The highest rate of teenage drug use in the industrialized world[31]

As if this wasn't enough, consider the fact that "21 percent of American nine-year-olds watch more than five hours of television per weekday—the highest percentage in the developed world."[32] What a sobering statistic! Millions of nine-year-olds watch *five hours* of television—so much of it poison—*per weekday*. We really are in a mess![33]

In our own blessed homeland, "Between 1990 and 1997, the percentage of births that are out of wedlock increased 16 percent. Between 1960 and 1997, the increase was 511 percent."[34] This means that *five times* as many babies are being born out of wedlock today than in 1960—and this despite the fact that most aborted babies are conceived out of wedlock. If we add in these conceived-but-never-birthed children, the out of wedlock figure is all the more staggering.

Focusing in on this situation in black America, we are faced with a paradox: While there has been an increase in civil rights over the last 40 years—this was actually one positive development that came out of the 1960s—there has been a terrible deterioration in the African-American family itself. Today, more than two-thirds of all black children are born out of wedlock, and the rate of moral decline here has been steep.[35]

In 1960, 23 percent of all births to blacks were out of wedlock; by 1965, that figure had risen only to 27.9 percent, while by 1970, it was up to 37.6 percent. But in the 1990s, it has averaged *better than 68 percent,* an increase of almost three-to-one from 1960. How can it be that this very same segment of our population is the most religious, with 82 percent of black Americans claiming to be church members, 43 percent stating that they attend church weekly, and 86 percent saying that they "view religion as a solution to today's problems"?[36]

Yet there are even more shocking figures than these. The percentage of white children born out of wedlock has risen far more dramatically! In 1960, out-of-wedlock births among whites were only 2.3 percent, rising only to 4.0 percent in 1965, 5.7 percent in 1970, and 7.3 percent in 1975. But by 1997, it had reached 25.8 percent—amounting to an increase of more than 1,000 percent—better than ten-to-one!—from 1960.[37] *All this means that across America, almost one in every three children is born out of wedlock.* In fact, over the last 40 years, the national birthrate has decreased within marriage and increased outside of marriage to the point that "in 1994, for the first time in American history, more than half of all firstborn children were conceived or born out of wedlock."[38]

This is all quite staggering, especially when you consider just how important a strong family unit is for the health of any civilization. Yet the family is unraveling.

> Of the approximately 65 million children under 17 in 1996, almost 28 million (43 percent) spent time in a single-parent family. About 8.25 million were born out of wedlock, about 16.7 million experienced the divorce of their parents, and an additional 3 million or so children were born out of wedlock *and* experienced the divorce of their parents.[39]

Satan is going after the youth! Consider these appalling statistics, quoted verbatim from William Bennett's study:

- Among women born between 1951 and 1955 [making them in their 40s in the 1990s], 23 percent were married to their partner at the time of first sexual intercourse. Among women born between 1971 and 1975 [making them in their 20s in the 1990s], 2 percent were married to their partner at the time of first sexual intercourse.[40] [That means that in my generation, only one in four women waited until marriage to have sex with their husbands, which is hardly a statistic to boast over. But in my daughters' generation, the number drops to *one in fifty!*]

- The percentage of high school senior girls who think "having a child without being married is experimenting with a worthwhile lifestyle or [is] not affecting anyone else" increased from 33 percent in 1976-1980 to 53 percent in 1991-1995.[41]

- In 1997, roughly 3 million teenagers—about one in four who are sexually active—acquired a sexually transmitted disease.[42]

- Seventy-six percent of all births to teenagers occur outside of marriage.[43]

- In 15 of our nation's largest cities in 1995, the teenage out-of-wedlock birth ratio was greater than 90 percent. The cities with the highest out-of-wedlock birth ratio for girls under 20 are Baltimore and Pittsburgh [both at 96.5 percent!].[44]

- In 1996, 8,000 children under six years old were using one of three commonly prescribed antidepressants—Prozac, Zoloft, or Paxil. That number rose 400 percent, to 40,000, in 1997. [Yes, this took place in just one year!][45]

Words truly are inadequate to express how deeply we have fallen. This is reality, my friend. Still, there is really only one thing that matters, and there is only one thing we must ask: Is there any way out? (Can America be changed?) The answer, I say, is absolutely yes. Our country *can* be changed. But it will take a revolution, and that revolution must begin *now*. Can I count you in?

Chapter Three

Dedication to the Cause: The Fundamental Principle of Revolution

Cannot the love of Christ carry the missionary where
the slave trade carries the trader?

DAVID LIVINGSTONE
WRITING FROM THE HEART OF AFRICA IN THE MID-1800S

We Christians have given Calvary to the Communists. They accept
deprivation and death to spread their gospel, while we Christians
reject any gospel that does not major on healing and happiness.

GEORGE E. FAILING

This experience of ours is really worth taking a couple of bullets for.
[If you do come,] don't think of returning, the revolution won't wait.

CHE GUEVARA
INVITING HIS OLD FRIEND JULIO "EL GAUCHO" CASTRO
TO JOIN HIM IN CUBA

To any whom the Hand Divine is beckoning: count the cost,
for He tells us to, but take your slate to the foot of the Cross
and add up the figures there.

AMY CARMICHAEL
WHO SERVED AS A MISSIONARY IN INDIA FOR 55 YEARS
WITHOUT EVER TAKING A FURLOUGH

I will open the Sudan to the gospel or die trying.

ROWLAND BINGHAM
INFLUENTIAL LEADER OF THE SUDAN INTERIOR MISSION

World history has been shaped by revolutionary movements, from the American Revolution in the late 1700s to the Islamic Revolution of the late 1900s, and from the eighteenth-century French Revolution to the twentieth-century Russian Revolution. Some have been relatively bloodless, like the Industrial Revolution that transformed England 200 years ago. Others have been terribly brutal, like Mao Zedong's Cultural Revolution that spread through Communist China, beginning in 1966. But every revolution has been fueled by certain principles, by some nonnegotiable essentials. Without these, revolution would never occur.

Jon Lee Anderson, in his lengthy study of Che Guevara, the violent Latin American revolutionary—who was called a "totalitarian terrorist" by a leading historian—lists "self-sacrifice, honesty, and dedication to the cause" as the "revolutionary principles [Che] seemed to exemplify."[1] Ultimately, Che's cause cost him his life, along with the lives of many others. Yet it was a price he was fully prepared to pay. Just consider some of the chapter titles in Anderson's biography (the first three of the following five titles are Che's own words): "God and His New Right Hand"; "The Sacred Flame Within Me"; "We Are the Future and We Know It"; "No Turning Back"; "Necessary Sacrifice." Yes, it seemed that Che, like hundreds of other revolutionaries, could do nothing less than give his life for his cause. For the revolutionary, the cause is worth dying for; nothing else is worth living for.[2]

Why is this dedication to a cause—this passionate, often selfless, sometimes murderous, always fanatical dedication—characteristic of revolutionary movements? It is because the revolutionary has an unshakable conviction that something is terribly wrong with society, that something very important is missing, that something major needs to change; indeed, that it *must* change and that it must change *now*. Listen to this articulate statement from an American counterculture pioneer (in other words, an LSD-using hippie!) living in the Haight-Ashbury district of San Francisco in 1967. I have highlighted two key sentences:

> The street scene has become an entrance into a phenomenon to which we all have been invited. The word has been passed throughout the country, compliments of the aboveground media, that there is a scene going down on Haight Street. The most receptive to the call are from middle-class urbia. *They leave jobs, armies, and schools to turn their lives and psyches inside out, all looking for some material to build a life with.* All of us started to realize, even in 17 or 20 short years, that the game of life played in school and supermarket U. leads only to styrofoam coffins and oblivious servitude. Most of us have been on the threshold of jumping into the accepted swim, but stop and ask for time, having already seen enough instinctively, if not intellectually. Few have talents or skills developed enough for personal satisfaction or for the marketplace; all are well trained towards indiscriminate consumption. *Yet the feeling persists—there must be something greater than this!*[3]

Yes, there must be something greater than this—than eating and drinking, working and sleeping, *existing*. There must be something greater than simply getting a good education so that you can find a good job and have a good family, so *your kids* can get a good education and find a good job and have a good family, so *their kids* can a get a good education . . . Is this really it? Is this why God put us here on Earth? There is so much suffering, so much pain, so much injustice, so much waste, so much senselessness. What is our divine purpose in the midst of all this?

Even during times of peace and prosperity, when all seems well, there are sensitive, seeking souls asking probing, unsettling questions: Why are we here? Since death is the final, unavoidable end for every one of us—and thus we are all born to die—what is the ultimate purpose of our peace and prosperity? Is it merely to birth another generation to live and die, as we have done and are doing? Is it merely to guarantee the reproduction and preserva- tion of the human species? Is it merely to survive but to survive with gusto? Why are we here?

Regardless of how satisfying and fulfilling our own lives may be, regardless of how hard we try to insulate ourselves from the suf- fering that surrounds us, the suffering is still there, shouting for our attention, shattering our illusion of security, assaulting our all- too-fragile happiness. How do we relate to the agony of our race?

Yes, even times of peace and prosperity are marred by the pain of a fallen world, and that pain often serves as the impetus that causes people to break away from the culture of the day and seek another way of life—even when all is "well." This is what happened in the 1960s in America, when men like Timothy Leary, the LSD-advocating Harvard professor, became the gurus of the hippie movement. The philosophy was simple: Turn on, tune in, drop out! The message was clear: There's more to life than middle-class America. There's more to life than smiling suburbia. So find a higher reality and check out of the rat race for a while. There must be something greater!

What is interesting is that American society had been fairly stable through the 1950s and early 1960s, yet social upheaval still came. And if upheaval can occur in the best of times, what happens during times of national calamity—times marked by poverty or famine or moral chaos or social collapse? Times such as these are fertile ground for revolution, and it is out of such soil that revolutionary movements often grow. "There must be more!" is the battle cry. On some level, it is a cry we can all affirm. We are people, not animals, made in the image of God, not in the image of fish or fowl. And we were made *for the Lord*. Without Him, we seek fulfillment in vain.

Step back and consider our origin and purpose. We were not created to copulate with endless sexual partners like so many dogs on street corners, to reproduce offspring without a family or a home. We were not created to shoot drugs into our veins or pour hard liquor down our throats until we pass out in a pool of our own vomit. We were not created to murder, rape, torture, and abuse one another. Our bodies were not made to become slaves to base cravings and humiliating addictions. God did not put us here so that we could devise new and improved methods of mass destruction or concoct increasingly bizarre ways to satisfy our fleshly lusts. Even animals don't sink to such depths. There is more to life than sports and sex, fashion and fun, rest and relaxation, money and materialism, education and entertainment. There is more!

Theologians often refer to a God-shaped void that is found in each of us, a void that only an intimate relationship with Him can fill. What happens when a generation becomes dissatisfied with life as it is—for good reason!—but doesn't turn to Jesus to fill that void? That generation will turn to something else— whether it be to false religions and cults, drugs and promiscuity, guns and violence, animals rights activism and environmental extremism, the cares and pleasures of this world, or a "noble" cause like economic justice brought about by the overthrow of a government.

One way or another, people will try to fill the emptiness in their lives with a cause that will rise to prominence (like the anti-war movement in the 1960s), or a meaning for life will be sought (like our current idolatrous plunge into materialism). Still, the void will not be filled.

There *is* something greater than earthly life in this world, but our society is looking for the wrong things in the wrong places. We who know the Lord must lead the way. We must forge the path. We must be the ones to renounce the gods of this world, repudiate the system of this world, and reject the values of this world. We must give ourselves wholly to the truly counterculture principles of the Master. We must demonstrate the real meaning of life and articulate the true purpose of our existence, making it clear that our lives are not measured by the abundance of our possessions (see Luke 12:15) or by being somebody great in the eyes of man (see 1 Cor. 3:18,19) or

THERE IS SOMETHING GREATER THAN EARTHLY LIFE IN THIS WORLD, BUT OUR SOCIETY IS LOOKING FOR THE WRONG THINGS IN THE WRONG PLACES. WE WHO KNOW THE LORD MUST LEAD THE WAY.

by having earthly success or achievements (see Jer. 9:23,24). The real meaning of life is to know Jesus and to make Him known (see John 17:3; Acts 20:24). Apart from knowing Him and making Him known, our lives are empty, aimless, and worthless.

Paul was not exaggerating when he wrote:

But whatever was to my profit I now consider loss for the sake of Christ. What is more, I consider everything a

loss compared to the surpassing greatness of knowing
Christ Jesus my Lord, for whose sake I have lost all
things. I consider them rubbish, that I may gain Christ
and be found in him, not having a righteousness of my
own that comes from the law, but that which is through
faith in Christ—the righteousness that comes from God
and is by faith. I want to know Christ and the power of
his resurrection and the fellowship of sharing in his sufferings, becoming like him in his death, and so, somehow, to attain to the resurrection from the dead (Phil.
3:7-11).

Paul knew what really mattered!

Nate Saint and Jim Elliot also knew what really mattered.
Saint and Elliot, along with three other American missionaries,
were martyred in 1956 by the Auca Indians in Equador. They recognized that life was far more meaningful, far more rich, far
more significant than most of us ever realize, even if we live to be
100 years old. As Nate Saint wrote:

People who do not know the Lord ask why in the world
we waste our lives as missionaries. They forget they too
are expending their lives and when the bubble has burst
they will have nothing of eternal significance to show for
the years they have wasted.[4]

Yes, everyone's bubble will burst one day. The dust will
return to dust and the spirit will return to God who gave it (see
Eccles. 12:7). On that day, only one thing will matter for you:
Did you fulfill the purpose of God? Did you make a lasting
impact for Jesus? Did you leave behind a blessed legacy for the
generation to come?

All the silly little things that seemed so important to us during our few years here on Earth will seem utterly insignificant when they are viewed in the light of eternity.

How wise it was for Jim Elliot to write these now-famous words: "That man is no fool who gives what he cannot keep to gain what he cannot lose." And how wise it was for him to lift up this petition before the Lord as a young man in college: "God, I pray Thee, light these idle sticks of my life and may I burn for Thee. Consume my life, my God, for it is Thine. I seek not a long life, but a full one, like You, Lord Jesus."[5] Oh, that all of us would lead truly full lives!

Deep in your heart, I believe you can sense the rightness of Jim Elliot's petition. At the same time, you may be wondering how in the world you can break away from the mundane routine of mere earthly subsistence. How can you lead a truly meaningful life? Sometimes it takes all of your energy just to make it—to pay the bills, to care for your family, to keep your sanity, to stay free from moral pollution. Sometimes it seems that all this lofty spiritual talk about revival, holy revolution, radical renewal, fulfilling the Great Commission, and impacting society is completely unrealistic and unattainable. Not so! With Jesus, it is totally realistic and attainable.

Don't buy into the lie that nothing can change, that your life or your family or church or society will always remain the same, that you will always be trapped in a cruel cycle, mired down in a mundane morass from which you can never extricate yourself. Don't accept that mentality! Determine to believe God afresh. Set your heart free to dream holy dreams. Set your mind free to hatch a plan of action.

All true revolution begins with a belief, with a dream, before it turns into action. The Lord has a plan of action for you! But it must flow out of your loyalty to Him, out of your dedication to His cause. He came to set the captives free, but they will remain in bondage unless we tell them the good news. Isn't now the time to go and proclaim liberty to the prisoners?

Stop for a moment and ask yourself some questions. How much do you owe the Savior? How much are you willing to give for His cause? How important are the things for which He died and the principles for which He sacrificed? And how great is His power to bring about change, to produce transformation, be it in your life or in the lives of those you touch? If God is God and if God is for us, where are the limitations? Aside from that which lies outside *His* will, are not all other limitations those that are imposed by *our own* wills?

John Wesley and an army of nameless lay preachers transformed England in the 1700s. The fruit of their labors was so undeniable that a prominent French historian, Professor Elie Halévy, claimed that "it would be difficult to overestimate the part played by the Wesleyan revival" in transforming England. He actually called it "the moral cement" of the society and stated that the revival explained "the miracle of modern England." Archbishop Davidson observed that it was "not too much to say that Wesley practically changed the outlook and even the character of the English nation"; and while British Prime Minister Lloyd George said that the Wesleyan movement was responsible for "a complete revolution effected in the whole country" of Wales, Prime Minister Baldwin said that it was impossible to explain nineteenth-century England without first explaining Wesley. He even claimed that "you cannot understand twentieth-century America, unless you understand Wesley."[6]

This was the man who was sometimes pelted with rocks and feces when he preached! This was also the man who said, "Give me 100 men who fear nothing but sin and desire nothing but God, and I will shake the world." Who will be the world-shakers in today's revival? Who will be the leaders in this generation's revolution?

The simple truth is that there would have been no John and Charles Wesley without their godly mother, Susanna, and without John and Charles, there would have been no Methodist Revival. Without that revival, there would have been no Industrial Revolution, and without that revival the violence of the French Revolution probably would have swept through England as well. We must remember that every life counts—the life of every praying mother, the life of every obedient son, the life of every soldier in God's army. Every life counts! The question is, Will you give your life for the cause? Will you offer yourself for the Master's service? Will you fight the good fight? Will you go for it?

"But nothing will change here in America!" you say. "Nothing *ever* changes."

I beg to differ! Consider the short history of our nation. It seems utterly outrageous to us today that women anywhere would be denied the right to vote. Yet 100 years ago, American women were denied this basic, democratic privilege. When the concept was introduced in 1869 by women such as Lucretia Mott, Elizabeth Cady Stanton, and Susan B. Anthony (some of whom were hardly Christian in their beliefs or practices), the idea seemed radical and revolutionary. In fact, it took more than fifty years—until 1920, to be exact—to establish this fundamental right as federal law. Today, *not* granting women this basic right seems primitive and repulsive. Things *can* change if we will only be faithful and stay our course. What seems outrageous in one generation becomes ordinary in the next. What was once revolutionary is now quite regular! As expressed by Mark Twain, "The radical of one century is the conservative of the next. The radical invents the views. When he has worn them out, the conservative adopts them." Well said!

Think of the enormous contributions made by black Americans to professional sports. The absence of these athletes from the sports world is unimaginable. What would basketball look like without Michael Jordan and Julius Erving, or baseball without Hank Aaron and Willie Mays, or football without Walter Payton and Jim Brown? Yet it was not until 1947 that Jackie Robinson broke the color line in baseball, enduring a hail of abuse and prejudice along the way. Decades earlier, voices had been raised—the passionate, articulate voices of black Americans—helping to expose bigotry and bias in our society. They had to stand their ground!

Listen to the words of W. E. DuBois, delivered in August 1906:

We will not be satisfied to take one jot or tittle less than our full manhood rights. We claim for ourselves every single right that belongs to a freeborn American—political, civil, and social—and until we get these rights we will never cease to protest and assail the ears of America. The battle we wage is not for ourselves alone but for all true Americans. It is a fight for ideals, lest this, our common fatherland, false to its founding, become in truth the land of the thief and the home of the slave, a byword and a hissing among the nations for its sounding pretensions and pitiful accomplishment.[7]

Not everything DuBois hoped for has fully come to pass, but America today looks radically different from the way it looked in his day. Much of his dream *has* been realized. Things *have* changed for the better in terms of civil equality.

Of course, most of the changes that have taken place in our society in the last few decades have been for the worse, as we saw with devastating clarity in the last chapter. But if things can *degen-erate*—through godless lives spurred on by devilish power—they can *regenerate* through godly lives inspired by the Spirit's power. Around the world today, there are cities and even nations (in Latin America and Africa, in particular) that are experiencing major transformation through the gospel, through God's people winning the lost, making real disciples, living as true believers, working in unity, and praying until Jesus moves. Why can't change come to our nation? Why can't it come to this generation? Why can't it come to *your* life, to *your* community, to *your* city?

America has had its moral highs and lows before (although we have never been this low before in terms of fallen standards and open sin), and there have been spiritual turnarounds in our history. That is not in question. The question instead is this: Will you dedicate yourself to the cause?

Jesus sent us on a mission with a definite commission, and until the job is done—we'll know it's finished when He returns—we have our work cut out for us. We have our job descriptions! Jesus commanded us to "go and make disciples of all nations, baptizing them in the name of the Father and of the Son and of the Holy Spirit, and teaching them to obey everything I have commanded you" (Matt. 28:19,20). Until that task is completed, its fulfillment remains our most pressing obligation. It is our primary assignment, our sacred responsibility, our holy trust, our revolutionary cause. It is a call, to borrow a phrase from the title of Dr. Bill Bright's autobiography, to come and help change the world.[8] That is why we are here. That is our glorious task.

How sad it is that Satan's servants are heeding *their* master's call to change the world, doing an exquisite job of seduction and destruction, working feverishly as Earth's clock counts down. They are owned and operated by the devil, and it is for his kingdom that they live and die. But the cost of following him is high! That once-wealthy gambler has forfeited his life earnings; that teenage stripper has forfeited her dignity; that divorced alcoholic has forfeited his wife and kids; that devoted witch has forfeited her soul. And all for what?[9]

Think of the extreme measures people will take in the pursuit of sin: stealing and killing to support a drug habit; lying, deceiving, and conniving to pursue an affair; going to the ends of the earth to experience an elusive pleasure. How far should we go and what price should we pay in the pursuit of spiritual obedience and service? The devil really doesn't care what words are sung and what professions are made as long as he gets the desired results: "All to Satan, I surrender, all to him I freely give." That's the kind of taskmaster he is. He's the one who has been fueling Earth's age-old rebellion and inspiring countless godless revolutions, and he demands complete obedience from those he captures. How loyal his followers are!

Consider the example of Chang Ta Pao, an illiterate Chinese peasant who became a leader in the Red Guard, the brutal youth army that rose up in response to Mao's teachings. Chang's story is told by Niu-Niu, a victim of Mao's Cultural Revolution. She was only a child of four when, in front of her eyes, her parents were brutally beaten and taken away. Their beautiful house was trashed and their possessions destroyed. Young Niu-Niu, her sister, Mimi, and their father's parents were relocated to a vacated hovel in another part of town, where their grandparents were subjected to humiliating labor and frequent beatings. Their crime? They had been rich and educated, part of the bourgeois society and therefore branded as criminals and enemies.

Much of the brutal treatment was dished out by Chang. He was involved in the attack on Niu-Niu's family, and he was responsible for much of the ongoing torment endured by her grandparents. Niu-Niu described what happened one day at a community gathering when she was just five years old. The memories remained vivid in her mind through the years:

It was a beautiful day. Everyone stood dressed in his or her best, solemnly waiting for the ceremony to begin. Finally, after a long delay, they all turned their heads to a man who was slowly mounting the steps to the platform.

"That's Chang Ta Pao," murmured my grandmother.

He wore an army cap, a handsome white shirt, khaki pants, and was holding something wrapped in red paper. Slowly he approached Mao's portrait and prostrated himself in front of it several times before he turned to the audience.

"Comrades! Today I am going to do something special to prove that my heart belongs to Mao. Comrades! Before the Liberation, I was miserable. It's Mao and the Communist Party that saved me. Yet even then the criminals and capitalists continued to harass me. . . . With the Cultural Revolution, Mao saved me for the second time. All that I have today, Mao gave me. That's why I swear before Heaven that I will give every drop of my blood for Mao. . . ." Short of breath, he was unable to continue, his eyes welling with tears. He was really crying![10]

The young revolutionary unwrapped his package, revealing a large pin of Mao; then he opened his shirt, bared his chest, and, to the shock of the onlooking crowd, stuck the pin directly into his flesh, resulting in his hospitalization. What pathetic, misguided devotion! Yet the story doesn't end there.

At a public meeting one day, he proudly announced that out of his love for Chairman Mao, he had named his newborn son Mao Zedong. This was an utterly unthinkable act in that culture (it was considered an insult to the honor of an emperor or supreme leader), and he was immediately denounced and disgraced for his foolish and ignorant zeal, being branded a criminal and consigned to hard labor for his "crimes." Now he performed meaningless acts of labor, harnessed like an animal and harassed like an enemy. And he felt he deserved the treatment! After all, he had disgraced his beloved Mao. His death was even more tragic than his life:

> Chang Ta Pao died a little while later. Like other gawkers, I went to see his body in the shack where his family had been "relocated" just as ours had been. I was still very young and horrified by the spectacle. The dead man was on his knees, his head on his chest. He had pierced his torso with another medallion of Mao. A piece of paper on his thigh read, "Forgive me, Mao." A fragment of his bloody tongue was sticking to the paper. He had slit his wrists with a kitchen knife and cut off his guilty tongue.[11]

Yes, just as he had pledged, this deluded revolutionary gave his blood for Mao. Such was his dedication to the cause. And what a perverse, destructive cause it was! (He also left behind his little baby boy and his young wife, who quickly lost her mind.) Mao meant everything to Chang Ta Pao. Dare I ask what Jesus means to us? Dare I ask how important His cause is to us? Can we, in truth and integrity, give *less* (not in terms of self-mutilation or self-destruction or suicidal or violent acts—perish the thought!— but in terms of healthy devotion, joyful sacrifice, and loving service) for the cause of Jesus?

Our society is deteriorating all around us and something is terribly wrong. Why? It is because we, the people of God, the army of the Lord Jesus, the messengers of liberation, the ambassadors of reconciliation, *we* have been sidetracked by the love of this world and distracted by the cares of this world. We have not changed this generation; this generation has changed us!

Rather than seasoning the world like salt and brightening the world like light, we now smell and taste like the world, and its darkness is snuffing out our lamps. Rather than setting captives free by the power of Jesus' blood, we ourselves are being ensnared and enslaved, making a mockery of that sacred blood. Rather than making disciples of sinners and teaching them the ways of God, we are being discipled by them, learning their ways, imitating their lifestyles, and conforming to their standards.

Really now, in the last 40 years, whose standards have changed more—those of the Church or those of the society? Who is looking like whom? A 1997 survey conducted by George Barna used 152 different items to compare the Church and the world. He found virtually no difference between the two.[12] We need a revolution!

If I could talk with you face to face, I would implore you, I would plead with you, I would urge you, I would exhort you to wake up to the reality of the day and age in which we live, to embrace the call to follow Jesus at any cost, and to give yourself to the Master's service, by life or by death.

Why am I and so many others of like mind so passionate about this? It is because we have hit bottom or, more frightfully, we have gotten low enough to see what the bottom could look like, and the view is absolutely terrifying. School shootings like Columbine could soon appear tame. Churches and synagogues could require metal detectors at the doors, just like airports and, tragically, so many of our schools. (There was a time when metal detectors were not needed at airports at all, and 30 years ago, the thought of metal detectors at schools seemed preposterous.)

In the coming days, child pornography could grow even uglier and more rampant. Our inner cities could become virtual war zones, while real family life could all but vanish from city streets. Trash-talk TV shows could stoop even lower—who would have ever thought they could stoop as low as they do now?—while people who even dare to suggest the need for some kind of moral standards could be rejected out of hand as dangerous and extreme. What I am saying is not that outlandish!

Who would have thought that physician-assisted suicide would be legalized in certain states in the late 1990s or that Jack Kevorkian could help terminate the lives of more than 70 people before finally going to jail? What is to stop us from becoming another Netherlands, where physicians have freely admitted to taking the lives of thousands of hurting or incapacitated patients—without even getting the patient's permission or the permission of the patient's family? The day could soon come in America when you will have to specify what kind of doctor you want—one who will cure you, not kill you!

Do you remember the description of life in America in 1961? (See the previous chapter.) What if a prophet of God stood up in 1960 and said, "Within ten years, there will be a wide-scale counterculture revolution marked by sexual liberation, widespread drug use, and the emergence of a homosexual movement, a feminist movement, a hippie movement, and an antiwar movement. And within eight years, John F. Kennedy, Jr., Robert F. Kennedy, and Martin Luther King, Jr., will all be assassinated." Would we have believed such a message?

I have looked with amazement at footage from the early days of classic rock, as clean-cut, neatly dressed youngsters—the young men wearing jackets and ties and the young women wearing skirts—sat in the audience and bounced to the music. Within three years, many of these same young people had long, unkempt hair and dressed in tie-died T-shirts, bell-bottoms, and sandals. Their minds had been "expanded" by LSD and hash, and they had dropped out of college and were living in communes. It really happened! Radical changes like that are ready to come to our society again, and if we don't seize the moment and lead the way, the devil certainly will. And if he does, look out. It will get *very* ugly. May we not get caught off guard again!

In 1993, I wrote that this generation could be the one that would see the blood of martyrs flowing right here in America. Ask our Christian teenagers if it has been flowing in their midst! Without radical cultural transformation, without sweeping national revival, without a Jesus-centered moral revolution, without a holy, nation-shaking move of God, it is virtually impossible for us to recover ourselves. But with the Lord's intervention, some of our wildest dreams for America can be fulfilled. Our most fervent hopes, our most passionate prayers, our most burning desires for this country can be realized.

"But," you ask, "who says we are called to change our society? Aren't we simply called to win the lost?"

My friend, do you realize what you're saying? When we win the lost, society *does* change, especially in times of spiritual outpouring. As I wrote in 1989:

When large numbers of sinners get saved, there is not so much sinning going on! Fewer murderers means lower murder rates. A decrease in thieves means a decline in theft. When drug dealers get delivered, drug dealing diminishes. In times of revival, bars are converted to churches, and pornographic theaters are used for evangelistic rallies. The owners have gotten saved!

This is not the only factor that impacts the society. God's people have come alive too! They are actively standing for righteousness. They are confronting sin on their jobs and ungodliness in their communities. Their lives have become truly holy. They shine forth God's light like a torch. Justice returns to the courts. Reverence returns to the schools. Jesus is Lord of this church![13]

AS BELIEVERS, WE ARE CALLED TO BE A PROPHETIC VOICE, TO EXPRESS THE HEART AND MIND OF THE SPIRIT, TO CONVICT, TO WARN, TO CRY OUT; TO COMFORT, TO HEAL, TO HELP.

Throughout history, the gospel has changed societies. Widow-burning was outlawed in India through the tireless efforts of William Carey.[14] Both slave-trading and unjust child-labor laws were abolished in England through the dauntless work of William Wilberforce. Around the world, the gospel has raised standards of education, of health care, of treatment of minorities, of human dignity. Whole books could be written on the subject. In fact, whole books *have* been written![15] And here in America, where nearly 100 million people profess to be evangelical believers, if *one-quarter* of them got *really right* with God it would quickly reverse our nation's moral decline. We are called to make a difference!

To say it again, our goal is revival, not survival—the transformation of our race, not the preservation of our race. As believers, we are called to advance God's kingdom on earth, "plundering hell to populate heaven," as Evangelist Reinhard Bonnke says. As believers, we are called to be a prophetic voice, to express the heart and mind of the Spirit, to convict, to warn, to cry out, to comfort, to heal, to help. This too will change a nation! And as exiles here in this world, we are called to bless and pray for the nation in which we live. As God said to the people of Judah exiled in Babylon, "And seek the welfare of the city where I have sent you into exile, and pray to the LORD on its behalf; for in its welfare you will have welfare" (Jer. 29:7, *NASB*; for a New Testament parallel, see 1 Tim. 2:1-4).

We can say without exaggeration that the direction of our nation hangs in the balance, and that's why so many are hearing the Spirit say, "Let's start a revolution!" That's why the words of William Booth's 100-year-old hymn "Send the Fire" have been set to contemporary music. The theme is so relevant. As one of the stanzas implores:

> God of Elijah, hear our cry—
> Send the fire!
> And make us fit to live or die—
> Send the fire today!
>
> To burn out every trace of sin,
> To bring the light and glory in,
> The revolution now begin—
> Send the fire today!

Through William and Catherine Booth and the Salvation Army, a revolution did begin, a revolution of gospel fire, gospel passion, and gospel sacrifice. We need another revolution today, a revolution more radical, more far-reaching, more impacting, more powerful, more anointed, more world-shaking. America is ready for it! Sin has reigned far too long; too many lives have been cut short and destroyed; too much darkness fills the land. It's time for the Church to rise up in the red-hot fire of revival! It's time for the Church to hit the streets in the demonstration of the Spirit. It's time for the world to see and know that Jesus is Lord, that He has truly risen from the dead, that the power of Satan has been broken.

God has uniquely positioned this generation to march in the front lines of the battle right up to the gates of hell. If we will follow the spirit of the apostles and martyrs and not count our own lives dear, if we will give ourselves unconditionally to make Jesus known, our nation will be shaken. It's time!

But let's be realists. The reason why Satan has been winning the battle for this generation is that his servants are more hungry, more committed, more serious, more devoted than most of the servants of the Lord. This must stop now! Let us *today*, in the words of eighteenth-century German religious reformer Count von Zinzendorf, "go and win for the Lamb the reward of His sacrifice."[16] He is so worthy and His work is so wonderful! Just think of the fruit of His labors: Hopeless sinners become holy saints. Lost perverts become loving parents. Murderers become missionaries, and the debilitated are liberated. The hurting are healed, the wounded made whole, and the outcasts finally find a home. Sin stains *are* lost in His life-giving flow. The work of Satan *is* destroyed. What a message we have! What a Master we have!

Our gospel is a gospel of liberty from sin and all of its entanglements, a declaration of freedom and forgiveness, a message of hope with the promise of heaven. It is a proclamation of amnesty, a pronouncement that almighty God is ready to change the most rebellious sinner into His very own son or daughter. It is not just good news, it is extraordinary news, almost unbelievable news. It is the best news human ears could ever hear. And it is our privilege to make it known! What stops us from proclaiming it? What hinders us from declaring it? Who or what is holding us back?

We have the most wonderful, revolutionary message the world has ever heard. Let us shout it from the rooftops. Let us live it on the campuses, in the workplaces, in the schoolrooms, on the streets, in the homes. Let us demonstrate to the world once and for all the true potential of the gospel of Jesus. Dare we live and die without finding out just what God could do through a truly dedicated life?

Naturally, there will be a battle as you live your life here on Earth. Many causes will vie for your affection and many projects will clamor for your attention. But only one of them is worthy.

Mao Zedong was wrong. Che Guevara was wrong. Timothy Leary was wrong. Jesus and His cause are right!

So count the cost, hatch a plan, and take the plunge. The revolution now begins!

Chapter Four

Subversive Speech:
The Language of Revolution

To a person endowed with prophetic sight, everyone else appears
blind; to a person whose ear perceives God's voice, everyone else
appears deaf. . . . The prophet hates the approximate, he shuns the
middle of the road. Man must live on the summit to avoid the abyss.
The prophet's word is a scream in the night. While the world is at
ease and asleep, the prophet feels the blast from heaven. . . .
The prophet is human, yet he employs notes one octave too high for
our ears. . . . Often his words begin to burn where conscience ends.

ABRAHAM JOSHUA HESCHEL
THE PROPHETS

If a so-called religious belief is not radical, we must suspect
that it is mere superstition. The profession of a religious belief is a
lie if it does not significantly determine one's economic,
political and social behaviour.

M. SCOTT PECK
THE DIFFERENT DRUM

The Christians form among themselves secret societies that exist outside the system of laws . . . an obscure and mysterious community
founded on revolt and on the advantage that accrues from it.

ACCUSATION BROUGHT AGAINST THE CHRISTIANS BY CELSUS,
SECOND CENTURY

Most of us are so familiar with the story of the crucifixion that it hardly strikes us as odd. After all, it was God's plan for His Son to die on the cross, and Jesus came for that very purpose, right? Yes, He did come to give His life, but the striking fact is that Jesus didn't simply die. He was *killed*. Why?

Why did people hate Him so intensely? Why did they plot and scheme to take His life? Why did they have so much hostility toward Him? Why did people oppose Him so viciously? Why did they reject Him and malign Him? Why did they nail the Son of God to a tree?

These are not just abstract, theoretical questions. Our Savior was perfect in every way. He was the very image of God in human form, the most flawless and complete expression of pure love the world had ever seen. He was goodness personified, faithfulness magnified, compassion exemplified. Why would anyone want to murder Him? What was it that was so threatening about Him? I know that He was often confrontational and this would have certainly stirred up opposition. But *murdering* Him?

Let's take this a step further. Why would anyone want to kill His followers? Why would anyone want to imprison them or hurt them or persecute them? Why would anyone want to burn to death a humanitarian missionary and his two boys? (This happened in January 1999, in Orissa, India.) Why would anyone want to torture and then behead a young Christian nursing mother? (This happened in the year 203 in Rome.) Why is it that as many as 2 million Christians were killed for their faith in the last 20 years of the twentieth century? These people were not thieves or murderers or liars or criminals. They were not rabble-rousers or troublemakers. They were simply followers of Jesus. Why did the world treat them with such harshness, such cruelty? Why were they treated the very same way their Lord was treated?

Certainly, there are many reasons for persecution. Some people are afraid of anything new or foreign, and often, that's how a new religious message or messenger can appear.[1] This sometimes results in violent persecution. In other settings, people get jealous when someone else gets the attention, and they try to snuff out the competition. (We know that jealousy was a factor in the rejection of both Jesus and His apostles: see Matt 27:18; Acts 5:17,18.) But there is more to the equation. There is more than a simple psychological or sociological explanation.

You might say the whole problem is that sinful human beings don't want God in their lives, and they will reject—with force if necessary—anyone who tries to impose His standards on them.

This is a major factor in persecution. Jesus taught that "everyone who does evil hates the light, and will not come into the light for fear that his deeds will be exposed" (John 3:20; cf. Eph. 5:11-14); we know that the prophets were scorned and rejected because they brought God's rebuke to a hard-hearted nation. To the extent that people don't want the Lord in their lives, they don't want His faithful servants either. That's why the Lord said:

> If the world hates you, keep in mind that it hated me first. If you belonged to the world, it would love you as its own. As it is, you do not belong to the world, but I have chosen you out of the world. That is why the world hates you. Remember the words I spoke to you: "No servant is greater than his master." If they persecuted me, they will persecute you also. If they obeyed my teaching,

they will obey yours also. They will treat you this way because of my name, for they do not know the One who sent me. If I had not come and spoken to them, they would not be guilty of sin. Now, however, they have no excuse for their sin. He who hates me hates my Father as well (John 15:18-23).

These, then, are some of the reasons why God's Messiah and God's messengers have been given over to slaughter like so many innocent sheep. But there is something else you must see. *Jesus and His followers have been rejected, and continue to be rejected, because they are a threat to this world's system.* The light is a threat to the darkness. Truth is a threat to lies. God's kingdom is a threat to Satan's kingdom. Holiness is a threat to sin. Freedom is a threat to bondage. Just ask the drug lords in Colombia who tried to kill Cesar Castellanos, the pastor of Mission Charismatica Internacional in Bogota, one of the world's fastest-growing churches. Jesus messed up their business! They were losing their clientele, their influence, their money, and their kingdom.[2]

That's why King Herod, upon learning that *another* Jewish king had just been born, did his best to kill the royal infant (see Matt. 2:13,16). There was only room for one king! And that's why the synagogue leaders began to plot how they might kill Jesus immediately after he healed a cripple on the Sabbath and violated their traditions (see Matt. 12:1-14). How dare He undermine the Establishment! And that's why the chief priests made plans to kill both Jesus and Lazarus after the Lord raised Lazarus from the dead and a large crowd came to see them (see John 12:9,10). Such miracles exposed the emptiness of religion without power! And that's why, when great crowds followed Jesus and hung on His every word, the religious leadership knew they *had* to find a sly way to put Him to death (see Mark 11:1-18; 14:1). They were about to lose their hold on the masses!

After the Lord's crucifixion, when reports began to spread of His resurrection, the leaders denied that He was alive (they couldn't try to kill Him again!), spreading their own report that His body was stolen from the tomb (see Matt. 28:1-15). If people were to find out He had risen, the man-made religious system would collapse!

Simply stated, Jesus was a threat. His message was a threat; His miracles were a threat; His lifestyle was a threat; His standards were a threat. He was, and still is, the embodiment of the anti-Establishment mentality—when the Establishment is anti-God. The fact is that *most* of this world's Establishment—whether it is the religious establishment or the entertainment establishment or the crime establishment or the media establishment or the sports establishment—is either hostile to God or devoid of God. That's why the gospel is such a threat to the world system, even though the gospel message is actually one of peace and reconciliation.

Consider for a moment that it was Paul the apostle who urged "that requests, prayers, intercession and thanksgiving be made for everyone—for kings and all those in authority, that we may live peaceful and quiet lives in all godliness and holiness" (1 Tim. 2:1,2). It was Paul who taught that "everyone must submit himself to the governing authorities, for there is no authority except that which God has established. The authorities that exist have been established by God. Consequently, he who rebels against the authority is rebelling against what God has instituted, and those who do so will bring judgment on themselves" (Rom. 13:1,2). And it was Paul who encouraged Titus to "remind the people to be subject to rulers and authorities, to be obedient, to be ready to do whatever is good, to slander no one, to be peaceable and considerate, and to show true humility toward all men" (Titus 3:1,2).

Yet Paul was accused by Roman citizens of "throwing [the city of Philippi] into an uproar by advocating customs unlawful for us Romans to accept or practice" (Acts 16:20,21). And Paul was accused in Ephesus of being one of those "who have subverted the whole world" (Acts 17:6, as rendered by F. F. Bruce).[3] And Paul was accused by his own Jewish people of being "the man who teaches all men everywhere against our people and our law and this place" (Acts 21:28). His presence in the Temple actually threw the whole city of Jerusalem into an uproar (see Acts 21:27-37; 22:1-24ff)! Throughout the book of Acts, attempts are made to take Paul's life.[4] Why?

The answer is found in Acts 17:1-7. There is something revolutionary here! We'll read the relevant context in full:

When they had passed through Amphipolis and Apollonia, they came to Thessalonica, where there was a Jewish synagogue. As his custom was, Paul went into the synagogue, and on three Sabbath days he reasoned with them from the Scriptures, explaining and proving that the Christ had to suffer and rise from the dead. "This Jesus I am proclaiming to you is the Christ," he said. Some of the Jews were persuaded and joined Paul and Silas, as did a large number of God-fearing Greeks and not a few prominent women. But the Jews were jealous; so they rounded up some bad characters from the marketplace, formed a mob and started a riot in the city. They rushed to Jason's house in search of Paul and Silas in order to bring them out to the crowd. But when they did not find them, they dragged Jason and some other brothers before the city officials, shouting: "These men who have caused trouble all over the world have now come here, and Jason has welcomed them into his house. They are all defying Caesar's decrees, saying that there is another king, one called Jesus."

Did you catch it? "These men who have caused trouble all over the world have now come here. . . . They are all defying Caesar's decrees, saying that there is another king, one called Jesus." Wow! It sounds just like the accusation lodged against Paul and Silas one chapter earlier: "These men are Jews, and are throwing our city into an uproar by advocating customs unlawful for us Romans to accept or practice" (Acts 16:20,21). And *this* sounds just like the accusation brought against Stephen in Acts 6:13,14: "This fellow never stops speaking against this holy place and against the law. For we have heard him say that this Jesus of Nazareth will destroy this place and change the customs Moses handed down to us."

Troublemakers! Revolutionaries! You are inciting rebellion by proclaiming a different king—thereby threatening Caesar's kingdom—and by advocating different customs—thereby threatening the social and religious order. You are guilty of subversive speech!

New Testament scholar F. F. Bruce explains the gravity of the charge brought against the believers in Acts 17:

A most serious complaint was lodged against the missionaries and their hosts. Jason and his friends were charged with harboring Jewish agitators, political messianists such as had stirred up unrest in other cities of the Roman Empire. Rome and Alexandria had recently experienced such trouble; now, said the accusers, the troublemakers had come to Thessalonica. Their seditious and revolutionary activity was not only illegal in itself; they were actually proclaiming one, Jesus, as a rival emperor to him who ruled in Rome.[5]

The Greek word actually used in Acts 17:6, translated into the word "subverted" by Bruce and into "turned upside down" by other versions, is found only two other times in the New Testament—once in Galatians 5:12, in the sense of "unsettle," and once in Acts 21:38, in the sense of "incite a revolt." According to the Greek scholar Adolph Deissmann, the verb means "to incite to tumult, stir up to sedition, unsettle," while a major Greek dictionary suggests meanings for the word as strong as "to cause people to rebel against or to reject authority."[6] We're on to something here!

Of course, we know that, in one sense, the accusations were entirely untrue. As Calvin noted, "This is also the maliciousness of the enemies of Christ, to lay the blame of tumults upon holy and modest teachers, which they themselves procure."[7]

The Methodist commentator Adam Clarke, who witnessed identical scenes in his own day, also noted that the unruly mob, "having made this sedition and disturbance, charged the whole on the peaceable and innocent apostles!"[8] How ironic! A few unsavory people get mad at the believers, round up some bad characters and stir up a crowd until there is a near riot, and then they lay the blame for the disturbance on the peace-loving preachers. And notice what Clark identifies as the main charge brought against believers: "Persecutors always strive to affect the lives of the objects of their hatred, by accusing them of sedition, or plots against the state."[9]

There it is again! Sedition. Plots against the state. Fomenting rebellion. Inciting revolt. This sounds like revolution!

"But now I'm confused!" you say. "If the charges aren't true, where is the 'revolution'? If the accusations are false, why make anything out of them?"

I'm glad you asked! You see, the specifics of the accusations are false, but the spirit behind them is true.

Paul and the apostles *were* advocating loyalty to Christ above loyalty to Caesar—even though the Lord's kingdom was not of this world—so when believers were ordered to bow down before Caesar or his image, they refused. They would not call him lord because they had another Lord.

The apostles *were* introducing different customs and practices, even if those practices were not actually forbidden to Romans or unlawful to Jews.[10] So when Paul and Peter had table fellowship with uncircumcised Gentiles—something unthinkable to a traditional Jew—or when they called Roman citizens to submit to Jesus as Lord—something considered either illegal or highly irregular—they were ridiculed and rejected, misunderstood and maligned.

The Lord's servants were a threat to the Establishment then, and the Lord's servants are a threat to the Establishment now. The gospel is subversive, because the world has set itself against God.

Commenting on Acts 16:20,21, New Testament and Semitic scholar Joseph Fitzmyer writes:

Paul is charged with preaching a non-Roman cult, a mode of worship and practices that Romans do not welcome. A Roman could not adopt Judaism without liability according to Roman penal code; Cicero, *De legibus* 2.8.19: "No one shall have gods for himself, either new or foreign gods, unless they are officially recognized" (*nisi publice adscitos*, i.e., acknowledged by the state).[11]

Do you see why conflicts arose? "No one shall have gods for himself, either new or foreign gods, unless they are officially recognized." Paul and Silas, the state doesn't recognize your gods!

Another top New Testament Greek scholar, A. T. Robertson, makes an interesting observation on the charges of subversion brought against the apostles in Acts 17: "There is truth in the accusation," he notes, "for Christianity is revolutionary, but on this particular occasion the uproar (verse 5) was created by the [Jewish leaders] and the hired loafers."[12] Yes, the uproar was the work of unruly opposition, but what stirred up the opposition was the revolutionary nature of the message!

Church historian W. C. Frend comments, "Paul was preaching a revolutionary religion of conversion and commitment to Christ, a new exodus based on a new Torah."[13] Take note of the words of these careful scholars: "Christianity is revolutionary"; "Paul was preaching a revolutionary religion." It is no less revolutionary and confrontational today.[14]

Juan Carlos Ortiz, with some literary flourish, sheds more light on the mind-set encountered by the first believers:

> The Greek word *kurios* ("lord") in small letters was how slaves addressed their masters. But if the word was capitalized, it referred to only one person in the whole Roman Empire. Caesar of Rome was *the Lord*. As a matter of fact, when public employees and soldiers met in the street, they had to say as a greeting, "Caesar is the Lord!" And the standard response was, "Yes, the Lord is Caesar."
>
> So, the Christians had a problem. When they were greeted with "Caesar is the Lord!" they answered, "No, Jesus Christ is the Lord!" That immediately got them in trouble. Not because Caesar was jealous of the name. It

was far deeper than that. Caesar knew that the Christians really meant that they were committed to another authority and that in the balance scale of their lives, Jesus Christ weighed much more than Caesar.

They were saying, "Caesar, you can count on us for some things, but when forced to choose, we will stay with Jesus, because we have committed our lives to Him. He is the first one. He is the Lord, the maximum authority over us." No wonder Caesar persecuted the Christians.[15]

How threatening it is to the Caesars of any age when Jesus outweighs them in importance and authority!

In the Islamic world, if a Muslim converts to another religion, his own family has the legal right to kill him. Conversion *away* from the alleged true faith upsets everything and is totally undermining to the whole system. Perhaps someone else will convert too!

In the Communist world, mere faith in God is a terrible threat to the stifling, atheistic system, while absolute allegiance to any "party"—like the Church—other than the Communist Party is considered high treason. No divided loyalties can be tolerated!

Therefore I say without hesitation: The gospel is subversive. It is the ultimate revolutionary message. It is the supreme countercul-

> THE GOSPEL IS THE ULTIMATE REVOLUTIONARY MESSAGE. IT SAYS WE ARE GOVERNED BY A HIGHER AUTHORITY, RULED BY ANOTHER POWER, AT HOME IN A DIFFERENT WORLD.

ture philosophy. It says this world is not our eternal home and this world's system does not rule us or govern us. We are governed by a higher authority, ruled by another power, at home in a different world. And this is the message we spread. This is the mind-set we espouse.

James D. G. Dunn, a leading New Testament commentator, makes this observation on the motivation for the attack against the Jewish apostles by the Thessalonian Jews who rejected their message:

> That which was a threat to their own peace and established way of life they accused of being a threat to the law and order of society at large. The claims of the exalted and soon coming Jesus upon personal life and relationships in his gospel were so far-reaching that they could be misrepresented as the claims of an earthly tyrant, and Jesus portrayed as a rival to Caesar.[16]

Looking at this through the eyes of Jews who did not believe Jesus was the Messiah, can you understand why Paul's preaching was "a threat to their own peace and established way of life"? Just think of how unnerving it must have been to Paul's coreligionists when he, the arch-persecutor of the Jesus movement, became that movement's most zealous advocate.

After following Jesus, his Messiah, for years, Paul tried to share his testimony with a large Jewish crowd outside the Temple in Jerusalem: "The whole city was aroused, and the people came running from all directions. Seizing Paul, they dragged him from the temple, and immediately the gates were shut. While they were trying to kill him, news reached the commander of the Roman troops that the whole city of Jerusalem was in an uproar" (Acts 21:30,31).

When he finally was able to speak and they really understood what he was saying, things got even worse! "They raised
their voices and shouted, 'Rid the earth of him! He's not fit to
live!' As they were shouting and throwing off their cloaks and
flinging dust into the air, the commander ordered Paul to be
taken into the barracks" (Acts 22:22-24). Even the Roman soldier had Paul's real identity confused: "Aren't you the Egyptian
who started a revolt and led four thousand terrorists out into
the desert some time ago?"[17]

"Troublemaker! Traitor! Rebel! He's no longer one of us.
Let's kill him!" How threatening this one man was. How unnerving his new allegiance was. How dangerous his new perspective
was. How menacing his new message was. "Paul, you are guilty
of subversive speech!" He was![18]

Look at how the early believers responded to the Establishment
when that Establishment set itself against God. We read in Acts
4 that the religious leadership tried to shut down Peter's preaching after the miraculous healing of the lame man in Acts 3.
These men were Sadducees—Jews who did not believe in the resurrection of the dead—and "they were greatly disturbed because
the apostles were teaching the people and proclaiming in Jesus
the resurrection of the dead" (Acts 4:2, emphasis added). How subversive!

After seizing the apostles and deliberating between themselves, "they called them in again and commanded them not to
speak or teach at all in the name of Jesus. But Peter and John
replied, 'Judge for yourselves whether it is right in God's sight to
obey you rather than God. For we cannot help speaking about
what we have seen and heard'" (Acts 4:18-20).

What the apostles were saying was "Sorry, but we're not complying. You can order us not to testify, but we *must* testify. We can do no other!"

Soon enough, the leadership, filled with envy because of the apostles' success, had them arrested and put in jail. "But during the night an angel of the Lord opened the doors of the jail and brought them out. 'Go, stand in the temple courts,' he said, 'and tell the people the full message of this new life.' At daybreak they entered the temple courts, *as they had been told*, and began to teach the people" (Acts 5:19-21, emphasis added).

The apostles simply did what they were told by the Lord, not by man. The Establishment said, "Don't speak!" The Lord said, "Speak!" So they spoke! And notice that the angel of the Lord was not intimidated by the fleshly control of man. "Go, stand in the temple courts," he said, "and tell the people the full message of this new life." How utterly subversive! And how brazen it was too—at the Lord's command.

This time the high priest was incensed: "'We gave you strict orders not to teach in this name,' he said. 'Yet you have filled Jerusalem with your teaching and are determined to make us guilty of this man's blood.' Peter and the other apostles replied: 'We must obey God rather than men!'" (Acts 5:28,29). So they flogged the apostles and "ordered them not to speak in the name of Jesus" (Acts 5:40). These leaders meant business! They were deeply religious men, and they were not about to let this heretical movement flourish during their watch. They were going to snuff it out—by force, if necessary.

And what was the attitude of the apostles? "The apostles left the Sanhedrin, rejoicing because they had been counted worthy of suffering disgrace for the Name" (Acts 5:41). At last! The world was treating them the way it treated their Master![19] And what was their response to the command not to speak in Jesus' name? "Day after day, in the temple courts and from house to house, they never stopped teaching and proclaiming the good news that Jesus is the [Messiah]" (Acts 5:42). How totally subversive!

In the year A.D. 123, the Roman government launched a severe crackdown against the Jews, culminating in A.D. 134, when all Jewish practices were forbidden, including circumcision, Torah study, and Sabbath observance. How did the rabbis respond? One of the noted leaders, Rabbi Hananiah ben Teradyon conducted *public* Torah classes, paying for it with his life. But this was no emotional, spur-of-the-moment decision. There was a rationale behind his actions, traceable back to Rabbi Akiva, the greatest rabbinic sage of that day (but not a believer in Yeshua), also martyred for his allegiance to Torah. The Talmud relates:

> Once the wicked Roman government issued a decree forbidding the Jews to study and practice the Torah. Pappus ben Judah came by and, upon finding Rabbi Akiva publicly holding sessions in which he occupied himself with Torah, Pappus asked him: "Akiva, are you not afraid of the government?" Rabbi Akiva replied: "You, Pappus, who are said to be wise, are in fact a fool. I can explain what I am doing by means of a parable: A fox was walking on a river bank and, seeing fishes hastening here and there, asked them, 'From whom are you fleeing?' They replied, 'From the nets and traps set for us by men.' So the fox said to them, 'How would you like to come up on dry land, so that you and I may live together the way my ancestors lived with yours?' They replied,

'You—the one they call the cleverest of animals—are in fact a fool. If we are fearful in the place where we can stay alive, how much more fearful should we be in a place where we are sure to die!' So it is with us. If we are fearful when we sit and study Torah, of which it is written, 'For that is thy life and the length of thy days' (Deut. 30:20), how much more fearful ought we to be should we cease the study of words of Torah!"[20]

I remember how embarrassed many of us felt as American believers when Richard Wurmbrand—a Jewish Christian brutally tortured for his faith during 14 years in Romanian prisons—asked us one time at a meeting: "When the Supreme Court banned public prayer in schools, why did you obey?" His gentle words were stinging! Here was a brother who was imprisoned three separate times for preaching the gospel. He was kept in solitary confinement for three years, beaten continuously on the soles of his feet, carved with knives and red-hot pokers, frozen to the brink of death, snapped in two like a broken doll—and still, upon his release from prison, he went back to preaching, not once, but twice. He could do no other. Why? It was because Jesus was His life.

It is one thing to submit to governing powers in every way possible, even when we strongly disagree. Peter himself counseled believers to "submit yourselves for the Lord's sake to every authority instituted among men: whether to the king, as the supreme authority, or to governors, who are sent by him to punish those who do wrong and to commend those who do right" (1 Pet. 2:13,14).

We, above all citizens, should be known as the most law-abiding, the most respectful of authority, the most honest, the most honorable, the most trustworthy. Jesus called us to be meek, to be merciful, to be peacemakers (see Matt. 5:5,7,9). However, when the governing powers—religious or secular— *require* us to *disobey* God, we must refuse to comply, even if it costs us our lives. At that time—when the government tells us we cannot share our faith or pray or baptize new converts or read our Bibles—we say with the apostles, "We must obey God rather than men!"[21]

What does this mean in terms of our contemporary culture? Or, to consider this from another angle, if Jesus were here in the flesh today—I mean, living among us in twenty-first-century America—what kind of opposition would He face? And from what quarters? What accusations would come against Him? Would it be the religious crowd—in particular, the hard-hearted leadership—that would attack Him and plot to kill Him? And what if Paul and the apostles were here? What kind of charges would be brought against them? How would their message and ministry pose a threat to the Establishment? On what basis would people claim they were trying to incite a revolt? A revolt against whom, against what?

In the midst of profanity-laden, brutal interrogation in Communist China, a young Christian woman named Sheng was verbally assaulted with these words:

> You bunch of _____ (swearing), you have fouled the atmosphere and brought trouble to the people and government of these two districts and three countries. You have brought disorder to our work. Don't you realize how serious are the crimes you have committed?[22]

This sounds just like Acts, doesn't it!

You see, during Mao's Cultural Revolution, there was an attempt to eradicate the "four outmoded ways," namely, "old culture, old customs, old habits, and old ways of thinking."[23] Ancestor worship was opposed. Buddha worship was opposed. Only Chairman Mao was to be revered. Loyalty to the party became more important than loyalty to one's own family. Everyone had to conform to Mao's established norm. And thus his revolution replaced allegiance to the old system with even greater allegiance to the new system.[24] All those who resisted paid dearly.

Where does Christianity fit in with all this? It doesn't! "Followers of Jesus, you have fouled the atmosphere and brought trouble to the people and government! You are undermining everything we are trying to do!"

As a little girl in Communist Chinese schools, Niu-Niu (and all the other students) began each day by chanting: "Good morning, Mao [Zedong]," after which they were required to answer four questions out loud: "Do you love Mao? Will you follow Mao all your life? Are you a good child of Mao's? Do you have something to confess to Mao?"[25] There was no room here for loving devotion to another, greater Master!

Joseph Fitzmyer gives a similar perspective from the ancient Roman world:

Because Paul has proclaimed Jesus as "the Messiah" (Acts 17:3), his opponents deduce that Jesus must be regarded as *basileus* [king], knowing how ill the title "king" would sit with Romans. The implication is sedition and high treason. . . . Compare the so-called Oath of Gangra from 3 B.C., in which the one who swears promises to support "Caesar Augustus, his children and descendants throughout my life in word, deed, and thought . . . that whenever I see or hear of anything being said, planned, or done against them I will report it."[26]

What loyalty—and to a mere human, at that! There is no room for competing kings here. The loyal follower of Caesar made it clear that he would stand against and expose anyone who tried to plot against his beloved leader. Through the centuries, God's people have faced similar opposition from the state—be it Greek, Roman, Islamic, or Communist:

> Let no one have gods of his own, neither new ones nor strange ones, but only those instituted by the State. No one may hold meetings at night in the city.[27]

> Of those who introduce new religions with unknown customs or methods by which the minds of the people could be disturbed, those of the upper classes shall be deported, and those of the lower classes shall be put to death.[28]

> These people [Christians], who have refused to sacrifice to the gods and do not obey the command of the Emperor, shall be scourged and taken away to be beheaded according to the laws.[29]

> When we [Christians] assert that he who ordered this universe is one God, then, incomprehensibly, a law is put in force against us.[30]

Tertullian (160-225) expressed the reaction of the godless government to the beliefs of the early Christians:

> We are charged with being irreligious people and, what is more, irreligious in respect to the emperors since we refuse to pay religious homage to their spiritual majesties and refuse to swear by them.

High treason is a crime of offense against the
Roman religion. It is a crime of open irreligion, a raising
of the hand to injure the deity . . . Christians are considered to be enemies of the State, enemies of the public
well-being. . . .

We wage a battle when we are challenged to face the
tribunals of law. There, in peril of life, we give testimony
for the truth. Guards and informers bring up accusations against the Christians as sexual deviants and murderers, blasphemers and traitors, enemies of public life,
desecrators of temples, and criminals against the religion of Rome.[31]

The anti-God Establishment tolerates no rivals! And the
Lord, on His part, tolerates no rivals either (rightly so!). His first
commandment to Israel was "You shall have no other gods
before me" (Exod. 20:3). He demands our exclusive loyalty.
Obeying Him in this regard creates some intense conflicts along
the way and deeply challenges the other systems we reject.

According to the philosophy of militant Islam—another
totalitarian regime—"weeds" must be plucked out of Allah's garden. Certainly, those calling on Muslims to reject the authority
of Muhammad and submit instead to the teaching of Jesus are
classified as weeds! Sayyid Muhammad Qutb, a prominent
Egyptian fundamentalist leader, explains the general concept:

The world is a beautiful garden created for Man by Allah.
The creator of the garden has sent us His directions for
its use in the form of revealed religion. What is the central message of these divine directions? It is, simply, to
root out the weed that grows wild in this garden and
that, if allowed to spring up and to spread, will smother

it to death. Now who is to stop the weed, to eliminate it [altogether]? The answer is every one of us. For every one of the believers must fight this war.[32]

It is not hard to imagine how threatening the gospel is in such a society. And it's not hard to imagine what happens to Muslims who leave "the straight path" (this is how they refer to Islam) and become devoted followers of Jesus the Son of God. If "killing a hypocrite who refuses to reform is more worthy than a thousand prayers"—according to the notorious Iranian judge, Ayatollah Muhammad Muhammed Guilani[33] —what is the reward for killing someone who renounced Islam in favor of Christianity? How meritorious is an act like that?[34]

THE GOSPEL MESSAGE SNATCHES PEOPLE FROM THE CLUTCHES OF THE DEVIL AND DELIVERS THEM SAFELY INTO THE ARMS OF FATHER GOD. SATAN HATES THAT WITH ALL HIS DIABOLICAL MIGHT.

The gospel snatches people from the clutches of the devil and delivers them safely into the arms of Father God. Satan hates that with all his diabolical might. How threatened he must feel when the Church arises in power! Here in America, at the beginning of the twenty-first century, Satan is feeling threatened by the gospel. His kingdom is coming under fire. His strongholds are being attacked. And that's why he is fighting back so fiercely.

But how, exactly, is Satan's kingdom being threatened in America? What demonic worldview is being subverted by the Word of God? Obviously, believers in America are not fighting against Communism or Islam. No. Those are not the worldviews being opposed by the gospel today in the United States. But there is *another* worldview in our country, a worldview more subtle than Communism or Islam—although it is surely just as satanic—that is directly threatened by the gospel, since the gospel calls for loyalty to another (heavenly) King and another (heavenly) kingdom. And this system will not go down without a violent fight.

What, then, is this system and who is it that would consider us a threat today? What system would fight us so fiercely? And why would anyone want to kill *us*? Why, for that matter, would a deranged, heavily armed teenager ask another unarmed teenager, "Do you believe in God?" before cutting her down in cold blood after she said yes? Those now-famous words, "Yes, I believe"—spoken in the midst of the Columbine massacre—probably cost two young women their lives. Why would faith in God be such a threat?[35]

Little by little, the world is beginning to treat us the same way it treated Jesus and Paul and Silas and Peter and Stephen, the same way it is treating countless persecuted believers all over the earth today. Why?

There are cultural idols we are called to smash, godless mentalities we are called to subvert. Two kingdoms are in conflict, two worldviews on a collision course, and we are caught up in the clash of the ages. Jesus is enlisting troops for this holy revolution, and the strongholds of this world are being threatened.

Now, breathe a word of prayer before you turn the page. What you read may threaten *your* world.

Chapter Five

Exposing the Gods of This Age: The Ideology of Revolution

When a prophet is accepted and deified, his message is lost. The prophet is only useful so long as he is stoned as a public nuisance, calling us to repentance, disturbing our comfortable routines, breaking our respectable idols, shattering our sacred conventions.

A. G. GARDINER

Our expectation of [God's] kingdom cannot be a passive waiting, a sweet, soft occupation with ourselves and our likeminded friends. No; if we truly expect God's kingdom we will be filled with divine power. Then the social justice of the future—with its purity of heart and divine fellowship—will be realized now, wherever Jesus himself is present. Our belief in the future must bring change to the present!

EBERHARD ARNOLD
GOD'S REVOLUTION

The prophet is an iconoclast, challenging the apparently holy, revered, and awesome. Beliefs cherished as certainties, institutions endowed with supreme sanctity, he exposes as scandalous pretensions.

ABRAHAM JOSHUA HESCHEL
THE PROPHETS

Shortly after Richard Wurmbrand was exiled from Romania following 14 years of brutal imprisonment for his faith, he was speaking at a home meeting in suburban America. When the meeting ended, one of the men present asked Pastor Wurmbrand, "Why is it that we don't have to deal with Communism here in America?"

This was an important question! After all, Wurmbrand had suffered unspeakable agony because of the Communists, and his wife, Sabina, had languished in a slave labor camp for years, separated from her husband and their son. Some of their best friends and colleagues had been killed for their faith, while others had been tortured and endured hardships beyond description. Why was it that America had been spared the horrors of Communism? Why was it that the Church here had escaped the fury of atheistic persecution? How did Pastor Wurmbrand respond?

We might have expected him to say, "It is because of your national heritage! It is because you have not built or accepted a Communist government, because there are too many believers in your country to allow such a thing to happen, because the Church has consistently cried out to God." Yes, he could well have responded like this, and to a great extent, he would have been correct. But that was not his answer. Instead he replied, "You don't have Communism here; you have something far worse. You have materialism!"

What chilling, unsettling words! Materialism worse than Communism? Materialism a greater menace to the Church than atheistic persecution? How can this be? Some radical Islamic leaders can explain.

You see, Muslim clergy do not presently consider the gospel to be the greatest threat to their religion, nor are Christians the primary targets of the Islamic holy war. After all, there is only one full-time Christian worker for every one million Muslims, and the slow-but-sure progress we are making is not gripping the attention of Muslims worldwide. What then is perceived to be the greatest threat to radical Islam? Western worldliness!

Listen to Ayatollah Fazl-Ali Mahalati:

> Islam was defeated by its own rulers, who ignored the Divine Law in the name of Western-style secularism. The West captured the imagination of large sections of our people. And that conquest was far more disastrous than any loss of territory. It is not for the loss of Andalusia [i.e., the parts of Spanish-speaking Europe once ruled by Islam] that we ought to weep every evening—although that remains a bleeding wound. Far graver is the loss of large sections of our youth to Western ideology, dress, music and food.[1]

Western ways are the real enemy! By Islamic moral standards, America is the great Satan, and Europe is America's closest ally in exporting godlessness. A newspaper correspondent writing for *USA Today* gave this insightful report of an evening he spent with Islamic terrorists in Egypt:

> As the night wears on, the militants grow more angry and more expressive. They turn their attention to the immorality of Westerners, whom they regularly refer to as "infidels." They cite figures on the divorce rate in the United States. They point to crime and drug use. They talk about America's preoccupation with sex. "You will never find these things where true Islam exists," argues Ziad Ali, 34. "Islam is the only answer, not Christianity, not Judaism, not Buddha. Without it, America is going

to hell." He points to a young Muslim woman outside the window below who is fully clothed from head to toe and even wearing gloves. Islamic practices vary from country to country but the norm is that women should cover their hair and bodies. . . . "That is how a woman must dress, not the way they dress in America, in Britain," Ali says. "In America, your women dress like harlots. They have no dignity. We want to change that here in Egypt so our harlots don't go to hell."[2]

Do you recognize the force of these words? "In America, your women dress like harlots"—and these Muslim extremists think that America is a Christian nation!

"But it's not a Christian nation," you may say. "Most Americans are not really born-again believers."

I agree! But you're missing two important points. First, there are tens of millions of professing believers in our land, yet the moral impact they make is negligible. Second, the lifestyle of most of those who really are believers is indistinguishable from the rest of the society. Trust me. These Islamic radicals would not be much more impressed with the standards of the American church than they are with the standards of our society at large. And what would these religious Muslims say if they heard that born-again Christians were more likely to go through a divorce than were non-Christians or that the divorce rate among atheists was lower than the divorce rate among evangelical Christians?[3]

Of course, as American followers of Jesus, we are appalled at the murderous violence of fanatical Islam. We are morally outraged when we hear of a Muslim terrorist blowing himself up on a crowded bus, killing and maiming men, women, and children. And when we read that he cried out, "Allahu Akbar!" ("Allah is great!")

before detonating the bomb, we shake our heads and think, *What hypocrisy!* And we're right! We have every reason to be outraged and appalled at such criminal behavior. Our feelings are completely justifiable. But do we realize that Muslims look at Christian America with similar feelings of moral outrage? Do we realize that many of their feelings are justifiable too?

> THE RELIGIOUS MUSLIM WORLD DOES NOT LOOK AT WESTERN CHRISTIANITY AS HYPOCRITICAL AS MUCH AS IT LOOKS AT IT AS PROOF THAT OUR RELIGION IS WORTH-LESS AND SHALLOW.

This is the sad indictment: The religious Muslim world does not look at Western Christianity as hypocritical as much as it looks at it as proof that our religion is worthless and shallow. As they compare the lifestyle of the average, committed American Christian with the lifestyle of the average, committed Muslim, they are convinced their faith is superior to ours. To put it bluntly, there is no need for a Wait Until Marriage movement among the religious Islamic youth! When Muslims look at those of us who profess to follow Jesus—the clothes we wear, the movies we watch, the standards we set, the prayers we pray, the decisions we make—they are appalled at our worldly ways. (The same could be said for religious Jews and even religious Hindus who see our brand of faith. It seems so shallow to them!)

That's why it is compromised Muslims who are the first targets of the Islamic holy war, as explained by Amir Taheri:

> The primary victims of Islamic terrorism are the Muslims themselves, for the emerging fundamentalist

movement throughout the Islamic world is still seeking
to establish political control of its own society before it
can mobilize the forces necessary for a global Holy War
against the City of War [meaning the non-Muslim
world]. Domestic enemies of Islam must be destroyed or
driven from power before the Partisans of Allah can
think of conquering other lands.[4]

It is for this reason that some Muslim radicals in Egypt
opposed their country's war against Israel, even though Israel
was the archenemy. And they were not surprised when Israel
crushed Egypt in just six days in June 1967. Why? Allah was not
with them, because Egypt had become too secular and worldly,
even opposing fundamentalist Islam. As one of the radicals
wrote from a military prison in May 1967:

> There is a lot of talk about war. Yet who is it who is going
> to fight? Those who prostrate themselves before idols,
> those who worship other deities than Allah? . . . Verily,
> God is not about to succor in battle people who have for-
> saken Him. . . . Can He bestow victory upon people who
> have been fighting Him, His religion, and His true
> believers, massacring and torturing them, inflicting
> upon them imprisonment and humiliation?[5]

Yes, it is worldly Muslims who are idol worshipers, worldly
Muslims who must be opposed.

Now, before anyone misunderstands my point, I want to
make it clear that I am not saying we should espouse Islamic
dress, nor am I saying that we should espouse the Islamic treatment of women, the Islamic system of justice, the Islamic ban on
music, the Islamic method of legislating religion, or the Islamic

philosophy of Jihad (violent holy war).[6] That faith is deadly and destructive, a far cry from life in the Spirit and liberty in Jesus, and it is a poor substitute for fellowship with the living God. For all its boasts, it brings people into bondage rather than freedom. I am not saying we should emulate Islam!

What I am saying is this: We are far more worldly than we know! We are far more compromised than we imagine! In fact, from a biblical standpoint, typical Muslim morality is closer to the Scriptures than is typical Christian morality (as practiced in the West); and the typical Muslim view of loyalty to God is closer to the Scriptures than the typical Christian view of loyalty to God (as lived out in the West).[7] That's why Islam considers Western worldliness to be its greatest enemy. How strange it is that we Christians in the West embrace this enemy with open arms.

But no more! A holy awakening is spreading through the land and our revolution begins right here by smashing the idols of this age, confronting the gods of this world, breaking their hold over the Church, exposing and expelling this subtle enemy from our ranks.

Do you remember one of the strategies of Mao Zedong's Cultural Revolution? The "outmoded ways" had to be eradicated. No more cultural idols! Only Mao's teachings would hold sway; only devotion to Mao—the Great Helmsman, the Sun, the Star—would be acceptable. Statues of Buddha had to be smashed; ancestor worship had to be eradicated. Competing ideologies would not be tolerated, and competing intellectual trends would be snuffed out—violently, if necessary. And snuffed out they were, costing tens of millions their lives. Such is the fruit of man-made, hell-inspired revolutions.[8]

But every revolution—whether peaceful or violent—will have a conflict with competing ideologies. Every revolution will have a battle with the idols of the age, and no revolution will feel the heat of battle more fiercely than the gospel revolution. We read about it in the book of Acts, where Paul's ministry clashed with the sinful kingdoms of this world. Because of Paul's teaching, coupled with miraculous demonstrations of the power of Jesus' name, the idol industry was losing business and the "great goddess Artemis" was losing worshipers. It caused such "a great disturbance" (Acts 19:23) that it led to a special planning meeting of the idol-makers union:

> "Men, you know we receive a good income from this busi-
> ness [said Demetrius, a silversmith with a thriving idol
> business]. And you see and hear how this fellow Paul has
> convinced and led astray large numbers of people here in
> Ephesus and in practically the whole province of Asia. He
> says that man-made gods are no gods at all. There is dan-
> ger not only that our trade will lose its good name, but
> also that the temple of the great goddess Artemis will be
> discredited, and the goddess herself, who is worshiped
> throughout the province of Asia and the world, will be
> robbed of her divine majesty." When they heard this, they
> were furious and began shouting: "Great is Artemis of the
> Ephesians!" Soon the whole city was in an uproar (Acts
> 19:25-29).

The gospel is subversive to idolatry! It says that "man-made gods are no gods at all." It proclaims Jesus as the one and only Lord, demanding complete allegiance to Him. All higher allegiances must be broken. That is revolutionary!

That's why Jesus said, "If anyone comes to me and does not hate his father and mother, his wife and children, his brothers and sisters—yes, even his own life—he cannot be my disciple" (Luke 14:26).

That's why He said, "Anyone who loves his father or mother more than me is not worthy of me; anyone who loves his son or daughter more than me is not worthy of me" (Matt. 10:37).

That's why He said to the man who wanted to bury his father and then follow Him, "Let the dead bury their own dead, but you go and proclaim the kingdom of God" (Luke 9:60), and to another would-be disciple, "No one who puts his hand to the plow and looks back is fit for service in the kingdom of God" (Luke 9:62). But this man had only wanted to go home and bid his family good-bye before becoming a follower of the Lord. How sternly Jesus rebuked him, and how stingingly His words rebuke us!

But don't they sound somewhat fanatical to our compromised Western ears? Can Jesus really mean what He said? Absolutely! He demands radical loyalty and ruthless love. His kingdom clashes with the kingdoms of this world; His holy revolution wages war against idolatry of every kind.[9]

That's why James could write, "Anyone who chooses to be a friend of the world becomes an enemy of God" (James 4:4); and John could state, "If anyone loves the world, the love of the Father is not in him" (1 John 2:15).

Paul exhorted all those who follow Christ,

Do not be yoked together with unbelievers. For what do righteousness and wickedness have in common? Or what fellowship can light have with darkness? What harmony is there between Christ and Belial? What does a believer have in common with an unbeliever? What agreement is there between the temple of God and idols? For we are the temple of the living God. . . . "Therefore come out from them and be separate, says the Lord. Touch no unclean thing, and I will receive you" (2 Cor. 6:14-17).

It is simply a matter of either-or, of serving one Lord or another. That's why Jesus taught emphatically that "no one can serve two masters. Either he will hate the one and love the other, or he will be devoted to the one and despise the other. You cannot serve both God and Money" (Matt. 6:24). It is impossible to serve two competing gods, and we will serve whatever we worship. That's why idolatry is so enslaving. We bow down to the gods we erect, as Jesus stated so emphatically: "No one can serve two masters."

When Yahweh gave the Ten Commandments to Israel, He began by saying, "I am the LORD your God, who brought you out of Egypt, out of the land of slavery. You shall have no other gods before me" (Exod. 20:2,3). Idolatry was Israel's greatest danger, and throughout Israel's history, idolatry was her greatest downfall. Because of that sin, a flood of evil engulfed them. When they lost their spiritual compass, they lost their moral bearings too.

"You shall have no other gods before me"—meaning in competition with Me, in place of Me, in front of Me, along with Me. "You shall not make for yourself an idol in the form of anything in heaven above or on the earth beneath or in the waters below. You shall not bow down to them or worship them; for I, the LORD your God, am a jealous God." (20:4,5).[10] The Lord alone was to be worshiped and obeyed. He would tolerate no rivals. And when they forsook Him, the fountain of living water, they opened the door to destruction: "This is what the LORD says: 'What fault did your fathers find in me, that they strayed so far from me? They followed worthless idols and became worthless themselves'" (Jer. 2:5).

Think of it! The unseen, eternal God delivered His people out of Egypt, but they exchanged worship of Him for the worship of images of gold and silver. Soon enough, they were not only worshiping worthless idols but serving them as well. False, man-made gods displaced the true God who made man. The Israelites became bound by the works of their own hands. How perverse! Yet this is what we have done too: We—meaning the believers, the born-again followers of Jesus, the blood-washed and redeemed people of God—have become idol worshipers, enslaved to the gods we have made.

"We have?" you exclaim. "How are we guilty of worshiping idols? I know that we have plenty of sexual sin in America, just like Israel did. And we have plenty of violence in America today, just like Israel did. We have plenty of injustice too, just like Israel did. But at least we don't have idol worship! At least we're not bowing down to gold and silver statues, like the Israelites did in Bible days and like the Hindus do today."

Really? Has human nature changed? Is it possible that we are faithfully keeping the first and greatest commandment—to love God with all our heart, soul, mind, and strength, refusing to bow down to idols of any kind—yet at the same time breaking all the other commandments on a regular basis—committing adultery, dishonoring our parents, ignoring the Sabbath, stealing, murdering, coveting, bearing false witness, taking God's name in vain? How can this be? It cannot!

Idolatry and sins of the flesh go hand in hand, and there is no way in this sex-saturated, pleasure-soaked society that we could be slaves to carnality and yet free from idolatry. One thing leads to another!

While Israel was staying in Shittim, the men began to indulge in sexual immorality with Moabite women, who invited them to the sacrifices to their gods. The people ate and bowed down before these gods. So Israel joined in worshiping the Baal of Peor. And the LORD'S anger burned against them (Num. 25:1-3).

Paul lists the acts of sinful human nature as, "sexual immorality, impurity and debauchery; idolatry and witchcraft; hatred, discord, jealousy, fits of rage, selfish ambition, dissensions, factions and envy; drunkenness, orgies, and the like" (Gal. 5:19-21). Where you have one you have another, like several symptoms that always accompany a particular disease. When that germ strikes your system, the other symptoms follow.

You will not commit murder if the Lord alone reigns supreme in your life. You will not be a fornicator if the Lord alone reigns supreme in your life. You will not break up your family if the Lord alone reigns supreme in your life. Our problem is that the Lord alone does not reign supreme in our lives. There are other gods among us! We Americans are a nation of idol worshipers, even if we claim the Lord as our God. Either the lusts of the flesh have lured us away from His lordship, or our fascination with other gods has led us into the lusts of the flesh. Either way, we have both immorality and idolatry in our midst. That's why God commanded the people of Israel to deal ruthlessly with idolatry when they entered the Promised Land: Don't worship the gods of the nations!

This is what you are to do to them: Break down their altars, smash their sacred stones, cut down their Asherah poles and burn their idols in the fire. For you are a people holy to the Lord your God. The LORD your God has chosen you out of all the peoples on the face of the earth

to be his people, his treasured possession (Deut. 7:5-6;
see also Exod. 23:24; Josh. 23:7).

What a clear directive: Idols and their altars are to be demol-
ished. Break them down; smash them to bits; cut them to pieces;
burn them up! Not surprisingly, whenever there was religious
reform in Israel and God's people turned back to Him, the first
thing they did was smash the idols in their midst, sometimes
pulverizing them into powder.[11] We must do the same! But
where do we begin? What are the idols God is calling us to
denounce and destroy?

An idol is anything that takes the place of God in your life—anything that you worship and adore in His stead. It is the thing that
absorbs you and dominates you, the thing that has your heart
and emotions, the thing that influences your will and guides
your life. It is that to which you give yourself, that which con-
sumes your energy and inspires your dreams, that which really is
the center of your life and the object of your adoration. That
is your god! That's why Paul wrote that greed (or covetousness) is
"idolatry" (Col. 3:5). Covetous desire is a deity!

Throughout the Word, we are warned against the lure of
materialism (see Deut. 8:10-20; Prov. 23:4,5; Matt. 6:19-26;
13:22; Luke 12:13-21; 16:1-31; 1 Tim. 6:6-19). But what do we do
if we have been raised in such a materialistic environment that
we are unaware of its influence over our lives? Who among us is
a willful, conscious, committed materialist? If you go to India
and say to an educated Hindu, "Why are you bowing down to a
piece of wood? That wood cannot save you!" he or she would
respond, "You don't understand. I'm not bowing down to wood

or stone. That is merely an earthly representation of the heavenly god I serve and adore." That's how it is with each of us. We don't realize we are also worshiping idols.

Professor Tony Campolo relates this amazing story. Before the collapse of the Soviet Union, he received a call from a friend with the Christian College Coalition, notifying him "that a group of top educators from the Soviet Union were coming to the United States" and that "they were interested in seeing the things religious groups here in the United States are doing in the way of social service." This was right up Campolo's alley, since he was not only an educator but the head of several inner-city ministries as well. So he rolled out the red carpet for his guests: "With great enthusiasm I took them to our various latchkey programs. I showed off our youth clubs and explained how we communicate Christian values to ghetto teenagers. Finally, I took them to a special Christian school we have established for disadvantaged children."[12]

The Russian guests—which included the heads of two of Russia's most prestigious universities, along with the deputy minister of education—took full advantage of their opportunity: "Everywhere these Russian visitors went they interviewed people—children and teenagers, as well as adults. Their questions were probing and astute. They listened with intensity and they took copious notes." And what were their impressions? Campolo gives the surprising report:

"Those teenagers are so materialistic!" was one response. Another added, "All that these young people talked about was making money." But the most unexpected answer came from the deputy minister of education, who reluctantly remarked, "I am somewhat disappointed in your children. Since they are Christians, I expected that they would be concerned about spiritual things. Instead, they are more materialistic than the Marxist youth in my country. They seem to be devoid of any lofty, idealistic vision."[13]

So it is not only the Muslims who are not impressed with the fruit of our faith. The Marxists are not impressed either![14]

Paul said that "we fix our eyes not on what is seen, but on what is unseen. For what is seen is temporary, but what is unseen is eternal" (2 Cor. 4:18). It seems we have gotten this reversed! Our eyes are fixed on the here and now, on what we can touch, taste, and feel—on things that will one day pass away. The material world is far more real to us than the spiritual. How many of us can relate to the mentality of Moses?

> By faith Moses, when he had grown up, refused to be known as the son of Pharaoh's daughter. He chose to be mistreated along with the people of God rather than to enjoy the pleasures of sin for a short time. He regarded disgrace for the sake of Christ as of greater value than the treasures of Egypt, because he was looking ahead to his reward (Heb. 11:24-26).

But we have our reward here in full! Heaven only becomes important to us during times of tragedy or great loss. Otherwise, this world is our totally comfortable home. As my friend Jeff Bernstein wrote a few years ago (after uprooting his wife and small children and moving to Russia and then to Kazakhstan, to do Jewish outreach):

> By the world's standards we Americans face the greatest temptation in respect to being lured away from God's

true riches by temporal treasures. Our refrigerators are filled with food as we relax in our climate-controlled homes, firing our remote controls at color TV and CD stereo systems, leaving only to drive our air-conditioned cars to the nearest Blockbusters [video store], later to load the latest movies into our VCR as we laugh and lounge on our comfortable couches. The rest of the world, in the meantime, struggles to survive another day.[15]

How then do we relate to earthly things? We may have an abundance, but those things can have no grip on us. We must be able to live with them (in which case they are used for God's glory and enjoyed as a blessing from Him) or live without them (in which case we enjoy the Lord just the same). But we must constantly be aware of the temporal, transitory nature of everything we have in this world, doing our best to never allow it to get such a hold on us that it steals or obstructs our eternal perspective.

It can be quite a battle! Our culture is incredibly materialistic. We are glutted with greed and consumed with covetousness. We never have enough! And the so-called American dream plays right into this mind-set. Where is the concept of "fulfilling our purpose for God" in this dream?

On June 13, 1808, Benjamin Rush, one of the signers of the Declaration of Independence, wrote a letter to John Adams, complaining of the deterioration in American society "since the Revolution." He quoted the words of an 81-year-old man who "knew America in her youthful and innocent days" but who felt that now "they had all become idolaters; they worshiped but one god it is true, but that god was GOD DOLLARS." With disgust Rush noted, "St. Paul places covetousness and uncleanness together as improper subjects of our conversation. But not only our streets but our parlors are constantly vocal with the language of a broker's office, and even at our convivial dinners 'Dollars' are a standing dish upon which all feed with rapidity and gluttony."[16] What would he think today?

It has been one of my greatest joys to talk with young couples who are about to leave for the mission field. They are full of life, energy, and holy ambition, and they want to make their lives count for the kingdom. "But what about the American dream?" I ask them. "After all, you've only been married for a few months!" "Dr. Brown," they respond with tears, "we've got to go!"

YOU CAN USE THIS MATERIAL WORLD FOR THE GLORY OF GOD—ENJOYING ITS BOUNTIFUL BLESSINGS AS A WONDERFUL GIFT FROM HIM—OR YOU CAN BE ENSLAVED TO IT AND ENGROSSED IN IT.

They are Great Commission Christians, not greedy, carnal Christians. They have smashed the idol of materialism and broken its hold over their lives. While they love America, they relate now to the words of Count Zinzendorf, who said, "That land is henceforth my country which most needs the gospel." After all, we're only passing through![17]

People who say such things show that they are looking for a country of their own. If they had been thinking of the country they had left, they would have had opportunity to return.

Instead, they were longing for a better country—a heavenly one. Therefore, God is not ashamed to be called their God, for he has prepared a city for them (see Heb. 11:14-16).

You can use this material world for the glory of God—enjoying its bountiful blessings as a wonderful gift from Him—or you can be enslaved to it and engrossed in it (see 1 Cor. 7:31). It's so easy to get entrapped!

Do you remember the Lord's parable of the sower? He spoke of the seed sown among thorns "which grew up and choked the plants, so that they did not bear grain" (Mark 4:7). This represents those who hear the Word; but the worries of this life, the deceitfulness of wealth, and the desires for other things come in and "choke the word, making it unfruitful" (Mark 4:19). How aptly this applies to the American church!

In the book *How Saved Are We?* I addressed this point:

> There are so many thorns all around us: the worries of this life, the pleasures of this world, the deceitfulness of wealth, and the desire for other things. Because of these thorns, most of us "do not mature" and the Word in us becomes unfruitful (Luke 8:14; Mark 4:19). Just think of what our lives would be like if these thorns were removed! We would no longer be dominated by worldly desires—by the insatiable desire to be someone, to have something, to go somewhere, to find our satisfaction everywhere but in Jesus.
>
> Yet we are catering our very gospel to carnality! We act as if the kingdom of God were a matter of eating and drinking, of wanting and having, of fancy cars and luxurious homes, of big bank accounts and expensive designer clothes. We have lost sight of the object of our faith—Jesus, the Son of God.

Oh, yes, God can and will supply all our needs, and there is nothing shabby about His provision. He is not glorified through our poverty and lack. He gains nothing by us groveling in debt. He is a God of infinite wealth, and He can afford to share it with us. All that we need is found in Him, and as we seek His kingdom first, it will all be provided for us. But God "will not aid men in their selfish striving after personal gain. He will not help men to attain ends which, when attained, usurp the place He by every right should hold in their interest and affection"[18] Material wealth is never to be our primary goal.

Of course, there is nothing wrong with having possessions. But there is something wrong with possessions having us! There is nothing wrong with being rich, as long as being rich is not the purpose of our being! But many of us are now trapped. We have taken our eyes off Jesus and put them on earthly treasures. The "deceitfulness of wealth" has tricked us again. It has stolen eternity from our hearts! Some of us have even become "fools"—we have stored up things for ourselves but are not rich toward God (Luke 12:20,21).

Two thousand years ago, Jesus sounded an alarm: "Watch out! Be on your guard against all kinds of greed; a man's life does not consist in the abundance of his possessions" (Luke 12:15). Paul too warned us clearly: "People who want to get rich fall into temptation and a trap and into many foolish and harmful desires that plunge men into ruin and destruction. For the love of money is a root of all kinds of evil. Some people, eager for money, have wandered from the faith and pierced themselves with many griefs" (1 Tim.

6:9,10). Let us not read these verses lightly. Our relationship with God could be at stake. Paul speaks of "temptation and a trap," of being plunged into "ruin and destruction," of "all kinds of evil," of "wander[ing] from the faith."

And so Paul exhorted Timothy in no uncertain terms: "But you, man of God, flee from all this [today we run after it!], and pursue righteousness, godliness, faith, love, endurance and gentleness" (1 Tim. 6:11). For "godliness with contentment is great gain. For we brought nothing into the world, and we can take nothing out of it. But if we have food and clothing, we will be content with that" (1 Tim. 6:6-8). But are we really content? Or are we like those Pharisees who loved money and sneered at Jesus when He taught against greed (see Luke 16:14)?

The book of Proverbs says that "there are three things that are never satisfied, four that never say, 'Enough!': the grave, the barren womb, land, which is never satisfied with water, and fire, which never says 'Enough!'" (30:15,16). Today we can add one more: the materialistic American church! We are like the two daughters of the leech who cry "Give! Give!" (Prov. 30:15). We never have enough![19]

Amazingly, there is an even more extreme form of the carnal prosperity message sweeping the land today, with an even greater emphasis put on worldly wealth and a stronger accent placed on the pursuit of personal riches. Millions of Christians are buying it hook, line, and sinker, adding yet another bizarre dimension to the spiritual confusion of the day. It's time to smash these idols!

We are about to confront some of materialism's greatest traps and temptations, some of the most powerful gods in our society. Let's see how revolutionary we really are.

Chapter Six

Smashing the Idols: The Passion of Revolution

When the LORD your God brings you into the land you are about to enter and occupy, he will clear away many nations ahead of you: the Hittites, Girgashites, Amorites, Canaanites, Perizzites, Hivites, and Jebusites. . . . Do not intermarry with them, and don't let your daughters and sons marry their sons and daughters. They will lead your young people away from me to worship other gods. Then the anger of the LORD will burn against you, and he will destroy you. Instead, you must break down their pagan altars and shatter their sacred pillars. Cut down their Asherah poles and burn their idols. For you are a holy people, who belong to the LORD your God. Of all the people on earth, the LORD your God has chosen you to be his own special treasure.

DEUTERONOMY 7:1-6, **NLT**

[The Romans] charge us [Christians] on two points: that we do not sacrifice and that we do not believe in the same gods as the State.

ATHENAGORAS
A SECOND-CENTURY CHRISTIAN LEADER

We are publicly accused of being atheists and criminals who are guilty of high treason.

JUSTIN MARTYR
BEHEADED IN A.D. 165

The kingdom of God is a new order founded on the fatherly love of God, on redemption, justice, and fellowship. It is meant to enter into all life, all nations, and all policies till the kingdoms of this world become the kingdom of the Lord.

ERIC LIDDELL
OLYMPIC GOLD-MEDAL WINNER
AND MISSIONARY TO CHINA

L ess than two months after the Columbine killings in Littleton, Colorado, *Time* magazine ran an extraordinary article on youth revival in America, titled "Is Jesus the Answer?"[1] It offered some penetrating insights into the battles teens faced and how those battles were being won through total devotion to Jesus:

> In middle and high schools, the blessing and curse of young Christians is that their faith requires them to buck peer pressure over temptations like drugs, alcohol and sex. By refusing to hide her Christianity, Cassie [Bernall] triumphantly sustained her confession in the face of the ultimate peer pressure—the barrel of a gun. . . . Wendy Zoba, author of the upcoming book *Generation 2K: What Parents and Others Need to Know About the Millennials*, says many youths appreciate a radical refutation of high school materialism: "Cassie captured in that moment a blind faith in something greater than instantaneous gratification."[2]

That is the key—bucking peer pressure and refusing to give in to temptation, radically refuting materialism, recognizing that there is "something greater than instantaneous gratification." Yes! Obedience to God is greater. Loving God is greater. Enjoying God is greater. This revelation will lead to a cultural revolution, enabling us to utterly renounce the lust of the flesh, the lust of the eyes, and the pride of life:

> Don't love the world's ways, Don't love the world's good. Love of the world squeezes out love for the Father. Practically everything that goes on in the world—wanting your own way, wanting everything for yourself, want-

GRATIFICATION IS NOT OUR GOD! MONEY IS NOT OUR MASTER! LUST IS NOT OUR LORD! THE FLESH IS NOT OUR FOCUS! OUR ALLEGIANCE IS TO ONE GOD, AND HIM ALONE.

ing to appear important—has nothing to do with the Father. It just isolates you from him. The world and all its wanting, wanting, wanting is on the way out—but whoever does what God wants is set for eternity (1 John 2:15-17, *THE MESSAGE*).

Are you ready to smash some idols? Having exposed the strongholds of materialism in the last chapter, it's time to confront and crush them one at a time. Gratification is not our god! Money is not our master! Lust is not our lord! The flesh is not our focus! Our allegiance is to one God, one Master, one Lord; and we must focus on pleasing Him—and Him alone. All competing ideologies must be defeated and denounced. So take out your spiritual hammer and let us begin. Idols, look out!

Let us smash the idol of *addiction to entertainment*.

What if a man from a remote, tribal village in Africa was miraculously transported to America? What if he had never seen running water, let alone telephones or cars or TV? And what if he was an idol worshiper or even a witch doctor? It would take him no time at all to identify the family altar in our homes—the TV!

He would be impressed by our devotion to this speaking, living god. Not only do we spend hours sitting before it, entranced by its beauty and mesmerized by its power, but all the members

of our family have idols of their own, enthroned on fitting
pedestals in the rooms where they sleep. And how amazed this
visitor would be with the level of devotion to this god found
throughout the society. Yes, lines actually form outside of its
temples where huge images of this god smoke and thunder
and yell and laugh and fornicate and kill. What a mighty
god and what a religious people! And how freely they give their
time and money—and heart and soul—to this god!

I ask you now, am I exaggerating? Are we not idol worshipers
when we spend more time watching TV and videos than reading
the Word and praying? Are we not idol worshipers when our
lives revolve around the latest sitcoms, documentaries, movies,
talk shows, and news? Are we not idol worshipers when we actually compromise our convictions for the sake of entertainment?
Who or what rules us? Entertainment today has a pervasive, suf-
focating, strangling impact on the church.

It wasn't always like this. One hundred years ago we had neither radio nor TV, yet our lives were full. (As one of my colleagues points out, you will never see a tombstone from the
nineteenth century with the epitaph: Became sick and died for
lack of TV!) When radio was invented, Americans enjoyed full
lives while listening to just a few radio stations. And in the 1950s
and 1960s, we did not suffer lack because all we had were a few
TV stations from which to choose (in black and white, at that).
But soon it was not enough. We needed cable TV. And then cable
wasn't enough, so we had to get a satellite dish—as if any of us
needed 150 channels to browse. Such is the seducing, beguiling
power of idolatry. First we make something into a god, then we
bow down and worship it, and then we serve it. Now we are
under its power!

The problem is not just the craze for entertainment—and I've
barely touched on video games, Internet browsers, CD players,

and the like.[3] The content of our entertainment is just as frightening. Do we realize how powerful this medium has become? Do we realize how deeply we are impacted and influenced by graphic hi-tech images of violence, sex, and the occult?[4] The graphics are so real, the animation so believable, the special effects so intense, that we can easily lose touch with reality, blurring the distinction between a video game and real life, between a movie character and ourselves. Soon enough, a teenager is playing out the role, mowing down classmates—just like he saw in the movies!—while a married man is having virtual sex over the Internet.

Satan has increased the attack, yet we are hardly increasing our vigilance and discipline.[5] But the more available sin is, the more self-denial we need. How we must repudiate the idol of entertainment!

Is there a place for rest and relaxation? There is not only a place for it, there is a need for it. What about radio, TV, and videos? If the material is not offensive to the Spirit and we keep things in moderation, there's obviously nothing wrong. We can be enriched and expanded by the content they carry, and they can be used as tools to propagate the gospel. How many millions of people have come to the Lord through the world-famous *Jesus* film? How many millions of people have been reached through gospel radio (and now, gospel Internet)?

Tragically, among American believers, entertainment plays a predominantly idolatrous and polluting role. Most of us would do better to have no TVs in our homes than to watch TV the way we do, in terms of both time and content. If entertainment is an idol in your life, smash it. Live without it for a few months and spend the time instead praying, studying the Word, blessing your family, witnessing to the lost, serving your church, visiting the sick, developing wholesome skills, learning a trade, furthering your practical education—anything but wasting endless hours a month and ingesting deadly poison every week. Get rid of this foreign god now! And if you can limit entertainment to that which is moral and constructive, you have made it a tool instead of an idol. Use it for the glory of God!

Let us smash the idol of *obsession with sports*.

This is one of the greatest idols of our day. We are fanatical-ly devoted to sports. We *live* for it, depressed for days when the home team loses and elated beyond words when they win it all. How our emotions and desires are caught up with sports! How our time is consumed by it—watching game after game, listening to passionate discussions on sports radio, scouring the newspa-pers for the latest stats and the hottest stories. In fact, in many cities in America, Sunday services must end promptly at noon lest there be a conflict with the NFL game starting at 1:00.

"But it's only a game," you say. No it's not! No one gets paid $6 million a year to play "only a game." No one is vilified by the national press for losing "only a game." No one schedules church services around "only a game." No one shoots a player to death for making a stupid play in "only a game."[6] It has become an idol, an obsession, an almost sacrosanct preoccupation, and the Christian world buys right into it.[7]

Yes, I believe sports is fun and often exhilarating—to play and to watch and to follow, and I do all of those things. But I believe even more that it has gotten totally out of hand in our society. There are more leagues than we can follow, more teams than we can track, more games, more events, more tournaments, more stars, and more hype. Sports has been so glorified that it has become almost deified. A slow-motion replay of a reverse slam-dunk seems almost supernatural. Wow! You would almost think that the angels of heaven stood in rapt attention, watching with wonder and awe.

We even have a theology of sports: We believe that the more Christian athletes a team has, the more that team will win. But does the "Lord's team" always win? The fact is that spirituality doesn't always equal success, and God's greatest lessons are often learned in the furnace of affliction, not in the spotlight of adoration. Maybe *losing* is sometimes God's best for His team. (How contrary this is to most *all* of our theology in America.) For a believer, which is more important: becoming like Jesus or winning? Is it true that "winning isn't everything," or is this just another meaningless moral platitude?

Of course, I'm glad when a Christian athlete on a winning team unashamedly gives the glory to God for his accomplishments. I'd certainly rather hear this than hear him take the credit himself (or worse yet, praise some other god or religion). But we make it something cosmic, as if it was almost a spiritual defeat when the Nigerian Muslim Hakeem Olujawon led his basketball team to two straight titles or when Michael Jordan, not known as a religious man, led his team to six championships. But when an NBA player recently praised Allah for his team's astonishing playoff win, it actually put things in perspective for us: It seemed silly to give Allah credit for helping someone win a basketball game! Did Allah really care about it all? And did he favor one team because of the presence of a (nominal) Muslim, while Jesus was too weak to help the other team (with a number of Christians) win that night?[8]

My point is simply this: Even fine, upstanding, highly moral Christian athletes buy into the idolatry of sports. Should we thank God that there are men and women serving as role models to our children? Yes! Should we be grateful that many of them use their high profile to spread the good news of Jesus? Of course! Should we begrudge them for making so much money when the industry gladly pays it? Certainly not!

But is it wrong for us to grieve when it is a top *Mormon* athlete—rather than a top Christian athlete—who postpones his professional career to spend two years on the mission field? And is it wrong for us to wonder where today's C. T. Studds are, foregoing the accolades of sports to give their best years to winning souls as opposed to winning games?[9]

And is it wrong for us to expect at least one outspoken Christian athlete to say, "Look, it's immoral of me to make $5 million a year for playing a game. I can live very well on $1 million a year, so I'm giving the rest to foreign missions and inner-city work." How this would renounce the idolatry of it all! (Perhaps some Christian owners could follow suit?)

Someone, somewhere has to make us believe that all this is really not that important. But when Christian athletes justify their pay with an appeal to Scripture, saying that the laborer is worthy of his hire (see Luke 10:7), what message are they conveying?[10]

Honestly, words escape me here. We have almost no clue of how obsessed with sports we are. Major U.S. cities have been heavily vandalized during victory parties; massive, confetti parades of celebration have been attended by millions; grown men have run down the streets with faces painted, dressed in bizarre outfits and uniforms or, sometimes, without them (I mean naked!)—all because someone excelled at kicking or hitting or throwing a ball or shooting a puck or driving a car or riding a horse. (Husbands, maybe our wives are more right about their perspective on sports than we realize—unless our wives are sportsaholics too!)

Our culture virtually revolves around sports, although sports does nothing, in itself, to further our purpose here on

Earth. It's just an amusement, a diversion, a way to develop skills, an outlet for energy. Yet we have made it into a god of gigantic proportions. And as idolatry progresses in a culture, it becomes more sophisticated and expansive—just like sports in our day. Contrast today's football—with its legion of coaches, scouts, and computerized schemes—with the relative simplicity of the sport 30 years ago.

Stand back and ask yourself, *If Jesus is really the Lord of my life and if heaven and hell are real, why am I so consumed and dominated by these silly games?* It is because we have made these games (which have *some* valid place in society) into gods, magnifying their importance, exalting their status, and lavishing them with time and money galore. And having made them into gods, we have followed the inevitable pattern of bowing down to them and serving them to the point that many of us literally cannot live without them. Smash these idols too. But be prepared for quite a battle here.

Let us smash the idol of *worldly fashion.*

It is one thing to dress like Islamic women; it is another thing to dress like worldly women (although Islamic dress is closer to biblical styles than is much of our contemporary Western dress). But just as many Christian men worship the idol of sports, many Christian women worship the idol of fashion. It is a powerful god! Why the great pressure to stay in style? (Who sets the trends anyway?) Why so much emphasis on makeup and appearance? Could it be that things have gone to an extreme here too? Could we imagine Jesus, like many of our churches, having fashion shows to help draw in the ladies?

Now, by saying this, I am not implying that Christian women must dress in drab clothes and wear their hair in buns.

Of course not! Nor am I saying they should be ashamed of their natural beauty or try to look their worst instead of their best. God forbid! But there is quite a difference between Christian femininity and worldly sensuality, just as there is quite a difference between marital intimacy and fornication. One is holy; the other is forbidden. One is a gift from God; the other is a temptation of the flesh. There is no excuse for confusing the two!

Immediately after Paul exhorted "men everywhere to lift up holy hands in prayer, without anger or disputing," he exhorted women to "dress modestly, with decency and propriety, not with braided hair or gold or pearls or expensive clothes, but with good deeds, appropriate for women who profess to worship God" (1 Tim. 2:8-10). Could it be that men, more than women, need to be reminded to pray, while women, more than men, need to be reminded to dress modestly? (I'm aware, of course, that there are plenty of praying men and lots of prayerless women, along with plenty of vain men and lots of modest women. I'm simply following Paul's points here, along with the prevailing issues in the Church.)

Peter also told Christian wives that "your beauty should not come from outward adornment, such as braided hair and the wearing of gold jewelry and fine clothes. Instead, it should be that of your inner self, the unfading beauty of a gentle and quiet spirit, which is of great worth in God's sight" (1 Pet. 3:3,4). Does this counsel strike you as offensive or chauvinistic? Is there a *greater* beauty that godly women can pursue? And is it symptomatic of a divided heart when we spend hours standing in front of the mirror and minutes kneeling before the Lord?

How many pairs of shoes do you really need? How many outfits? How many color combinations? How much money was spent on outfits that now hang limply in your closet, worn once or twice (if at all), but purchased with passion because you *had* to have them, because they were the latest rage, because everyone was wearing that style—and now it's obsolete!

We must also remember how obsessed our culture is with perfect bodies—from head to toe, regardless of age, it seems—and this obsession has led to a plague of anorexia and bulimia ("I'm so fat!") along with a thriving plastic-surgery industry, specializing in everything from breast implants to liposuction. This is so unfair to women today. They feel as if they must measure up to a cover-girl's figure or a supermodel's shape, since anything less is ugly and subpar. And the pressure on teens to conform is especially great.

How unbiblical this is! And how ungodly it becomes when women who call on Jesus as Lord cast off His lordship in their dress, wearing clinging jeans, low-cut blouses, revealing skirts, or sensual dresses. Where is the modesty in this? And why should brothers in church services have to guard their eyes because of the dress of their Christian sisters? God's house should be a sanctuary!

It's one thing to welcome sinners in our midst, regardless of how they look or smell, or to patiently wait for young believers to grow in grace. It's another thing for women, who have been saved for years, to strive to be sensual, to draw attention to their bodies for the viewing pleasure of the opposite sex (and I don't mean their husbands). If we're going to make a mistake in dress, let's make it on the side of modesty.[11] It's better to be out of style than out of the will of God. Our self-worth is not measured by our looks or the quality of our clothes.

Richard Wurmbrand once said, "In the free world, attending churches, I sometimes say to myself, 'If the day of God's judgment were a fashion show, many in this congregation would be saved.'"[12] How true! Let's break the power of this idol—the idol of fashion, of overemphasis on outward appearance, of sensuality, of conformity to the world—over the people of God. His favor brings a beauty of its own.

Let us smash the idol of *fleshly indulgence.*

Missiologists have often confronted North Americans with some disturbing statistics. Although we make up less than 5 percent of the world's population, we consume more than 90 percent of its resources. We really are a continent of consumers! Where does all this money go? On what do we spend our funds (or, at least, our "excess" funds)? And what do we do with verses like James 4:3, "When you ask, you do not receive, because you ask with wrong motives, that you may spend what you get on your pleasures"? This describes so many of us!

Consider these alarming facts:

- "In 1998, the average American spent 99.5 percent of his after-tax income" (compared to 91 percent in 1975, meaning that almost 10 percent of our after-tax incomes went into savings then compared to ½ percent today).[13] We make more money, we spend more money, and we have little or nothing to show for it except ever-increasing personal debt.
- "Americans spend more than $9 billion every year on pornography. The number of hard-core pornography video rentals increased from 75 million in 1985, to 490 million in 1992, to 686 million in 1998."[14] We are becoming increasingly enslaved.
- "Americans spent $638.6 billion on legal gambling games in 1997 and lost about $51 billion of that amount (which is more than the recording, video-

game, movie, cruise-ship, spectator sport, and theme-park business revenues combined). Approximately 2.5 million adult Americans are pathological gamblers; another 3 million have been classified as problem gamblers."[15]

- *The Journal for the American Medical Association* now speaks of the "epidemic" of obesity in America, according to a report published in 1999. The authors of the report note that "the prevalence of obesity . . . increased from 12.0% in 1991 to 17.9% in 1998. A steady increase was observed in all states; in both sexes; across age groups, races, educational levels; and occurred regardless of smoking status." The authors further point out that "the increasing prevalence of obesity is a major public health concern, since obesity is associated with several chronic diseases"—including cardiovascular diseases and diabetes. It is also estimated that obesity-related deaths may account for as much as 6.8% of American health care costs.[16] And, as if this news wasn't bad enough, the authors of the study believe that their figures are actually too low and that the obesity rate is actually *higher* than what they have reported.[17] The bottom line is that about one out of every five Americans is obese (is it even higher in the church?), a figure that has risen dramatically in the 1990s. This is not a good sign! Our stomachs are not to be our gods.

In guerrilla war, large midday meals are discouraged, because "such meals in the afternoon can render the guerrilla lethargic, thus reducing his attention to detail and level of alertness. (The sleepy guerrilla who just consumed a big lunch is sometimes said to have fallen into a food coma.)"[18] Could it be that some of us through food overdose have become food comatose? Could it be that gluttony has reduced our attention to detail and our level of spiritual alertness?

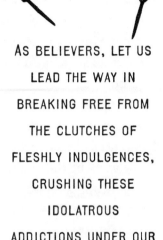

AS BELIEVERS, LET US LEAD THE WAY IN BREAKING FREE FROM THE CLUTCHES OF FLESHLY INDULGENCES, CRUSHING THESE IDOLATROUS ADDICTIONS UNDER OUR FEET—FOR GOOD.

R. A. Torrey said,

> Power is lost through self-indulgence. The one who would have God's power must lead a life of self-denial. . . . I do not believe that any man can lead a luxurious life, overindulge his natural appetites, indulge extensively in dainties, and enjoy the fullness of God's power. The gratification of the flesh and the fullness of the Spirit do not go hand in hand. . . . There are devils today that "go not out but by prayer and fasting."[19]

As believers, we are called to discipline, saying yes to the Spirit and no to the flesh. Let us lead the way in breaking free from the clutches of fleshly indulgences, crushing these idolatrous addictions under our feet—for good. Amen! That feels better already.

Let us smash the idol of *secular academics*.

Many of the greatest colleges in the world were founded by believers, for the glory of God, including Harvard, Yale, and

Princeton in America, along with Oxford and Cambridge in England. Many people around the world have learned to read and write through the efforts of Christian missionaries (who in some cases actually had to invent the alphabet and writing system too).

Many of the most important breakthroughs in health and science have come through the work of committed believers. Ignorance is not a virtue, nor is education a vice. Where would we be without the ability to read and write and communicate and develop? Who would want to downplay the importance of learning? Certainly not me! I spent some of my most fulfilling years engrossed in university studies, and I have devoted even more fulfilling years to teaching in or directing Bible schools and colleges. Thank God for literacy and the pursuit of knowledge.

Yet academics have become an idol to so many in our culture today. This idol needs to be repudiated as well. Most Christian teens end up attending secular colleges in America, even though the atmosphere there is often immoral and the professors are often anti-God in their philosophies. Yet it is to college our teens must go. Why? Because they need to get a degree![20] Why? Because everyone has to get a degree; because you can't get a good job without a degree; because you will not enter adult life rounded and balanced without a degree. Yet so often, college experience doesn't prepare us or improve us for life or enrich or expand our horizons. Rather, it is often something to be endured, leaving a huge financial debt in the end.

I have found it illuminating to survey college graduates (who are today believers) about their experiences in secular colleges. Did it help them fulfill their purpose in God? Did it ultimately enrich and benefit their lives? Only a small minority say yes.[21] Yet many of these same believers will insist that *their* kids go to secular college. Why? Because everyone has to get a degree! God forbid that your kids enroll in a specialized vocational program that will help them do inner-city work, or that the Bible college they want to attend is not listed in the nation's top schools.[22]

How utterly worldly this mind-set is! How it smacks of bowing down to the system of this age and how it measures itself by the standards of flesh and blood. It is especially ugly when it becomes a matter of prestige for the parents, as if sending our kids to a famous—although godless—school makes the parents look better. It is especially binding when a particular culture *demands* that we send our kids to such schools, regardless of the financial burden entailed. This is idolatry!

Christian schools can fall into this same trap. They can bow down to the same idol. Unless they offer certain courses and meet certain guidelines, they will lose their accreditation. If they lose their accreditation, they will lose potential students, and their degrees will not be recognized by other universities, which will make Christian education look bad. How so? Because the Christian college failed to live up to the standards of the state. But why must the state (or accrediting agency) set the standards? What if that school has a unique purpose and function? What if it needs to major on things the state considers minor, and minor on things the state considers major? Why must it conform? To offer degrees, of course! This too is idolatry.

Why must we prove that we are just as smart, just as educated, just as astute, just as academically excellent as the world? To whom are we proving this and what does it prove? In the long run, will it really produce that much fruit for the gospel? Where does the Word hint at this kind of orientation? (Isn't it interesting that neither Harvard nor Yale are accredited? They *set* the standard rather than submit to it!)

Even godly seminaries can be snared here, spending hundreds of hours combating liberal heresies (although most of the people to whom these graduates minister will never even know these heresies exist) or making sure that its graduates are of the highest intellectual caliber without also guaranteeing they are strong in the experiential knowledge of God. Jesus is more interested in using people who know Him than in using people who merely know about Him.[23]

Christian college students—especially if you are on a secular campus—may I ask you some personal questions? Do you long to be accepted by those who would reject Jesus if He showed up at your school? Are you pursuing academic excellence and seeking to demonstrate the reasonableness of your faith in order to avoid the sting of the Cross and its folly? And will your college degree simply be a stepping-stone to a graduate degree (be it in education or medicine or music or physics or law or theology) after which you will have proved to your parents (or family or self) that you have somehow "made" it? Then what? How does all this relate to the plan of God for your life?

I personally long for the day when God will raise up an army of highly educated, deeply intellectual, and mentally sharp radicals—men and women like Pascal, with minds on fire and souls aflame. It will be wonderful to hear them refute the cultists and confute the atheists, providing us with a revolutionary strategy to take this generation for Jesus and shake this society for the King.

My own life has been shaped by my educational experiences, and I would not be able to do most of the things I now do in Jewish ministry (especially apologetics) or biblical scholarship without that training. But it is only a tool, not an idol, and I willfully—joyfully—"go to [Jesus] outside the camp, bearing the disgrace he bore. For here we do not have an enduring city, but we are looking for the city that is to come" (Heb. 13:13,14). There it is again: We are only passing through![24]

Educators, smash the idols of worldly acceptance and make your faith known with boldness mixed with compassion and grace. Refuse to compromise truth! Students, don't let rationalism steal your zeal and don't allow the pursuit of knowledge to quench your faith. Do what God has called you to do, utilizing whatever tools He gives you along the way but keeping fellowship with Him at the top of your list.

So what if the unsaved scorn you. They scorned Paul and Wesley too, both of whom were brilliant, learned men. Paul and Wesley scorned the wisdom of this age!

> For the message of the cross is foolishness to those who are perishing, but to us who are being saved it is the power of God. For it is written: "I will destroy the wisdom of the wise; the intelligence of the intelligent I will frustrate." Where is the wise man? Where is the scholar? Where is the philosopher of this age? Has not God made foolish the wisdom of the world? (1 Cor. 1:18-20).

As the Lord made crystal clear, "What is highly valued among men is detestable in God's sight" (Luke 16:15). This can apply to academics too! We must take the higher ground here. The church of Jesus must help define what education is all about.

On that great day of accounting, we will stand before our God—not our professors, not our accrediting agency, not our board of regents. We must bow down to no god but Him, regardless of the cost. That is how idolatry is defeated.

These, then, are some of the idols in our midst, and either we smash them or we serve them.[25] What about you? What will it be? As for me and my house, we will serve the Lord (see Josh. 24:15). On with the revolution!

Chapter Seven

Moving Music
and
a Militant Message:
The Sounds of
Revolution

Whenever the spirit from God came upon Saul, David would take his harp and play. Then relief would come to Saul; he would feel better, and the evil spirit would leave him.

1 SAMUEL 16:23

While the harpist was playing, the hand of the LORD came upon Elisha.

2 KINGS 3:15

As they began to sing and praise, the Lord set ambushes against the men of Ammon and Moab and Mount Seir who were invading Judah, and they were defeated.

2 CHRONICLES 20:22

Secular music, do you say, belongs to the devil? Does it? Well, if it did I would plunder him for it, for he has no right to a single note of the whole seven. . . . So consecrate your voice and your instruments. . . . Offer them to God, and use them to make all the hearts about you merry before the Lord.

WILLIAM BOOTH
FOUNDER OF THE SALVATION ARMY

How can you be so dead when you've been so well fed?
Jesus rose from the grave, and you—you can't even get out of bed!

KEITH GREEN
FROM HIS SONG "ASLEEP IN THE LIGHT"

Music is an incredibly powerful medium, a tremendously effective tool for good or for evil. During the counterculture movement of the 1960s, rock music was the principle carrier of the message, as Irwin and Debi Unger observe:

> Rock 'n' roll was the theme music of psychedelia. A merger of black rhythm and blues with jazz and country, it was the sound of youth revolt that began with Chuck Berry and Elvis Presley. In the form of "acid rock," along with strobe lights, LSD, and marijuana, it accompanied unbuttoned counterculture celebrations in San Francisco's Fillmore auditorium and its imitators east and west. In 1964, Bob Dylan, a nasal former "folkie," composed the anthem for the era: "The Times They Are A-Changin'."[1]

And how the times did change! When Os Guinness wrote his book *The Dust of Death*, he did well to add the subtitle *The Sixties Counterculture and How It Changed America Forever.*[2]

Yes, the 1960s radically changed America, and music was a central factor in that change. In fact, when author Herbert Schlossberg wrote his endorsement for the 1994 printing of *The Dust of Death*, he noted that "the 1990s cannot be understood without knowing what happened in the 1960s," which means that the 1990s cannot be understood without knowing the impact rock music had on that fateful season in our history.[3]

I can testify to this firsthand. Rock music had a dramatic impact on me as a teenager. I would not have used drugs if not for rock music; I would not have become an antiauthority rebel if not for rock music; I would not have pursued a godless lifestyle if not for rock music. This was the experience of so many in my generation.

"Music was a great unifier," says Paul Krassner. "When I had my radio show, I asked people to call in and tell me what it was in their lives that kind of woke them up. And more than a few said getting stoned and hearing the Beatles. It was an awakening on a mass level, and that's what it was about. It was like some kind of fairy story, people waking up."[4]

Did you catch those words "an awakening on a mass level . . . like some kind of fairy story, people waking up"? That's exactly what happened! Having lived through it myself, and looking back at it 30 years later, I can say that it *was* an awakening of almost "fairy story" proportions. But it was an awakening primarily owned by hell, not heaven, as Satan rushed in to fill a void in young, seeking hearts while much of the Church slept away the night.

What were the ingredients that fueled this counterculture awakening? Drugs and rock music, or "getting stoned and hearing the Beatles," in the words of the callers to Krassner's radio show. It is therefore no surprise that the defining moment in the counterculture movement, the crowning moment of the era, was a drug-happy, sex-filled, music-fest called Woodstock. It really was a "happening," and it helped validate the whole "make love not war" philosophy. But without rock music, there would have been no Woodstock. It was simply a massive festival of rock, attended by 400,000 people.

Os Guinness describes the power of these musical festivals:

Far more than a passing fashion or style of music, the festivals uniquely expressed a generation's utopian wistfulness. One high point was in Monterey in June 1967 with Eric Burdon, Janis Joplin, The Who, Ravi Shankar, Otis Redding, and Simon and Garfunkel. After three days, even the police were wearing flowers, and those not high on grass or acid were high on idealism. If that was the beginning, Woodstock in August 1969 was the orgasmic climax of love, peace, and music. Hailed as an important landmark in the awakening of the collective unconscious, it was later blown up to mythical, cosmic proportions by the film on Woodstock, which broke down distinctions and made all who saw it true participants.[5]

One of the young seekers of that era later changed his name to Baba Ram Dass, reflecting his lasting identification with counterculture religion. Speaking about a collection of photos from the 1960s published in 1987, he had this to say of those turbulent times:

> These photographs are nostalgia, pure and simple: memories of a time of Divine Funk. Yet they chronicle a moment in history when there was a mushroom explosion of consciousness and a resulting increase in life force. And through that explosion we broke out of the prison created by the worship of our intellect. As we went out of our minds, we met once again our own innocence. We rejoined the Universe—a Universe no longer separated from us by the chasm of dualistic thought. And freeing ourselves of the rational mind as ultimate arbiter of reality freed us simultaneously of the constrictions of Puritan values and the Protestant work ethic. We had opened once again the cookie jar of possibilities—political, social, sexual, and spiritual. It was all up for grabs.[6]

Now I know this may sound like philosophical mumbo-jumbo to some, but there is a message here that cannot be missed: The 1960s were a time of exploration and experimentation, of flirting with the forbidden and toying with taboos, of breaking boundaries and bursting bonds. The "cookie jar of possibilities—political, social, sexual, and spiritual"—was opened wide, and everything was now "up for grabs."

Listen again to the Ungers:

> The Sixties delegitimized all sources of authority—governments, universities, parents, critics, experts, employers, the police, families, the military. In this decade's wake, all hierarchical structures became more pliant, all judgments and critical evaluations and "canons" less definitive and acceptable. The decade also witnessed the "liberation" of whole categories of people who have been previously penalized for their race, age, physical fitness, gender, or sexual preference. . . . In mid-1967, San Francisco's Haight-Ashbury district became the locale of a spontaneous "hippie" experiment in living informed by LSD. The new movement proclaimed itself a "counterculture," a liberated alternative to the life and institutions of "square" America.[7]

And rock music helped make most of this happen! Rock music was the trendsetter, the door opener, the pathfinder. Rock music, in and of itself, was a culture and a lifestyle, a living carrier of the anti-Establishment message. It provided an atmosphere within which a new way of thinking could be developed, and a backdrop against which new concepts could be conceived. It was the ideal means for propagating the new message. Nothing drills a theme into hearts and minds like music! Nothing is memorized better than when it is put to music.[8] Nothing impacts a person more than when it is put to music.

Think of lyrics you remember from childhood songs—with no formal attempt at memorization—and compare that with poems you tried so hard to memorize. Which do you still recall? Those which were learned to music! Or put on some mournful music while you go about your business at home, and watch how easy it is to become melancholy and sad. Then put on some cheery, vibrant tunes and the whole room lights up. Even a movie with a powerful plot is greatly enhanced by the right musical soundtrack. Without it, the movie seems tame. (For moviegoers of old, think of *Rocky II* without "Eye of the Tiger." Rocky's early morning jogs don't seem so dramatic anymore, and his quest for the heavyweight title loses some of its epic proportions. But with the music, it's a different story!)

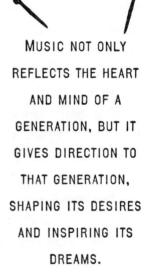

MUSIC NOT ONLY REFLECTS THE HEART AND MIND OF A GENERATION, BUT IT GIVES DIRECTION TO THAT GENERATION, SHAPING ITS DESIRES AND INSPIRING ITS DREAMS.

Music can change our moods and our emotions. Music can change our outlook and our perceptions. Music can change a society. It not only reflects the heart and mind of a generation (like the swing music of the Roaring Twenties or the rap music of the Nineties) but it gives direction to that generation, shaping its desires and inspiring its dreams. There is power in the beat (whether it be the pounding beat of disco or the hypnotizing beat of the waltz); there is power in the lyrics (whether they repeat a simple theme or tell a lengthy story); there is power in the melody (you will associate it with certain memories and messages for years to come); there is power in the playing (you can become absorbed or carried away by powerfully played music).[9]

Music has the unique ability to catch the listener up, to take us into a different place and time. It has the power to transport us into another realm and, when coupled with mind-altering drugs, it has the power to transform (in the worst sense of the word). It certainly warped and twisted me!

Before I knew the Lord, my two favorite activities in life were to get high and play drums with my band or to get high and go to a rock concert with my friends. What a highlight those concerts were! I measured time by the days between concerts, dreaming about them in advance and recounting them in detail when they were over. And what an assault on the senses those concerts were, overwhelming both eyes and ears with the sights and sounds. The shrieking lead guitar, the driving drums, the pounding bass, the howling vocals, the pulsating light show, the frenetic movement of the flamboyant rockers—how captivating all of it was! How I longed to be like those rock stars! And how I actually *became* like those stars, growing my hair long, smoking pot, dropping LSD, shooting speed, breaking laws, scorning authority, living to satisfy the flesh, *giving myself* to the music.

Even though I was absorbed with the music and rarely listened to the words (some of which were so bizarre as to be completely meaningless), the overall message was clear: Do your own thing! Live to party! Down with the Establishment! As expressed in extreme form by Jim Morrison, one of the rock kings of the day and a casualty of the movement at the tender age of 27: "I am interested in anything about revolt, disorder, chaos—especially activity that seems to have no meaning."[10]

Somehow, this chaotic, discordant message resonated with our generation. Somehow, this was our theme. Somehow, the dark side appealed to us, and no one expressed it better than the Grateful Dead, singing what was one of my favorite songs (with words that I actually *did* catch): "A friend of the devil is a friend of mine." Rock music meant change, and change was the god of the hour. Out with the old! In with the new! Rock expressed this so well.

It is one of the ironic "coincidences" of that era that three of the most influential musical leaders, three of the cultural heroes, three of the most gifted artists all died at the same age: Jimi Hendrix, the master of the electric guitar, dead September 18, 1970, age 27; Janis Joplin, the soulful singer of blues-rock, dead October 4, 1970, age 27; Jim Morrison, the rebel poet and leader of the Doors, dead July 3, 1971, age 27. Their loss is still fresh in my mind. Something died in all of us at that time, as it seemed that somehow "the new" was failing. How our mighty ones had fallen!

Of course, some of us thought this was cool. Such were the casualties of the partying lifestyle! But Eric Clapton, one of the rock icons who survived, had a different perspective on the passing of Hendrix and Joplin: "Their deaths were almost necessary sacrifices.... It'll be a long time before I shall feel at peace again. I just wish 1970 would hurry up and go away. It's all been a disaster."[11] The euphoria was quickly fading, as Guinness makes plain:

> "A great spiritual awakening is breaking out," said the disc jockey at the Isle of Wight [concert in 1970] as peace signs waved and hundreds of thousands of hands were linked.... Three days later, as violence erupted, the same DJ was cursing. Three weeks later, a trio of the original Monterey stars were dead, all in tragic circumstances related to drugs.[12]

It was around this time that the worldwide "Jesus People Movement" began, bringing multiplied thousands of seekers and radicals and hippies and druggies and rockers and activists into the Kingdom. At last, we discovered the *true* Reality, the *legitimate* Higher Consciousness, the *one and only* Absolute Truth. And what happened to our musical creativity? Some churches (like the Calvary Chapels on the West Coast) cultivated it, birthing a whole new genre of gospel music. Other churches (like the traditional Pentecostal church in which I was saved) incorporated it, making for an interesting mix (should I call it "Sunshine in My Soul" with a snap, or "Power in the Blood" with pizzazz?). Most churches stifled it.

On the one hand, stifling it was fine. All of our associations with rock music had been sinful, and there was no alternative Christian music to which we could listen. So without anyone telling us to, we got rid of our rock albums after a few months in the Lord. Plus, Jesus was our portion, and in Him we had all we could ever need.

What extraordinary joy we experienced singing those simple choruses and little ditties (as we later came to call them) with their ultrapredictable words. We were so filled and blessed that we renounced drugs and drink virtually overnight, and saying good-bye to our music was not that painful.

On the other hand, the stifling of musical expression—or simply the lack of appreciation for its potential—was tragic. The creativity was not redirected and the powerful medium of music was hardly used to touch our generation.

But if that was tragic, something far more tragic has happened in the decades since. Christian rock has grown by leaps and bounds, and still it has hardly been used to impact this generation. It has become professional, it has become slick, it has entertained, it has merchandised—but it has hardly impacted.

What a shame! It could have been used so powerfully. What an indictment of the contemporary Christian music scene!

My own life was shaped by rock music—by the sounds of rock, by the stars of rock, by the songs of rock. The devil used it to help fashion me for destruction, and I was headed straight for hell, if not for the intervening grace of God. Satan knew full well how to exploit music to the max. But what have we done? We have shown so little vision for the life-changing power of music; we have given so little attention to the soul-transforming power of music; we have failed, by and large, to use it as a revolutionary tool. Yet it has the potential to change this generation! A spiritual Woodstock could be around the corner if we only let the Lord shape our sounds and mold our messages.

But no! Contemporary Christian music, with rare exception, has sold out to what is economically correct, to a marketable message and a sellable star. Where are the prophetic voices in the contemporary music scene? We need more groups who truly *minister* through the medium, challenging this generation to leave all and follow the Master. Why are they so few and far between? And what is the spiritual purpose of Christian ballads sensually sung by glamorous vocalists (are they being sung to Jesus or to a boyfriend?) or ridiculous rap that is strong on coolness but weak on content? Is it not primarily carnal entertainment designed to turn a profit?

WHY IS THE CHURCH FOREVER COPYING THE WORLD? WHY DO WE TAKE THE MUSIC OF THE WORLD AND PUT SOME CATCHY LYRICS TO IT INSTEAD OF JOINING A "NOW" MESSAGE WITH SOME "NOW" MUSIC TO RADICALLY IMPACT A LOST GENERATION?

"But you're being unfair!" you say. "Young people need an alternative to secular rock, and contemporary Christian music provides it."

Hardly! They don't need something empty and shallow to take the place of the music and message of the world. They need something with substance. They need something from heaven!

Music is not merely a mixture of harmony, melody, and rhythm. It's a powerful medium given to us by God. If Satan could inspire an *un*holy musical revolution, why can't the Spirit inspire a *holy* musical revolution? Why is the Church forever copying the world? And why do we simply take the music of the world and put some catchy lyrics to it instead of joining a "now" message with some "now" music to radically impact a lost generation? (If we *are* going to use some of the music of the world, as William and Catherine Booth and a host of others have done, then let us make the message count all the more.)

Where are the musicians who will truly repudiate the music *industry* —the money-driven, greed-motivated, celebrity-making, flesh-exalting contemporary music industry—and simply follow Jesus? Why must it all be hyped, packaged, and marketed to the masses in its most saleable—and toothless—form, as opposed to distributed in its purest, most powerful and pointed form? (Remember, what is really prophetic doesn't always sell!)[13]

Where are the Keith Greens of today, who will put their heart and soul into the message and use the music to further that message, who will develop a radical style and spirit of their own that will infuse this young generation with a radical call to radical discipleship? For lost musicians (like Jimi Hendrix), music was an extension of their own souls. When they played, they played with body, soul, and spirit—their instruments functioning as an extension of their own person. For many of them, even with their drugs, immorality, and dabbling with Eastern religion, rock was more than an entertainment industry. And in this they have been more devoted and idealistic than many a contemporary Christian artist. How can this be?

Here is a word for every Christian recording artist or performer reading this book: Perhaps you began in the Spirit, using your talents and gifts for the glory of God. But as soon as you were "discovered," the playing field changed and you had to learn the new rules of the game. Successful promotion became more important than secret prayer. Image became more important than intimacy. Marketing became more important than the message. Sales became more important than souls. Yet God cannot be mocked, and having begun in the Spirit, we are not made perfect in the flesh (see Gal. 3:3, *KJV*).

You have prostituted your gift and sold it for money! You could have been changing lives. You could have been a radical role model. You could have helped spark a revolution. But now, what fruit remains? What do you have to show for all your efforts—your endless weeks on the road and your endless hours in the studio? And what has happened to your relationship with God? Has it become a casualty to success and stardom? I appeal to you to return to your roots. I appeal to you to use your gift for the glory of God. Don't let money drive you. Be driven by the call. Be driven by the message. Be driven by God, not greed. Break with the system. Become a counterculture Christian, not a casualty of the contemporary scene.

As an author, traveling speaker, and Bible school president, I too know the pressure of "bringing in the bucks." But I write from personal experience: I would rather die or go hungry than compromise principle. And if it is not enough to have Jesus pleased with me, then I'm in the wrong line of work. In fact, in our own ministry offices, our staff is not allowed to use the word "product" for any of our materials (books, tapes, or videos). We have ministry materials to sell and distribute for the edification of the Church and the expansion of the Kingdom, but we are not a business with "product" that we must market. Yet this is the mentality of so much of today's contemporary Christian music industry.[14]

Christian musicians and songwriters and vocalists, however, are not the only ones at fault. The church as a whole plays a large part in this, in particular, among the leadership. We have not made musicians welcome in our midst, consigning them for the most part to noncreative, nonexpressive positions that merely scratch our musical itch or fill some holes in our program. Where are the "chief musicians" among us?[15] Why do we give so little attention to something of such great importance in the Word?

Scripture tells us that in 2 Kings 3:1-19, without a minstrel, Elisha could not receive a prophetic word from God, while in 1 Samuel 10:5, the traveling group of prophets had musicians in their midst. King David, whose playing of the lyre as a young man chased oppression from King Saul (see 1 Sam. 16:14-23), esteemed music so highly that he set aside *four thousand* Levites to praise the Lord with the musical instruments he provided for them (see 1 Chron. 23:5; Neh. 12:36), while one of the most beloved portions of the Scriptures, namely, the psalms, was written to be *sung*.[16] (This continued right into the Early Church, where the book of Psalms formed the primary songbook of the first believers. To this day, the psalms are chanted during traditional Jewish prayer.) Solomon learned well from his father's example, investing lots of money in musical instruments for the Temple (see 1 Kings 10:12).

The New Testament exhorts us to "speak to one another with psalms, hymns and spiritual songs. Sing and make music in your heart to the Lord" (Eph. 5:19), which ties in directly with being thankful in Ephesians 5:20, while heaven itself will be marked by the sounds of music and "new songs" (see Rev. 5:9-13; 14:2,3; 15:1-4; there really will be harps there!). Absence of the sound of music was a sign of judgment in the Word (see, for example, Lam. 5:14; Ezek. 26:13; Rev. 18:22), while joyful music characterized days of favor and restoration (see Jer. 31:4,13). And just as natural celebrations were marked by music (see Gen. 31:27; Luke 15:25), so also were spiritual celebrations marked by music (see Neh. 12:26,27). In light of all this, Psalm 150:1-6 makes perfect sense:

> Praise the LORD. Praise God in his sanctuary; praise him in his mighty heavens. Praise him for his acts of power; praise him for his surpassing greatness. Praise him with the sounding of the trumpet, praise him with the harp and lyre, praise him with tambourine and dancing, praise him with the strings and flute, praise him with the clash of cymbals, praise him with resounding cymbals. Let everything that has breath praise the LORD. Praise the LORD.

Even verses such as the following now fall into place for us:

> Every stroke the LORD lays on them with his punishing rod will be to the music of tambourines and harps, as he fights them in battle with the blows of his arm (Isa. 30:32).

> Praise the LORD. Sing to the LORD a new song, his praise in the assembly of the saints. Let Israel rejoice in their Maker; let the people of Zion be glad in their King. Let

them praise his name with dancing and make music to him with tambourine and harp. For the LORD takes delight in his people; he crowns the humble with salvation. Let the saints rejoice in this honor and sing for joy on their beds. May the praise of God be in their mouths and a double-edged sword in their hands, to inflict vengeance on the nations and punishment on the peoples, to bind their kings with fetters, their nobles with shackles of iron, to carry out the sentence written against them. This is the glory of all his saints. Praise the LORD (Ps. 149:1-9).

Yes, even God's wars are fought to the sound of music and praise!

After consulting the people, Jehoshaphat appointed men to sing to the LORD and to praise him for the splendor of his holiness as they went out at the head of the army, saying: "Give thanks to the LORD, for his love endures forever." As they began to sing and praise, the LORD set ambushes against the men of Ammon and Moab and Mount Seir who were invading Judah, and they were defeated (2 Chron. 20:21,22).

Some of the most wonderful encounters with God we have as believers come in the context of anointed music, as we draw near to Him during times of vibrant praise and glorious worship. It seems as if heaven comes down among us, as if we are transported into a different realm—a holy, sacred realm as opposed to the hellish, sinful realm into which we journeyed through drugs and carnal rock. Yet so many ministers refer to the "song service" as part of "the preliminaries!"

This musical segment of the service, which is actually a special time of celebration and adoration, has become something to be patiently endured until we get to the *really* important parts of the meeting: the offering and the preaching! In many services, it is not uncommon to spend more time making announcements (and/or taking offerings) than worshiping the Lord. This is out of order. Are not *all* these elements—worshiping, giving of our hard-earned money, receiving the Word—important in the sight of God, one for meeting with Him, one for consecrating our funds to His work, and one for hearing His directives? And isn't it true that the atmosphere created through worship will largely determine how we respond in giving and how we hear the Word? And isn't it true that the goal of our worship is simply worship, meaning worship and adoration of our King? Isn't worship, in that sense, an end in itself?

Yet so many of our churches have trivialized the ministry of music and the importance of worship. Just ask some worship leaders and professional Christian musicians for a candid response. They will back this up, having no trouble expanding on what has just been said.

Isn't it time for all of us to make a concerted effort to recover the potential of anointed music and song in the churches and in the homes, in the pews and on the streets, in the studios and in the schools? The counterculture revolution of the 1960s only succeeded with the help of satanically inspired music and mind-altering drugs. Could it be that today's Jesus revolution can only succeed with the help of Spirit-inspired music and a life-altering encounter with God? What else will produce the necessary change in our perspective?

It's obvious, of course, that drugs played a large role in fostering the rock revolution, warping—not expanding—our consciousness, making us more prone to fleshly experimentation, divorcing us from reality.[17]

Drugs have also been used in certain religious rites and revolutionary movements. In fact, there is a fascinating tradition behind the word "assassin," going back to the days of Hassan al-Sabah (died 1124), an Islamic radical who has been called almost a model revolutionary. His religious brotherhood was devoted to propagating an extreme form of Islam, and his followers were prepared to kill or be killed for the cause. (Those who specialized in murderous terrorism were called the *fedayeen*.)

> To despise death was one of the highest values promoted in the tightly knit community; the poet Nasser Khosrow wrote:
>
> > Man's fear of death is an illness
> > Whose only medicine is the science of the Faith.
>
> But was "the science of the Faith" enough to make the *fedayeen* kill and die without hesitation? Almost certainly not. The *fedayeen* were subject to long periods of intense propaganda in which they took part in a series of initiation ceremonies. . . . The *fedayeen* must also have been initiated in the use of narcotics [in particular hashish]. . . . The term *hashasheen*, or smokers of hashish, began to be applied to Hassan's followers soon after Nizam al-Mulk's murder [al-Mulk was a prominent opposing leader]; it stuck, and later entered Western languages as "assassin."[18]

So an assassin was a smoker of hashish, helped by narcotics to kill for the faith. What a deadly combination! In the context of the 1960s, rock music and drugs had a different kind of deadly effect, but it was deadly nonetheless.

Of course, revolutionary movements have existed without the influence of music or drugs. In fact, the greatest revolutionary tool is probably the printed page. But this generation, I am sure, will not be reached without moving music and a militant message, anointed and empowered by the Spirit.[19]

And while it is absolutely true that life in the Spirit bears little or no resemblance to drug-induced dazes or drink-induced stupors, it is equally true that young people today don't want empty words or religious talk. They want *reality*, and life in the Spirit is *real*: It has substance, it produces change, and it brings people into contact with the living God. Just "having church" doesn't do it. The MTV generation needs more. (Most adults need more too!) And the Lord is ready to give more.

What a glorious prospect: Our meetings *filled* with the presence and power of God, as holy music blends with powerful truth and ascends like incense to the Throne. Prophetic messengers shaping the consciousness of a young, disillusioned generation, their message carried by music that will never be forgotten. These are the sounds of the coming revolution. If you listen well, you might hear them now.

Chapter Eight

Uncompromising Holiness: The Standard of Revolution

I will be careful to lead a blameless life—when will You come to me?
I will walk in my house with blameless heart. I will set before
my eyes no vile thing. The deeds of faithless men I hate;
they will not cling to me.

PSALM 101:2-3

Be imitators of God, therefore, as dearly loved children and live a life
of love, just as Christ loved us and gave himself up for us as a fra-
grant offering and sacrifice to God. But among you there must not be
even a hint of sexual immorality, or of any kind of impurity, or of
greed, because these are improper for God's holy people. Nor should
there be obscenity, foolish talk or coarse joking, which are out of
place, but rather thanksgiving. For of this you can be sure: No
immoral, impure or greedy person—such a man is an idolater—has
any inheritance in the kingdom of Christ and of God.

EPHESIANS 5:1-5

We are allergic to sin.

E. STANLEY JONES, AMERICAN MISSIONARY TO INDIA

A holy life is a voice; it speaks when the tongue is silent and is either
a constant attraction or a perpetual reproof.

ARCHBISHOP ROBERT LEIGHTON
SEVENTEENTH CENTURY

How little people know who think that holiness is dull. When one
meets the real thing . . . it is irresistible. If even 10 percent
of the world's population had it, would not the whole world
be converted and happy before a year's end?

C. S. LEWIS

Islam's Holy War is a struggle against idolatry, sexual deviation,
plunder, repression, and cruelty.

AYATOLLAH KHOMEINI

Every revolution has a battle cry, a central theme, a rallying call. Every revolution has a standard it raises high and a banner it unfurls, declaring its agenda, solidifying its ranks, unifying its goals.

For the American Revolution, the battle cry was: *Rebellion to Tyrants Is Obedience to God.*

For Communism, the battle cry has been: *Workers of All Countries, Unite!*

For Islam, the battle cry remains: *There Is No God But Allah, and Mohammed Is His Prophet.*

Our revolution has a battle cry too. It is our central theme, our rallying call. It is the standard we raise high, the banner we lift up for the world to see. It declares who we are and announces where we are going, setting forth our agenda and our goals. It is our counterculture message, our confrontational word, the unshakable foundation of our radical reformation. It is our antidote to the devil's poison and our answer to the world's confusion. It is our strength, our sword, and our shield as we advance against the forces of hell.

What is our battle cry? What is the standard we raise high? It is *Holiness to the Lord.*

That is our call to arms! That is the requirement for every soldier in the army. That is the banner under which all of us march. That is the heart of the revolution!

It is the message that transforms entire generations.
It is the message that makes broken lives whole.
It is the message that destroys injustice.
It is the message that puts the family back together.
It is the message that sets captives free.
It is the message that restores dignity and self-respect.
It is the message that brings God near.

It is the message that drives sin away.

And it is a message that will be resisted!

Is that why we are often tempted to water the message down? Is that why we feel so much pressure to lower the standard? Is that why we are sometimes ashamed to declare boldly and plainly what we believe? Yet our message is the message of life! Our message is the message of liberation! How can we compromise even one syllable of our God-given, God-backed, God-blessed standard?

Consider the standard of Communism. It has been held high without shame for more than 150 years. When Marx and Engels forged *The Communist Manifesto* in 1847, they called for Communists to come out of the closet, beginning with the now (in)famous words: "A spectre is haunting Europe—the spectre of Communism. All the powers of old Europe have entered into a holy alliance to exorcize this spectre." Yes, things had reached the point that "communism is already acknowledged by all European powers to be itself a power." Therefore, only one logical course of action remained: "It is high time that Communists should openly, in the face of the whole world, publish their views, their aims, their tendencies, and meet this nursery tale of the Spectre of Communism with a manifesto of the party itself."[1]

What confidence in their system! What belief in their message! What commitment to their cause! This was their great commission. Just look at the expressions Marx and Engels used. There was urgency: "it is high time." There was no shame: Communist beliefs must be declared "openly, in the face of the whole world." There was a definite agenda: they were to "publish their views, their aims, their tendencies." (In fact, they planned to publish the work immediately in English, French, German,

Italian, Flemish, and Danish!)[2] The approach was confrontational: they would proudly and loudly set forth their platform and "meet [the] nursery tale of the Spectre of Communism with a manifesto of the party itself."

They would combat myths and lies with truth—their own perverted brand of truth. And since everyone blamed Communism for everything anyway, expecting and believing the worst, the Communists might as well confirm the fears and suspicions: "We *are* everywhere, and we're as radical as you think." (My believing friend, can't we learn something from this?)

The concluding words of this little world-changing book make clear that it was, in fact, a manifesto, not merely a philosophical proposal or a theoretical treatise. It was a call to battle!

> The Communists disdain to conceal their views and aims. They openly declare that their ends can be attained only by the forcible overthrow of all existing conditions. Let the ruling classes tremble at a communistic revolution. The proletarians have nothing to lose but their chains. They have a world to win.
> WORKERS OF ALL COUNTRIES, UNITE![3]

It is no wonder that Communism spread with such vigor and power in the twentieth century, at one time bringing almost half of the known world under its sway. Its proponents really believed in their message. The world system had to be changed, and the Communists knew how to change it. Revolution! The forcible overthrow of all opposition! They were so convinced they were right that they wore the badge of rejection and reproach with honor: We disdain to conceal our views and aims! The more you reject us the more we gain strength. It proves how right we are and how blind you are. Onward at any cost! Such was the spirit they espoused, and it has been espoused by Communists until today. In India, Communists sign their party vows with their own blood. That's commitment!

In my hand I hold one of the most influential books of the twentieth century: *Quotations from Chairman Mao Tsetung,* also known as Chairman Mao's "Little Red Book."[4] On the front page one phrase is written in all red caps: WORKERS OF ALL COUNTRIES, UNITE! The Communist standard was being raised again. The call to arms was being sounded. Mao urged his people to raise the banner high:

> Thousands upon thousands of martyrs have heroically laid down their lives for the people; let us hold their banner high and march ahead along the path crimson with their blood! . . . Be resolute, fear no sacrifice and surmount every difficulty to win victory.[5]

Onward with the revolution! So said Chairman Mao, and almost 1 billion Chinese were brought into bondage. But such was the courage of Communism. Its staunch adherents were and are true believers who "heroically laid down their lives for the people." What does this say about us—about our devotion, our commitment, our confidence in the rightness of our cause?

We must ask ourselves honestly, truthfully, How is it that we can be so ashamed of our message, so timid with our revolutionary standard? Why must we apologize for preaching holiness and living holiness, for proclaiming God's way as the only right way? Why are we embarrassed by our motto, intimidated by the opposition of the world, unwilling to proclaim it for all to see?

God is the one who made us, and His instruction manual for human beings requires holiness for proper functioning. Holiness is health. Holiness is wholeness. Holiness is wellness. Why do we hide this truth?

Communism has been unashamed! Communism has been zealous and passionate, burning with a missionary spirit of its own. And Communism has extended its kingdom at the cost of blood—oceans of blood![6] Yet we are often ashamed.

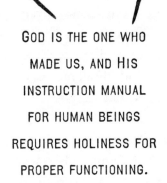

Without God on their side, these Marxist zealots made more people into Communists within decades than the Church made into believers within centuries. Without the hope of heaven, they were willing to lay down their lives for the cause. Without a message that can liberate from guilt, they were unashamed to proclaim their beliefs for the world to hear. Without the expe-

GOD IS THE ONE WHO MADE US, AND HIS INSTRUCTION MANUAL FOR HUMAN BEINGS REQUIRES HOLINESS FOR PROPER FUNCTIONING.

rience of forgiveness or the love of God, they considered no sacrifice too great for the sake of Communism. As Chairman Mao said, "Be resolute, fear no sacrifice and surmount every difficulty to win victory," and they did! What does this say about us?

"We disdain to conceal our views and aims," Marx and Engels wrote. Yet we often conceal ours, trying to convince worldly people that our views are not really extreme, that our faith is completely reasonable, that our aims are not radical at all. Nonsense! As Christians, we believe that everyone who rejects our message will be sentenced to eternal punishment by God. That's extreme! We believe that anyone who does not know the Lord, is a child of Satan. That's extreme! We believe there is no other way to the Father except through the Son. That's extreme! We believe it is our mission in life to reach the entire world with the gospel of Jesus, calling all people to believe in Him. That's extreme! And we believe that God's Word is the standard by which everyone will be judged, in which case, all who have not been born again are ungodly sinners. That's extreme![7]

Does this mean we do not use wisdom and sensitivity when sharing our faith? Certainly not! Does it mean we do not try our best to explain why we believe what we do? Not at all! Does it mean we do not pray for grace and favor when dealing with the world? By all means, no! We need all the grace and favor we can get. But in more cases than we would care to admit, the more clearly that people understand our message, the more decisively they will reject us and mock us.

The Communists, when mocked, took this as a badge of honor. As Mao explained, "The Communist Party does not fear criticism because we are Marxists, the truth is on our side, and the basic masses, the workers and peasants, are on our side."[8] Yet when criticism comes against us for our faith, we wear it as a badge of shame. Something is wrong with this picture!

The Marxists boldly confessed Communism and publicly identified themselves as Communists. So many of us timidly confess Christ in public while boldly professing Him in private (in church services, where it's safe), identifying ourselves as Christians when there's no risk involved. They held their banner high and freely added their blood to the "path crimson with [the earlier martyrs's] blood." So many of us hold our banner low for fear of appearing fanatical and don't even dream of adding our blood to the path crimson with the blood of millions of martyrs, not to mention the blood of our Savior. What does this say about us? What does this say about the strength of our beliefs and the depth of our convictions?

The fact that the power of Communism began to crumble at the end of the twentieth century is not due to a lack of dedication or effort or strategy. Rather, as Professor Robert Coleman observes: "The collapse of communism . . . is not due to its strategy, but to its moral and spiritual bankruptcy. Human beings cannot accept permanently a way of life that denigrates their personhood in the image of God."[9]

But we have a message that is morally and spiritually rich! We have a message that liberates, renewing fallen people in the image of God! We have a message that will set people free! Why do we hold back? HOLINESS TO THE LORD must be proclaimed and published and preached and pronounced. HOLINESS TO THE LORD must be declared! Holiness is God's answer for a dying world. Holiness is the way out and the way back. Holiness is our only hope! It is our weapon against sin and Satan, our arsenal against every unclean power and force, every lie and lust, every wicked thought and way.

There is no message more radical, more revolutionary, more prophetic, more dynamic, more dangerous to hell than the message of HOLINESS TO THE LORD. It is a message that flies in the face of this sin-soaked generation. *It is the ultimate counterculture message* and, not surprisingly, it is a message that is hated and attacked.[10] As Joseph Parker, a contemporary of Spurgeon, said so powerfully:

The man whose little sermon is "repent" sets himself against his age, and will for the time being be battered mercilessly by the age whose moral tone he challenges. There is but one end for such a man—"off with his head!" You had better not try to preach repentance until you have pledged your head to heaven.[11]

The message of holiness, of repentance, of turning from your sins, of getting right with God is *not* a message for the cowardly or the compromised. But it is a message for the serious and the sold-out, a message that restores and transforms. It is a message that must be carried by everyone in God's revolution—a message that has been lifted high in every generation where the Spirit has moved.

Every prophet was a holiness preacher. Every apostle was a holiness preacher. Every true revivalist has been a holiness preacher. (It has been rightly said that every revival is a revival of holiness.) Every true reformer has been a holiness preacher. (By definition, a reformation must bring reform—doctrinal, moral, spiritual, social.) Every true revolutionary—I mean Christian revolutionary—has been a holiness preacher. This is how we topple the society!

"Topple the society?" you say. "What do you mean?"

I do *not* mean the physical overthrow of our government, nor am I endorsing a state of anarchy, chaos, or social collapse. I do *not* mean the abolition of law and order or the end of democratic rule. In fact, Christian revolution has great respect for God-ordained authority and seeks to bring stability, not instability, to society.

What I *do* mean by toppling the society is the pulling down of anti-God strongholds through the bold, unashamed, compassionate, immovable, unshakable proclamation of the message of holiness in word and deed, calling a godless generation to repentance, reformation, restitution, and restoration. Holiness alone can make our society whole!

What exactly is holiness? Holiness is the love of God incarnate, the purity and righteousness of God expressed through man. It is the character of God lived out in flesh and blood. Holiness is soundness and health—mental and emotional, spiritual and moral. Holiness is life—and I mean *real* life. Holiness is truth—pure and unadulterated, crystal clear and undefiled. Whereas sin is corruption and decay, holiness is wholeness and wellness. Where sin pollutes and poisons, holiness refreshes and invigorates. Holiness is the beauty of Jesus made manifest in us and through us. A holy individual is a blessed individual. A holy family is a blessed family. A holy society is a blessed society. A holy generation is a blessed generation.

Sin is our enemy. The flesh is our enemy. The devil is our enemy, opposing everything that is good, fair, lovely—anything that reflects the image of God. The devil is a perverter, a destroyer, a deceiver; and sin is the means by which he accomplishes his evil works. This world system marches to his beat—throbbing with lust and unclean desires, pounding with greed, injustice, violence, idolatry, witchcraft, drunkenness, murder, cruelty . . . the list goes on and on. Society is in a mess because of sin!

Why are there broken homes? Sin. Why are there drug addicts and alcoholics? Sin. Why are there jails and prisons? Sin. Why are there suicides and murders? Sin. Why are there unwanted pregnancies and abortions? Sin. Why are there abused children and battered wives? Sin. Why are there thefts and rapes? Sin. Why are there adulterers, fornicators, homosexuals, and lesbians? Sin. Why are there false religions and cults? Sin! Why did Jesus come into the world? To save us from our sin, to take away our sin, to destroy the power of sin, to deliver us from the clutches of sin. So it is written in the Word!

She will give birth to a son, and you are to give him the name Jesus, because he will save his people from their sins (Matt. 1:21).

The next day John saw Jesus coming toward him and said, "Look, the Lamb of God, who takes away the sin of the world!" (John 1:29).

Now He has appeared once for all at the end of the ages to do away with sin by the sacrifice of Himself. . . . Christ was sacrificed once to take away the sins of many people (Heb. 9:26,28).

For we know that our old self was crucified with him so that the body of sin might be done away with, that we should no longer be slaves to sin (Rom. 6:6).

Everyone who sins breaks the law; in fact, sin is lawlessness. But you know that he appeared so that he might take away our sins. And in him is no sin. . . . He who does what is sinful is of the devil, because the devil has been sinning from the beginning. The reason the Son of God appeared was to destroy the devil's work (1 John 3:4,5,8).

[He] gave himself for us to redeem us from all wickedness and to purify for himself a people that are his very own, eager to do what is good (Titus 2:14).

This is the purpose of God! "He himself bore our sins in his body on the tree, so that we might die to sins and live for righteousness; by his wounds you have been healed" (1 Pet. 2:24). Yes, "You have been set free from sin and have become slaves to righteousness" (Rom. 6:18). This is God's eternal plan: "For he chose us in him [Jesus] before the creation of the world to be holy and blameless in his sight" (Eph. 1:4). Do you grasp the force of these words? The very reason the Lord chose us in His Son was *so that* we would be holy and blameless in His sight. Otherwise, we are of no value to Him.

Our God is absolutely holy. He is the perfect expression of everything good and right, eternally free from sin in any form. His angels are holy, heaven is holy, and the New Jerusalem is holy (see Rev. 3:7; 4:8; 6:10; 14:10; 15:4; 16:5; 21:2,10; 22:11). Only the holy make it in!

> Blessed are those who wash their robes, that they may have the right to the tree of life and may go through the gates into the city. Outside are the dogs, those who practice magic arts, the sexually immoral, the murderers, the idolaters and everyone who loves and practices falsehood (Rev. 22:14,15).

> And a highway will be there;
> it will be called the Way of Holiness.
> The unclean will not journey on it;
> it will be for those who walk in that Way;
> wicked fools will not go about on it.
> No lion will be there,
> nor will any ferocious beast get up on it;
> they will not be found there.
> But only the redeemed will walk there,
> and the ransomed of the LORD will return.
> They will enter Zion with singing;
> everlasting joy will crown their heads.

Gladness and joy will overtake them,
and sorrow and sighing will flee away (Isa. 35:8-10).

It is only the "blessed and holy" who participate in the first resurrection, meaning the resurrection of the saved (see Rev. 20:6). The unholy are lost; they will never enjoy the blessing of heaven. They will never see the smile of God—only His wrath—in the world to come. What a terrible shame!

If sin could be present in heaven—even in the smallest, most minute degree—it would no longer be heaven. What makes heaven so wonderful is holiness: It is a place without sin. That's why there will be no prisons in heaven, no gun-toting police in heaven, no funeral parlors in heaven, no hospitals in heaven—because there's no sin there. It's a holy place, marked by harmony, beauty, tranquillity, joy, love, vision, fulfillment, and endless worship. It is what we were made for!

Here on the earth, there is a fierce battle between flesh and Spirit, between the system of this world and the kingdom of God, between this age and the age to come. We stand between two worlds—not just two ideologies—and we bring a message that is not just a counterculture message but rather a counter-age message. Jesus "gave Himself for our sins to rescue us from the present evil age, according to the will of our God and Father" (Gal. 1:4). How revolutionary! The powers of the age to come have broken into this age, and those two ages are in conflict. There is a clash of values, of standards, of ethics, of ideals. Will we bow the knee to God alone, refusing to compromise, or will we bow the knee to this world, relaxing our convictions for the sake of our companions?

Compromise will not work in a revolution, and we must raise our standards to reflect His: "But just as he who called you is holy, so be holy in all you do; for it is written: 'Be holy, because

I am holy'" (1 Peter 1:15,16). To compromise is to side with the enemy. To compromise is to sow confusion and discord. To compromise is to fight against your own side and your own self. Holiness without compromise is the key. God hates foreign mixtures. Therefore, "let us purify ourselves from everything that contaminates body and spirit, perfecting holiness out of reverence for God" (2 Cor. 7:1). What a radical aim!

How far would Communism go if its leaders and followers were secret capitalists? How far would Islam go if its leaders and followers were secret Hindus? How far will our holiness revolution go if we—its leaders and followers—are secret, willful sinners?

We can only liberate captives if we ourselves are free. We can only war in the Spirit if we defeat the flesh. This is how we must live. This is how we must fight. Paul called Timothy to "endure hardship with us like a good soldier of Christ Jesus," pointing out that "no one serving as a soldier gets involved in civilian affairs—he wants to please his commanding officer" (2 Tim. 2:3,4).

Even the soldiers in Mao Zedong's Communist Army (called the Chinese People's Liberation Army) in 1947 were ordered to abide by strict ethical principles and not get involved in civilian affairs:

The Three Main Rules of Discipline are as follows:
1. Obey orders in all your actions.
2. Do not take a single needle or piece of thread from the masses.
3. Turn in everything captured.

The Eight Points for Attention are as follows:
1. Speak politely.
2. Pay fairly for what you buy.
3. Return everything you borrow.

4. Pay for anything you damage.
5. Do not hit or swear at people.
6. Do not damage crops.
7. Do not take liberties with women.
8. Do not ill-treat captives.[12]

Now, God only knows to what extent the soldiers heeded this counsel, but those who did showed more integrity than many a Christian today—not to mention many a minister. (Just look again at points 1 and 7!) Yet we are called to be soldiers in the Lord's army (see Phil. 2:25; Philem. 2), to please Jesus—not Mao or Khomeini or Lenin, but the Lord—our commanding officer. Therefore, we *cannot* get involved in sinful affairs. They distract us, they counteract our efforts, and they undermine our work.

We don't watch filthy movies, we don't lie and cheat, we don't steal and oppress, we don't fornicate and get high, and we don't practice sin, because all of that is of the enemy and the world—the very system we're opposing. That is part of the culture we are renouncing, part of the age we are transcending, part of the mind-set we are rejecting. We are not of this world! We have been born again, born from above, and we are now seated with Jesus in heavenly places, dead to the old, alive to the new. We are now hidden with the Messiah in God (see Col. 3:1-4). How revolutionary!

We are not just men and women with a different social agenda or a different set of beliefs; we are a different kind of people, a people indwelt by God Himself, a people who already have one foot in heaven. That is how we live in this world: as heavenly people spreading a revolutionary message of forgiveness and transformation through the power of the blood of Jesus.[13]

Paul also wrote that "if anyone competes as an athlete, he does not receive the victor's crown unless he competes according to the rules" (2 Tim. 2:5). The rules of our game can be summed up in one word: "Holiness"! Holiness is separation *from sin* and separation *to God*. Without holiness, we can't win the race. Without holiness, we'll never receive the victor's crown. That's why we live as we do. Sin to the believer is like injury to an athlete. It cripples, it cramps, it hinders, it hurts. Sin to the believer is like a traitor to an army. It leads to death and destruction. Fellow soldiers, be diligent! Fellow athletes, stay in shape! This is how we must live.

Our revolution is a revolution of separation, as sinners are set free from their sins and called to serve the Lord. Our revolution is a revolution of grace, as people receive new life and a fresh start, with a perfectly clean slate and no strikes against them because of what someone else (Jesus!) did for them.

There will be fierce opposition to our message and real persecution because of our lifestyle. We don't totally fit in this world! We make people uncomfortable. We mess up people's guilt-free parties. We shine the light into dark corners where the unsaved hide in their sin. This is not appreciated! And the light shines in our own lives too, where we must make choices every day, refusing to give ground to the enemy, refusing to surrender an inch of moral turf, refusing to cave in to the onslaughts of sin, refusing to define holiness based on the world's dictionary.

But we fail miserably here! This is our Achilles' heel, the weak spot of our revolution: We ourselves are not holy! We ourselves look so much like the world and live so much like the world that we are hardly distinguishable from the world. How then can we change the world?

"But we have to become like the world in order to win the world," you say.

Never! If we become like the world in order to win the people of the world, to what are we winning them? Cultural sensitivity is one thing. Compromise is another. And yet so many Christians justify moral compromise in their lives. So many try to explain why their views on sin do not resemble God's views on sin. And the excuses are so pathetic, especially when you remember that Jesus died to save us from our sins. *Anything* that justifies the presence of willful sin in our lives is an enemy of the Cross and an insult to the blood of Jesus. That is something to consider![14]

IF WE BECOME LIKE THE WORLD IN ORDER TO WIN THE PEOPLE OF THE WORLD, TO WHAT ARE WE WINNING THEM? CULTURAL SENSITIVITY IS ONE THING; COMPROMISE IS ANOTHER.

Of course, we say that we don't want to be religious, but we never define what "religious" really means. And we are quick to point out that we don't want to be legalists, but we fail to explain what *non*legalism is.[15] The simple truth is that there is *no good reason in the sight of God* for any of us to look for an excuse to sin or to equate Christian liberty with freedom to sin or to justify habitual sin or to downplay the ugliness of sin. Sin is the only thing that can cut our revolution short. Sin is the only thing that can stop us from reaching our goal. Sin must be rejected and resisted. Sin must be trampled under our feet.

Do we still have to battle with sin? Yes! Do we sometimes feel buffeted and battered by temptation? No doubt! Do we sometimes fall short of the mark? Absolutely! And is our Father quick to forgive us when we turn to Him in repentance and faith? Yes! But none of this means that we tolerate sin, justify sin, or excuse sin. Sin is the enemy! I would rather have someone call me a legalist (although I am no more a legalist than I am a ballet dancer) or have someone call me religious (although I am no more religious than I am ten feet tall with purple hair) than have someone call me a compromiser. Never!

In 1999, a friend began sending me copies of a Christian magazine from Europe devoted to the theme of renewal and revival. Every issue was filled with exciting testimonies of what the Spirit was doing in the land. Every issue featured edifying teachings by national leaders and often carried inspiring stories of godly examples from the past. Every issue was devoid of hype and the exaltation of man. And every issue carried a lethal dose of poison.

Poison? In a renewal magazine?

Yes! There was a hateful foreign mixture, a destructive mingling of the clean with the unclean, a terribly dangerous joining of the sacred with the profane, a grievous merging of the work of the Spirit and the work of the devil. You see, in Europe, there are very few (if any) prominent Christian radio stations devoted to playing contemporary Christian music, so Christian artists and groups can be heard on secular radio. This, of course, can be a godsend, since these believers have the opportunity to get their message out where it is needed (provided they have a message). But this can also be a trap, since many European Christians make no distinctions in their listening habits, enjoying secular music with a sinful message alongside Christian music with a saving message. Sadly, this European revival and renewal magazine plays right into this trap—or to be perfectly honest, sets a trap of its own—by devoting several pages to music reviews that include the latest secular music.

But what's wrong with that? you may be thinking. *Must we be totally ignorant of what the world is singing and writing and hearing and seeing?*

Certainly not! But that is not the problem here. This magazine is not primarily attempting to critique the nonbelieving artists from a believing viewpoint, interacting with their songs and showing their need for the Savior. To the contrary, the reviewers often rave about the music of some of today's most worldly, sensual, godless stars. How can this be?

What believer in close fellowship with God would allow music by Madonna into his or her home? Taking this a step further, what committed believer would dream of praising one of her recording projects? (Remember, this is the same woman who published an entire book of her explicit pornographic photos, the same woman famous for singing her lewd, sometimes anti-Christian songs with a large cross around her neck.) Yet this renewal magazine, this otherwise fine publication inspired by an outpouring of the Holy Spirit (yes, *Holy* Spirit), praises Madonna's songs on its pages without even a hint of discomfort or embarrassment. Worse yet, it praises contemporary artists even more vile than Madonna (a woman we should certainly pray for and pity).

For example, in the fall 1999 issue, it contained a review of the latest release of Alanis Morissette, a woman whose totally in-your-face sexual lyrics shocked the *secular* recording industry. Her lyrics cannot be repeated here without violating clear biblical teachings (such as Eph. 5:1-12). This is a woman who surely needs the Lord. Speaking of her CD *Supposed Former Infatuation Junkie,* the reviewer exclaims:

If you feel in the mood for melodies that twist and turn with no warning and for lyrics that expose a level of honesty that could become uncomfortable, then Alanis is your woman. [Yes, you read that rightly!]. . . *Supposed Former Infatuation Junkie* cannot be considered as background music. But it certainly contains songs that will affect you to your very core—if you dare let them! . . . She has an incredible gift to turn her racked emotion into a verbal and musical language that may just relate to your own life. [Can you believe this?] Powerful stuff! . . . Heavy, fragile, beautiful, angst-ridden—and definitely not for the faint-hearted. But I love it![16]

This review is on the very same page where the reviewer pens some insightful, challenging words about groundbreaking Christian music. No wonder we have been losing the cultural war. There is compromise in our ranks. There is disease in our Body. There are counterrevolutionary attitudes in our midst. How this must grieve the Lord! He died to get this junk out of our lives. He knows how destructive sinful music can be (just remember the last chapter!). And yet we, His purchased flock, His blood-bought brothers and sisters, gulp down the very poison that sapped His lifeblood. May it not be![17]

In January 2000, a ministry student in our school forwarded an e-mail to me that he described as "a sad, yet (ironically) hysterical [message] from a 'Christian,' warning of the atrocities of a recent, R-rated movie called *Dogma*—[a movie] known for its foul language, perverseness, and sacrilegious nature."

What made the original e-mail so shocking or, in the student's words, "sad yet (ironically) hysterical" was that it came from the wife of a concerned Christian couple who wanted to alert readers *not* to see this movie *after seeing it themselves.* (Actually, it was so bad they had to walk out—but only after enduring 45 minutes!)

First, why did they go to see an R-rated movie? If a movie is not suitable to be viewed in public with other believers—for example, at a church gathering—then it's not suitable to be viewed at all, and this includes virtually all R- and PG13-rated movies, not to mention many PG movies.

Second, why did they subject themselves to 45 minutes of profanity, violence, nudity, and sexual jokes? Here is their description of what they saw (naming some of the movie's actors, who played angels):

> In the 45 minutes we watched the movie, they had an angel pull his pants down to show he was not anatomically correct and then make several references about it; Matt Damon (one of the angels) shot seven people (he shot the people because he found a loophole on how to get into heaven after killing people); Chris Rock fell from the sky stark naked; at least four or five profane words were spoken in every sentence, and they did away with [a] crucifix and had another portrayal for Jesus (he was winking and giving a thumbs-up sign). They also had a derogatory slang term they were using for Jesus.

Yet this couple watched almost an hour of this garbage before leaving and apologizing to God. How insensitive we have become!

Worse still, movie reviewers in Christian magazines—even leading evangelical magazines such as *Christianity Today*—will often discuss the contents of profane, violent, sensual movies without saying "And believers have no business seeing such trash!" Rather, they will review the movies as works of art, drawing various moral lessons or commenting on the movie's moral bankruptcy, also naming their favorites for the year, assuming that their readers will also view some of the same flicks.[18]

Where, then, do we draw the line? Why not review blatant pornography, unless, of course, XXX are films lacking in artistic merit and devoid of a message. (Forgive the sarcasm.) And what does the Word mean when it calls us to "come out from among them and be separate" (2 Cor. 6:17)?

Jude gave us clear counsel: "Be merciful to those who doubt; snatch others from the fire and save them; to others show mercy, mixed with fear—hating even the clothing stained by corrupted flesh" (Jude 22,23). Yes, hating it, not praising it; loathing it, not loving it. And if we are called to hate "even the clothing stained by corrupted flesh," how should we feel about movies stained by profanity, videos stained by nudity, sports stained by gratuitous violence? As Edwin A. Blum commented on Jude's words, "Perhaps the figure is that their depravity has made them infectious. Christians are to show mercy as in the first case, but now *they are to be fearful lest the infection spread to them.*"[19]

Sin spreads like a deadly infection! Yet we justify watching filth, listening to filth, digesting filth, reading filth by saying it's not that bad or, worse yet, by saying that it helps us relate better to the world. What folly! That's like encouraging Christian men to have sex with other men in order to better relate to gays, or encouraging our daughters to undress in public in order to better relate to strippers, or encouraging pastors to shoot dope in order to better relate to drug addicts, or encouraging prison chaplains to kill someone to better relate to murderers.

"But," you say, "there are people who got saved after we went to the movies with them—without judging them or criticizing their standards—while others came to the Lord after we sat in the bar with them and had a drink—without getting drunk, of course. If people get saved, that's all that matters."

Says who? If the ends justify the means, then maybe we should start a ministry called Prostitutes for Jesus (or Call Girls for Christ or, better yet, Streetwalkers for the Savior). After all, the only ones who go to prostitutes are sinners, so the ladies would be reaching out to the lost. And these sisters would be able to touch the men in their hour of need, really "giving themselves" to the ministry in a selfless way. And then when they were finished and the men were feeling guilty, the hookers could lead them in the sinner's prayer. (I've just come up with the best name yet for the ministry: Hookers for Him!)

Sorry, friend, but the ends don't justify the means, and I question the depth of any salvation that did not call the sinner to turn from sin. Yet how can we call sinners to turn from sin when we join them in their sin? It has never worked and it never will. Satan is the author of this soul-winning by-any-means deception. It must be utterly renounced!

I say again: We need a revolution of holiness. We need a return to holiness. We need a rediscovery of holiness. Without holiness, there is no true happiness. As John Wesley rightly said, "They who bring most holiness to heaven will find most happiness there."[20] Without holiness, there is no true fulfillment. (It is those who hunger and thirst for righteousness who are filled.) Without holiness, there is no true freedom. (Only those who are free from sin really know what freedom is.) We must boldly proclaim HOLINESS TO THE LORD.

Do you remember the climax of the Communist Manifesto? It said this:

> The Communists disdain to conceal their views and aims. They openly declare that their ends can be attained only by the forcible overthrow of all existing conditions. Let the rulings classes tremble at a communistic revolution. The proletarians have nothing to lose but their chains. They have a world to win.
> WORKERS OF ALL COUNTRIES, UNITE![21]

What a blatant satanic counterfeit of God's call to arms. The real call sounds like this:

> The Christians disdain to conceal their views and aims. They openly declare that their ends can be attained only by the spiritual overthrow of all devilish conditions. Let the ruling demons tremble at a Christian revolution. The prisoners of sin have nothing to lose but their chains. They have eternal life to win.
> WORSHIPERS OF ALL COUNTRIES, UNITE!

And around what standard do we unite? HOLINESS TO THE LORD. That is our battle cry! True holy war is a war *for* holiness and a war *of* holiness, and God's battles are won on holy ground (see Josh. 5:13-15). The Lord only fights for the one "who has clean hands and a pure heart, who does not lift up his soul to an idol or swear by what is false" (Ps. 24:4). That is the one who "will receive blessing from the LORD and vindication from God his Savior. Such is the generation of those who seek him" (vv. 5,6). God is ready to back His holy troops. He is ready to march in our midst. He is ready to give us this generation. Are you ready? Are you holy?

In 1983, Winkie Pratney gave this pointed challenge, a challenge that speaks even more pointedly today. We need only add the word "revolution" to drive the point fully home:

> When the question is asked: *"What hinders revival [and revolution]?"* one of the simple answers is this: *We do not have men and women who are prepared to pay the same price to preach the same message and have the same power as those revivalists [and revolutionaries!] of the past.* Without these firm believers, the community can never be changed. Our concern is conciliatory, our obedience optional, our lack theologically and culturally justified. *Quite simply, it costs too much!*
>
> We say we want revival [and revolution!]. But who today is prepared to live a life of absolute obedience to the Holy Spirit, tackling sin in the Church as well as the streets, preaching such a message of perfection of heart and holiness of life—a message feared and hated by the religious and street sinner alike. Are we prepared?[22]

Are we? If so, help me hoist the banner, raise the standard, and get on with the revolution!

"Give Me Liberty or Give Me Death": The Driving Force of Revolution

Let's face it: the reason you are in a guerilla war is because you either want to overthrow the existing corrupt government, be it Communist, Socialist, Fascist, or what have you, and establish a democratic government that is truly by and for the people, or because your country has been invaded by a foreign army and you are bent on destroying them at all costs.

GUNNERY SERGEANT BOB NEWMAN
UNITED STATES MARINE CORPS

The people never give up their liberties but under some delusion.

EDMUND BURKE
EIGHTEENTH-CENTURY BRITISH STATESMAN

Resolved, that the women of this nation in 1876, have greater cause for discontent, rebellion and revolution than the men of 1776.

SUSAN B. ANTHONY
NINETEENTH-CENTURY SUFFRAGETTE

In the beauty of the lilies Christ was born across the sea,
With a glory in his bosom that transfigures you and me,
As he died to make men holy, let us die to make men free,
While God is marching on.

JULIA WARD HOWE
THE "BATTLE HYMN OF THE REPUBLIC"

What causes people to revolt? What sparks a popular uprising? What captures the imagination of the masses, transforming them from peaceful citizens into violent revolutionaries? It is the cry for freedom and justice, the cry for liberty and equal rights. It is a cry heard around the world.

Freedom! So many promise it, but so few deliver it. So few even know what it really is. But whoever can promise freedom can gain a following. This has been the appealing power of many a revolution. It has been the lure of Communism, the bait that Marxism has used to capture multitudes: Working classes unite! Throw off your shackles! Cast off your bonds! Determine your own futures! Gain freedom for yourselves and your children!

As expressed so clearly in the closing words of *The Communist Manifesto,* "The workers have nothing to lose but their chains."[1] Everyone wants to lose their chains! But did Communism produce what it promised?

Frederick Engels, one of the authors of *The Communist Manifesto,* was so convinced of the liberating power of its message that 40 years after the first edition was printed, he predicted economic emancipation would bring about the emancipating of "society at large from all exploitation, oppression, class distinctions and class struggles."[2] Not only would the working classes be liberated, but *all* classes would be liberated, all the oppressed set free. How wrong Engels was! Communism has not liberated the masses, it has enslaved them by the hundreds of millions.[3]

One century earlier, the passions of the French Revolution were ignited by the publication of another cry for freedom, the concise three-page document *The Declaration of the Rights of Man and Citizen.* "Equality for all! Liberty for all!"[4] But this declaration did not deliver freedom either. It *could* not deliver. Something fundamental was missing. It did not grasp the root problem. It did not understand the key. What is it that really enslaves? What is it that really liberates? What is the key to freedom?

It was the cry for freedom that led to the American Revolution, something recognized by Malcom X: "Look at the American Revolution in 1776. That revolution was for what? For land. Why did they want land? Independence."[5] Our forefathers wanted freedom from oppression and tyranny. Independence was the goal! And how was it expressed? The national leaders drew up a declaration of independence, inspired in part by one of the greatest speeches in American history, delivered by Patrick Henry in 1775. His closing words left the hearers in stunned silence, followed by a rousing show of their support. America was founded on these very words!

> Is life so dear or peace so sweet, as to be purchased at the price of chains and slavery? Forbid it, Almighty God! I know not what course others may take, but as for me, give me liberty or give me death!

This says it all! We must have liberty, we must have freedom—even at the cost of life itself. Without freedom, life is no longer worthy of the name. That's why many influential leaders have declared their willingness to pay the ultimate price for freedom.[6] Consider the words of two Black leaders, Nelson Mandela and Malcolm X. At his 1964 trial for sabotage in Pretoria, South Africa, Mandela ended his opening statement by saying:

> During my lifetime I have dedicated myself to this strug-gle of the African people. I have fought against white domination, and I have fought against black domina-tion. I have cherished the ideal of a democratic and free

society in which all persons live together in harmony and with equal opportunity. It is an ideal which I hope to live for and to achieve. But if needs be, it is an ideal for which I am prepared to die.[7]

Malcolm X put it like this: "If you're not ready to die for it, put the word 'freedom' out of your vocabulary. . . . . The price of freedom is death."[8]

Freedom! So many have fought for it. So many have died for it. Even in the closing days of the twentieth century, people were dying for their freedom. Just look at the country of Chechnya. Russia was hitting this breakaway republic with all its might, and still, the Chechnyan soldiers fought back. General Mashkadov, a Muslim leader, was amazed at the tenacity of his troops: "I can only wonder at the strength with which my men fight. . . . All we can do is fight on, to show not only that we want our independence, but that we are willing to die for it."[9]

People will die for freedom. People will only sink so low before they say "Enough is enough! I cannot live any longer under such conditions. I *will not* live any longer under such conditions. Give me liberty or give me death. Life without liberty is not worth living."

This is how the Maccabean revolt began almost 2,200 years ago. Enough was enough! The Jewish people had suffered at the hand of Antiochus Epiphanes IV for years. Their lifestyles were restricted and their faith was mocked. Still, they complied and went along. After all, they were outnumbered and out-armed, and the breaking point had not yet been reached. And then it came! Antiochus had the gall to sacrifice a pig on the Temple altar, and that was more than the people could take.

The truths expressed by Patrick Henry—although not to be spoken for two millennia—resonated in the hearts of these

Maccabean freedom fighters: "Is life so dear or peace so sweet, as to be purchased at the price of chains and slavery? Forbid it, Almighty God! We know not what course others may take, but as for us, give us liberty or give us death!"[10]

The uprising had begun! After a protracted struggle of many months, the victory was secured and the Temple purified. (We commemorate this event in the Jewish holiday called Hanukkah.) But what would have happened if Antiochus had not been so brazen in provoking the Jewish people? What if he had not gone that far? It is possible that freedom would never have come. The people only fought when they reached the breaking point. The defining moment came when they said, "Enough is enough!" At some point, people are willing to die to be free.

I found a particularly tragic, gruesome example of a breaking point being reached in a book I was reading on martyrdom. In the 1990s, a Canadian couple went on a horrific rampage of violence and perversion, sexually abusing and then torturing to death a number of young women. The crimes they committed— and videotaped—were repulsive beyond words. After raping and abusing one of the teenage girls, they ordered her to perform an even more humiliating sex act, but she refused to comply. They reminded her of the consequences: She would suffer an agonizing death, just as the others girls had, just as they had shown her on videotape. "Some things are worth dying for!" she exclaimed, before they snuffed out her life.

To live under such conditions, to preserve life at the expense of one's honor, to accept life at the price of humiliation and bondage—this was too high a price to pay. Sometimes the only choice, be it individually or corporately, is "Give me liberty or give me death!" Yes, there are some things worth dying for, while at other times even life itself—dragged down into chains and slavery—is hardly worth living for. Only freedom satisfies.

It was craving for freedom that sparked the French Revolution, craving for freedom that sparked the American Revolution, craving for freedom that sparked numerous Communist revolutions, and still, lasting freedom has not come. What is missing? For all the passion of the French Revolution, for all the noble aims of the American Revolution, for all the promises of Communism, people remain enslaved and bound. Why?

Consider the history of America. More than 75 years after the Declaration of Independence was signed, slave trade was still flourishing in our land. It was not yet the land of the free and home of the brave. Hundreds of thousands were held captive.[11] But voices rose up in protest: There must be freedom for all!

One of the most militant—and sometimes extremist—voices was that of William Lloyd Garrison, a "poorly educated, failed journalist and publisher" who "found his calling in the abolitionist movement" and in 1831 "began publishing a rather radical antislavery paper" called *The Liberator*.[12] (This is reminiscent of the radical women's rights paper published by Susan B. Anthony and Elizabeth Cady Stanton called *The Revolution*.[13]) Although *The Liberator* "never attracted a circulation of more than three thousand, it became the driving force toward the abolition of the institutions of chattel servitude."[14] A short poem Garrison wrote captured the hearts of New Englanders and helped pave the way for freedom of the slaves:

> They tell me, Liberty! that in thy name
> I may not plead for all the human race;
> That some are born to bondage and disgrace,

Some to a heritage of woe and shame,
And some to power supreme, and glorious fame:
With my whole soul I spurn the doctrine base,
And, as an equal brotherhood, embrace
All people, and for all fair freedom claim!
Know this, O man! whate'er thy earthly fate,
God never made a tyrant nor a slave:
Woe, then, to those who dare to desecrate
His glorious image!—for to all He gave
Eternal rights, which none may violate;
And, by a mighty hand, the oppressed He yet shall
save.[15]

How true! All human beings are made in the image of God, and therefore one man is not created a tyrant—as if he was somehow entitled to cruelly oppress other human beings—while another man is created a slave—as if he was somehow less human than the next. No! Such degraded concepts can destroy the very fabric of a nation, as Abraham Lincoln recognized, recalling the words of Jesus, "If a house is divided against itself, that house cannot stand" (Mark 3:25). Lincoln said, "I believe this government cannot endure permanently, half slave and half free."[16] No! Rather, as he stated in his annual message to Congress (December 1, 1862), "In giving freedom to the slave, we assure freedom to the free,—honourable alike in what we give and what we preserve."[17] Freedom for the oppressed meant freedom for all.

Yet even the freeing of the slaves set in motion with the signing of the Emancipation Proclamation did not bring harmony and peace. It did not stop the terribly costly Civil War, and our nation was left bloodied and bruised for decades. When the twentieth century dawned, our nation was still marred by massive social inequality for blacks, for women, and for others. Where could freedom be found?

One of the most eloquent spokesmen for black equality was W. E. DuBois, an advocate of freedom-by-force when necessary.[18] For him, a white man like John Brown was a hero of freedom whose death was not in vain. (Brown was the antislavery leader who believed he was on a divine mission to liberate captives, using murderous force in the process.) Listen to the passionate call of DuBois:

> We do not believe in violence, neither in the despised violence of the raid nor the lauded violence of the soldier, nor the barbarous violence of the mob. But we do believe in John Brown, in that incarnate spirit of justice, that hatred of a lie, that willingness to sacrifice money, reputation, and life itself on the altar of right. And here on the scene of John Brown's martyrdom we reconsecrate ourselves, our honor, our property to the final emancipation of the race which John Brown died to make free.[19]

Yes, John Brown made the ultimate sacrifice (killing others as well), just as many Americans made the ultimate sacrifice in our country's Revolutionary War (also killing others in the battle). And DuBois and his colleagues fought valiantly for freedom for all for "the final emancipation of the race." And still it did not come! Everyone wants emancipation. Everyone wants freedom. Everyone wants liberty. Every revolution promises it. But none can fully deliver it.

Almost 60 years after DuBois delivered his speech, an even more famous black American leader delivered an even more famous speech. It was Dr. Martin Luther King, Jr., preaching to more than 200,000 at the Lincoln Memorial in 1963. (Is it a coincidence that I write these very pages on Martin Luther King Day, January 16, 2000?) Who among us has not heard his words?

> When we let freedom ring, when we let it ring from every village and every hamlet, and every state and every city, we will be able to speed up that day when all God's children, black men and white men, Jews and Gentiles, Protestants and Catholics, will be able to join hands and sing in the words of that old Negro spiritual, "Free at last! Free at last! Thank God Almighty, we are free at last!"

The cry went out once again! "Let freedom ring! . . . Free at last!" Sixty years earlier, DuBois had proclaimed: "We reconsecrate ourselves, our honor, our property to the final emancipation of the race." Twenty years before that, Engels prophesied the emancipating of "society at large from all exploitation, oppression, class distinctions and class struggles." One hundred years earlier, Patrick Henry had cried out, "Give me liberty or give me death!" Yet total emancipation, true liberation, lasting freedom has not come. Why?

Before the American Revolution, Christians turned to the Word of God to support their political views. In fact, verses such as 2 Corinthians 3:17 (Paul: "Where the Spirit of the Lord is, there is liberty") and John 8:32 (Jesus: "Then you will know the truth, and the truth will set you free") were preached from pulpits throughout the land. As stated then by Charles Turner of Duxbury, "The Scriptures cannot be rightfully expounded without explaining them in a manner friendly to the cause of freedom."[20] But was Paul speaking of political freedom? Was Jesus referring to social liberty? Hardly.[21] Yet our forefathers were on the right track in turning to the Scriptures. The Bible is the ultimate book of liberation, God's handwritten freedom manifesto.

Freedom! It is one of the great themes of the Word, the cornerstone of the Old Testament and the foundation of the New. Freedom! The Scriptures alone understand human slavery and the Scriptures alone have the cure. It is only in the Word that we have a real declaration of independence, only in the Word that we find the ultimate emancipation proclamation. Of course, our nation's Declaration of Independence made a great difference in history, giving birth to our blessed country, and Lincoln's Emancipation Proclamation resulted in the abolition of a horrific, destructive practice. These two documents had a real liberating effect. But the liberating effect of the Word of God is infinitely greater. Jesus came to set all captives free—free indeed!

IT IS ONLY IN THE WORD THAT WE HAVE A REAL DECLARATION OF INDEPENDENCE, ONLY IN THE WORD THAT WE FIND THE ULTIMATE EMANCIPA-TION PROCLAMATION.

All of us crave freedom. None of us would choose slavery for ourselves or our loved ones. None of would welcome oppression, bondage, exploitation, or captivity. All of us long for liberty. All creation groans for it! Slavery is degrading, debasing, destructive. It robs human beings of their dignity and strips them of their self-worth. It makes them subject to the whim and will of tyrants. It brings them into bondage to heartless masters who rule their lives with cruelty and malice. It turns their daily existence into a nightmare of misery and despair. Slavery is a fruit of sin.

In a perfect world, there would be no slavery. There will certainly be no slavery in heaven, no captives in chains, no prisoners in shackles. But here, on this sinful, fallen planet, Satan has made slavery his domain. He is the ultimate slave master, the bondage maker par excellence. He is the inspiration behind every demented dictator, the driving force behind every demonic despot. He loves to degrade and destroy. He loves to take people captive, enslaving them to his will, making them subject to his filthy ways (see Rom. 6:16; 2 Tim. 2:26). But Jesus sets the prisoners free! He came to this world to liberate slaves—of Satan, of sin, of fear, of death. Freedom! That was the goal of His ministry:

> To the Jews who had believed Him, Jesus said, "If you hold to my teaching, you are really my disciples. Then you will know the truth, and the truth will set you free." They answered Him, "We are Abraham's descendants and have never been slaves of anyone. How can you say that we shall be set free?" Jesus replied, "I tell you the truth, everyone who sins is a slave to sin. Now a slave has no permanent place in the family, but a son belongs to it forever. So if the Son sets you free, you will be free indeed" (John 8:31-36).

> *It is for freedom that Christ has set us free.* Stand firm, then, and do not let yourselves be burdened again by *a yoke of slavery* (Gal. 5:1, emphasis added).

Freedom! This was also the great theme of the Hebrew Scriptures. It began with the exodus from Egypt, when God liberated a whole nation of slaves and called them to Himself. Freedom! This was the great hope of the prophets, as they looked forward to the day when God would liberate the whole world from the curse of sin and guilt. Freedom! This is something of great importance to the Lord. Just consider how far He has gone and how much He has given to set His people free.

The Israelites had been subject to hard service in Egypt, living and dying with no future, no hope, no vision. Endless weeks faded into endless months, and endless years wore into endless decades, and still, there was no relief in sight: "The Israelites groaned in their slavery and cried out, and their cry for help because of their slavery went up to God. God heard their groaning and he remembered His covenant with Abraham, with Isaac and with Jacob. So God looked on the Israelites and was concerned about them" (Exod. 2:23-25). Their slavery got His attention. Their bondage captured His heart. Soon they would be free!

The Lord's people were not made to serve the Egyptians, to do the will of a foreign nation and to languish in a land of foreign gods. The Lord's people were not made to live and die without a sense of purpose and destiny, to bring new generations into the world only to see them live lives of hopelessness and despair. His people were made for Him! "Is Israel a servant, a slave by birth? Why then has he become plunder?" (Jer. 2:14) This was not to be! The nation of Israel was God's firstborn son (see Exod. 4:22), called to serve Him and Him alone, and the Lord was jealous to reclaim the devotion of His son. And so, in one sovereign display of power, recorded in Psalm 77:14-20, He set His firstborn free:

You are the God who performs miracles; you display your power among the peoples. With your mighty arm you redeemed your people, the descendants of Jacob and Joseph. Selah. The waters saw you, O God, the

waters saw you and writhed; the very depths were con-
vulsed. The clouds poured down water, the skies
resounded with thunder; your arrows flashed back and
forth. Your thunder was heard in the whirlwind, your
lightning lit up the world; the earth trembled and
quaked. Your path led through the sea, your way
through the mighty waters, though your footprints
were not seen. You led your people like a flock by the
hand of Moses and Aaron.

What an awesome God! He visited Egypt with 10 extraordinary plagues. He shook an entire nation. He split the sea and
brought His people through on dry land, killing the Egyptians
when they tried to pursue. Why? Because He is the Liberator, the
Redeemer, the Deliverer; because He refuses to allow His people
to remain in captivity when they cry to Him for help; because He
is the great Emancipator. As the Scripture says, it is "because the
LORD loved you and kept the oath he swore to your forefathers
that he brought you out with a mighty hand and redeemed you
from the land of slavery, from the power of Pharaoh king of
Egypt" (Deut. 7:8). This is something He never wanted Israel to
forget.

I am the LORD your God, who brought you out of Egypt,
out of the land of slavery (Exod. 20:2).

Remember that you were slaves in Egypt and that the
LORD your God brought you out of there with a mighty
hand and an outstretched arm. Therefore the LORD your
God has commanded you to observe the Sabbath day
(Deut. 5:15).[22]

The people of Israel were meant to serve Yahweh, not their enemies and not the gods of their enemies. Turning from the Lord meant returning to slavery. This was their pattern in Moses' day: "They refused to listen and failed to remember the miracles you performed among them. They became stiff-necked and in their rebellion appointed a leader in order *to return to their slavery*" (Neh. 9:17, emphasis added).

This was their pattern almost a thousand years later: "How deserted lies the city, once so full of people! How like a widow is she, who once was great among the nations! She who was queen among the provinces *has now become a slave*" (Lam. 1:1, emphasis added). What a terrible mistake, what a tragic error! Queens are not meant to be slaves. Yahweh's people are not meant to be captives.

But God's plan for Israel was not simply redemption from slavery. It was redemption to Him. It was redemption to dignity and honor, to calling and purpose, to priesthood and holy service. Look carefully at these two passages that sum up the purpose of divine liberation:

I am the LORD your God, who brought you out of Egypt so that you would no longer be slaves to the Egyptians; I broke the bars of your yoke and enabled you to walk with heads held high (Lev. 26:13).

You yourselves have seen what I did to Egypt, and how I carried you on eagles' wings and brought you to myself. Now if you obey me fully and keep my covenant, then out of all nations you will be my treasured possession. Although the whole earth is mine, you will be for me a kingdom of priests and a holy nation (Exod. 19:4-6).[23]

You are no longer bowed down under a yoke of bondage. Stand tall and walk with your heads held high. You are no longer a nation of slaves. You are Mine—My treasured possession, a kingdom of priests, a holy nation. What a transformation! But such is the character of God. Such is the nature of His liberating power. And such is the ultimate expression of His liberating heart of love that came through His Son.

This time it was not for Israel alone but for all mankind: "For he has rescued us from the dominion of darkness and brought us into the kingdom of the Son he loves [Jesus!], in whom we have redemption, the forgiveness of sins" (Col. 1:13,14). God gave His Son to rescue us from slavery, to deliver us from the dominion of darkness, and His Son gave Himself for our souls. Liberty!

Now, think again of the human slave trade. Think of a healthy young father being ripped away from his wife and children, chained like an animal, shipped across the ocean in conditions not fit for a rat, and then reduced to hard labor for life, with no future, no hope. How hateful this is! But sin's slavery is worse. It promises satisfaction and fulfillment. It produces pain and misery. Sin never satisfies. Instead, sin leads to more sin; sin leads to worse sin; sin leads to degradation and humiliation, to slavery and bondage. Sin destroys. Sin kills.[24] And Jesus liberates us from sin!

Consider the Lord Jesus, our Savior, our Deliverer, our Redeemer. He was liberation in action, freedom on the move, and the theme of setting the captives free formed the very platform of His ministry. That's why He based His inaugural sermon on a classic liberation text from the Hebrew Scriptures, declaring His agenda almost like a politician declares his candidacy and sets forth his campaign objectives. Here is Luke's description of that incredible, historic moment (4:16-21):

He went to Nazareth, where he had been brought up, and on the Sabbath day he went into the synagogue, as was his custom. And he stood up to read. The scroll of the prophet Isaiah was handed to him. Unrolling it, he found the place where it is written: "The Spirit of the Lord is on me, because he has anointed me to preach good news to the poor. He has sent me to proclaim freedom for the prisoners and recovery of sight for the blind, to release the oppressed, to proclaim the year of the Lord's favor." Then he rolled up the scroll, gave it back to the attendant and sat down. The eyes of everyone in the synagogue were fastened on him, and he began by saying to them, "Today this scripture is fulfilled in your hearing."

"Today" marked the beginning of a whole new era. Today—not tomorrow, not the next century, not sometime in a future generation—but today this glorious Scripture is fulfilled. This is the hour for good news to be preached to the poor. This is the hour for freedom to be proclaimed to the prisoners. This is why Jesus was anointed with the Spirit. This is why the Messiah was sent. This was the object of His mission, reaching its final destiny on the cross, where Jesus shed His blood to set us free from sin so that we could spend eternity serving Him.

Jesus had one agenda, one purpose, one goal: freedom! And it was for our freedom He shed His blood. That's why He chose that one specific text from Isaiah when He stood up to read in His synagogue.[25] No other passage provided a better job description of the Messiah, and now, at long last, His time had come. He was announcing the beginning of that great Messianic era, the time of the prophetic jubilee, the day when the debt of sin would be cancelled and the shackles of sin broken off.[26] It was the time of liberty!

Centuries earlier, in Leviticus 25, God had ordained that once every 50 years, on the Day of Atonement, the Israelites were to "proclaim liberty throughout the land to all its inhabitants" (v. 10). All debts would be cancelled. All slaves would be freed. All property would return to its original owners. It was the year of jubilee. What a wonderful concept! In fact, these very words—"proclaim liberty throughout the land"—were inscribed on our Liberty Bell. But it appears that Israel never did it! That's why Isaiah prophesied of the day when a greater jubilee would come, a great proclamation of liberty. Jesus took these words on His lips and said that *now* was the time of fulfillment.

What gracious words proceeded from His mouth! He spoke of good news, of freedom, of recovery of sight, of release, of divine favor. More wonderful still, He declared that the objects of God's favor were the poor, the prisoners, the oppressed, the blind—in other words, the down-and-outers, the rejects, the castaways. It was to such people that Jesus came, and it is among such people that revolution occurs.

This makes perfect sense. Who else is longing for radical change? Who else is yearning to break with the system and cast off the status quo? Certainly not those who are content and self-satisfied. Why would they want to change their current estate? Why would they want to start a revolution? It is not the free who revolt but the slaves.

Revolution appeals to the disillusioned, the dissatisfied, the disenchanted, the outcasts, the ostracized, the overlooked. It presents its case to the disappointed, the discontented, and the disgruntled, to the misunderstood, the misused, and the abused. It finds a home in the hearts of the dispossessed, the discouraged, and the disenfranchised. Such people crave revolution—for freedom, for liberation, for change, for the right to self-determination. This is what causes revolts in society. Prisoners get restless. Slaves become intolerant. The oppressed demand their rights. Captives insist on their freedom. And when revolts spread from community to community, when people get a taste of freedom, when unjust laws are challenged, a revolution is afoot.[27]

Historians tell us that when King Louis XVI learned of the fall of the Bastille—this was one of the sparks that ignited the French Revolution—he said, "It's a big revolt," to which a friend of the king replied, "No, Sir, a big revolution."[28] There is quite a difference! A revolution is a revolt that keeps advancing, a protest that keeps expanding, an uprising that is sustained, an insurrection with vision and goals. All of this has a spiritual counterpart!

We are accustomed to seeing revolts in the church (in a holy, sanctified sense). We say, "Enough is enough!" We become restive, getting more and more hungry and thirsty for a fresh visitation from heaven, fed up with business as usual in the house of God. We begin to despise the way we have been living, disgusted with fleshly addictions and entrapments, sickened by our lack of effectiveness in reaching the lost and in seeing them set free. And for a short time we have a breakthrough. We cast off the bondage of sin through the power of the blood of Jesus and we begin to bear fruit for Him. Even some lost sinners are saved.

But then it ends. Why? Because it was a revolt, not a revolution, a momentary expression of dissatisfaction, not a determined resolution. It lacked long-term vision and was devoid of a strategy that would say, "Whatever it takes, whatever the cost or consequences, we are going to see the purposes of God fulfilled in our lives and through our lives. We are going to follow the Master's battle plan and make disciples of the nations, proclaiming liberty for the prisoners and recovery of sight for the blind. We are going to set this captive generation free!"

That's the kind of talk that births a revolution. That's the kind of talk that leads to action. And who joins a "holy war" such as this? Who are the first ones to enlist in the battle? The poor, the prisoners, the oppressed, and the blind! All who recognize their need are candidates for liberation. Dissatisfaction is the key.

Think back again to America in the 1960s. What led to the counterculture revolution? What sparked such dissatisfaction, such disillusionment? Why did children from middle- and upper-class America repudiate the goals of their parents? Sometimes the exact breaking point is hard to pinpoint, but it is always reached one step at a time, little by little, almost imperceptibly. And then suddenly, without warning—*snap!*

I once sat on a platform in Tuni, India, getting ready to preach to the assembled crowd. Joining me on the platform were two colleagues from America, along with our Indian interpreter. Suddenly there was a snap, and the platform dropped once, and then again. We had no idea it was that unsteady! We had walked on it the night before, and that evening we had been sitting in our chairs for some time. But we couldn't see under the surface. A little too much weight in just the wrong place and—boom!

That's how it is with a society. Things fester under the surface, and we don't see it. Warning signs begin to crop up, but we pay no attention. Then, suddenly, a revolution is at hand. What happened? The breaking point was reached.

Think back to America in the 1960s. On the one hand, there was great affluence, as our country rebounded from the war years with a vibrant, growing economy in the 1950s. But affluence itself can be a trap. When young people have too much, when families become materialistic, when challenge and vision are low, restlessness can set in. This was part of the fragile under-pinning in the early 1960s.

And then the great shock came in 1963: President Kennedy was assassinated, and a nation's security was shaken. More uncertainty followed, especially on the college campuses where the Vietnam war was severely criticized. No longer were we proud to be in a war. No longer would we tolerate the nightly figures of American casualties. In fact, we got to the point where we no longer believed the figures reported on the news. Americans felt they were getting duped! Kennedy's successor, Lyndon Baines Johnson, was bombarded by youthful protesters chanting, "Hey, hey LBJ/How many kids did you kill today?" Soon enough, LBJ was out of office.[29]

By 1968, when America was rocked by the assassinations of Martin Luther King, Jr., and Robert F. Kennedy and by the riots at the Democratic convention in Chicago, the foundations were already unglued. The revolution had begun. As noted previous-ly, "The decade [of the 1960s] witnessed the 'liberation' [note that word!] of whole categories of people who [had] been previ-ously penalized for their race, age, physical fitness, gender, or sexual preference."[30]

But not all this liberation was good or healthy. Some of it was simply the result of casting off standards. Some of it was just plain rebellion. Some of it was inspired by the pit. How trag-ic it was—I must say it again—that Satan's people, not the Lord's people, were the revolutionaries, proclaiming "liberation" for the captives. It was no liberation at all! Yet we failed to see how near the breaking point was in that revolutionary generation.

Among David's warriors were "men of Issachar, who under-stood the times and knew what Israel should do—200 chiefs, with all their relatives under their command" (1 Chron. 12:32). We need such men and women today. Do we really understand the times? Do we know what we should do? Do we realize how near we are to another breaking point? Do we realize how deeply our society is crying for true liberty?

The twenty-first century in America begins with both expectation and uncertainty. There is a certain feeling of confidence, as our country has emerged as the world's sole superpower. The stock market has hit all-time highs month after month, and unemployment rates are down. Yet behind this feeling of excitement is a realism that something is ready to snap. There is great uncertainty in the land!

In 1999, the leader of our nation adamantly and repeatedly lied to us on national TV and was impeached, dragging us down with him. That certainly breeds uncertainty! The Columbine slaughter was only one of several shocking massacres—even if it was the most terrible of them all—sending parents, students, and teachers reeling, and breeding insecurity and fear.

The tragic deaths of John F. Kennedy, III, and golfer Payne Stewart, the threat of terrorism on our turf, the suspicious crash of Egypt Air flight 990, and the trade riots in Seattle all contributed to the feeling that things are not well. Even the (exaggerated) Y2K concerns added to the tension and anxiety.

Add to all this the state of the family in America: clinics offer DNA testing to determine who the real father is; millions of kids do not know both of their parents; millions of others are in day care more than in their own homes; others come home from school every day to an empty house and are left to fend for themselves. Talk about uncertainty! When the family unravels, society comes apart at the seams.

Thomas Jefferson said it well: "Any woodsman can tell you that in a broken and sundered nest, one can hardly expect to find more than a precious few whole eggs. So it is with the family."[31] Or, as expressed by Patrick Henry, "For good or for ill, the estate of the family will most assuredly predetermine the estate of all of the rest of the culture."[32] That is why, in the midst of affluence, there is dissatisfaction and disillusionment. Our foundations are shaky and unstable!

The society in which we live is filled with bondage and oppression. People are held captive to addictions and lusts, bound by fear and depression, tormented by guilt and sorrow, racked by pain and sickness, plagued by anxiety and dread. In the message of the Cross, we have what they need. In the message of the gospel, we have the key to their freedom. We can spark a revolution. But if we don't—I tell you again—the enemy will.

PEOPLE ARE CRYING OUT FOR LIBERTY. WILL WE OFFER THEM TRUE FREEDOM, OR WILL SATAN BEAT US TO THE PUNCH YET AGAIN, OFFERING HIS DESTRUCTIVE COUNTERFEIT?

It was the demented dream of Columbine killer Eric Harris that he and Dylan Klebold would ignite a murderous uprising: "We're going to kick-start a revolution," he said—a revolution of the dispossessed.[33] The family of Rachel Scott, one of the victims of Harris and Klebold, sees things otherwise. They believe that "Rachel's death was a Christian martyrdom—an act of God meant to spark a spiritual revolution in young people."[34] A revolution is coming. Which will it be? A revolution of the dispossessed, bringing suffering and death in its train, or a revolution of righteousness, liberating captives in its flood tide?

People are crying out for liberty. They are hurting and confused, not knowing which way to turn, not knowing who will lead them out. What will we do? Will we offer them true freedom, or will Satan beat us to the punch yet again, offering his destructive counterfeit? I say we take this revolution to the streets and proclaim liberty to the captives in Jesus' name. Freedom is the word for the hour! This was how the Son of God spent His life, as Peter spoke of "how God anointed Jesus of Nazareth with the Holy Spirit and power, and how he went around doing good and healing all who were under the power of the devil, because God was with him" (Acts 10:38). How clear this is! He set captives free because God was with Him and the Spirit was on Him. What else could He do? And what else can we do?

We are called to the ministry of liberation, the ministry of deliverance, and it is to eternal, glorious liberty that we are destined. All creation awaits the total freedom we will one day enjoy: "For the creation was subjected to frustration, not by its own choice, but by the will of the one who subjected it, in hope that the creation itself will be liberated from its bondage to decay and brought into the glorious freedom of the children of God" (Rom. 8:20,21). The entire creation longs for freedom!

James spoke of looking "intently into the perfect law that gives freedom" (Jas. 1:25), while Paul taught that through Messiah Jesus, "the law of the Spirit of life set [us] free from the law of sin and death" (Rom. 8:2). Freedom! Peter exhorted his readers to "live as free men, but do not use your freedom as a cover-up for evil; live as servants of God" (1 Peter 2:16). He warned them to beware of the false teachers who "promise [people] freedom, while they themselves are slaves of depravity—for a man is a slave to whatever has mastered him" (2 Pet. 2:19). True freedom is found only in Jesus, the one "who loves us and has freed us from our sins by His blood" (Rev. 1:5). True freedom is found only in the Spirit. Yes, "where the Spirit of the Lord is, there is freedom" (2 Cor. 3:17).

Only the life-changing power of the gospel will ultimately change a society for good. Only new hearts will bring forth the new life that the oppressed so long for and desire. Only the Spirit of God will truly liberate captives! But if we do not rise up and act, Satan will. The dissatisfaction is rising. The discontent is growing thick. Revolution is near, either heaven-sent or hell-bent, and only we have the truth that will set slaves free. As expressed by Rutherford L. Decker,

> Faith fosters freedom.
> Without faith there can be no freedom.
> Losing their faith men lose their freedom.
> When faith is revived freedom follows.[35]

Our Lord and Master calls us to continue His work. Therefore let us go and proclaim liberty to the captives through the blood of the Cross and the power of the Resurrection. Let us rediscover the revolutionary power of the gospel. Let us announce it boldly in the public squares and on the streets. Let freedom ring! The price has been paid. The chains have been broken. The prison doors have been opened wide. Captives, come forth! The Son of God has come to set you free—free indeed, free at last. On with the revolution!

Chapter Ten

Take Up Your Cross, Put Down Your Sword: The Jesus Way to Revolution

A Christian who . . . becomes a revolutionary will serve as a revolutionary catalyst in the Church; and by the multiplication of revolutionized Christians, the Church will become a revolutionary catalyst in society; and if society is sufficiently revolutionized, a revolution of violence will no more be needed than a windmill in a world of atomic energy.

VERNON C. GROUNDS
CHANCELLOR OF DENVER SEMINARY

[Jesus—] a man who was completely innocent, offered himself as a sacrifice for the good of others, including his enemies, and became the ransom of the world. It was a perfect act.

MAHATMA GANDHI

Every step of progress the world has made has been from scaffold to scaffold, and from stake to stake.

WENDELL PHILLIPS
NINETEENTH-CENTURY AMERICAN SUPPORTER OF
ABOLITION OF SLAVERY

The tyrant dies and his rule ends, the martyr dies and his rule begins.

SØREN KIERKEGAARD
NINETEENTH-CENTURY DANISH THEOLOGIAN AND PHILOSOPHER

Take up the cross, preach the Gospel and you will be filled with peace.
Jesus leads me down the heavenly road and it is joy without measure.
Even though we have met with persecution and tribulation,
the cross is my glory and crown.

A SONG WRITTEN AND SUNG BY CHINESE CHRISTIANS
AFTER BEING TORTURED AND PARADED IN PUBLIC

"Revolution." It is a violent word, a forceful word, a word often associated with blood. One could almost say that without the shedding of blood, there can be no revolution. Someone always dies!

This was a principle emphasized in the fiery speeches of Malcolm X, a man who scorned the nonviolent approach of Martin Luther King, Jr.[1] According to Malcolm X, there was no such thing as a nonviolent revolution:

> Look at the American Revolution in 1776. That revolution was for what? For land. Why did they want land? Independence. How was it carried out? Bloodshed. Number one, it was based on land, the basis of independence. And the only way they could get it was bloodshed. The French Revolution—what was it based on? The landless against the landlord. What was it for? Land. How did they get it? Bloodshed—was no love lost, was no compromise, was no negotiation. I'm telling you, you don't know what a revolution is. Because when you find out what it is, you'll get back in the alley, you'll get out of the way. The Russian Revolution— what was it based on? Land; the landless against the landlord. How did they bring it about? Bloodshed. You haven't got a revolution that doesn't involve bloodshed. And you're afraid to bleed. I said, you're afraid to bleed. . . .
>
> I cite these various revolutions, brothers and sisters, to show you that you don't have a peaceful revolution. You don't have a turn-the-other-cheek revolution. There's no such thing as a nonviolent revolution. . . . You don't know what a revolution is. If you did, you wouldn't use that word.

Revolution is bloody, revolution is hostile, revolution knows no compromise, revolution overturns and destroys everything that gets in its way. . . . You don't do any singing, you're too busy swinging. It's based on land. A revolutionary wants land so he can set up his own nation, an independent nation.[2]

Muslim extremists have also stressed that there can be no revolution—in their case, an Islamic revolution—without bloodshed. For them it is a must! It is clearly expressed by Ayatollah Fasl-Allah Mahalati:

But he who takes up a gun, a dagger, a kitchen knife or even a pebble with which to harm and kill the enemies of the Faith has his place assured in Heaven. . . . An Islamic state is a state of war until the whole world sees and accepts the light of the True Faith.[3]

The opening words of the Hamas Manifesto are equally clear:

The ten fundamental principles of faith of Hamas are as follows:

1. Hamas swears to conduct a holy war over Palestine against the Jews until Allah's victory is achieved.

2. The land must be cleansed of the filth and evil of the tyrannical conquerors. . . .

And how will these goals be realized?

Blood must flow. There must be widows, there must be orphans. Hands and limbs must be cut and the limbs and blood must be spread everywhere in order that Allah's religion stand on its feet.[4]

How brutally clear!

No one expressed this philosophy more decisively than Ayatollah Khomeini, the man responsible for engineering the overthrow of the Shah of Iran, and the first leader of that nation's ultrafundamentalist government. For the Iranian Muslims, he was the Imam, the hidden leader, revealed in the end times to establish Allah's kingdom. Imam Khomeini represented a militant version of Islam, completely rejecting the non-violent approach of most Muslims. His goals were clear: "Islam's Holy War is a struggle against idolatry, sexual deviation, plunder, repression, and cruelty," and he was confident that "those who study Islamic Holy War will understand why Islam wants to conquer the whole world. All the countries conquered by Islam or to be conquered in the future will be marked for everlasting salvation." His methods were equally clear:

Those who know nothing of Islam pretend that Islam counsels against war. Those [who say this] are witless. Islam says: Kill all the unbelievers just as they would kill you all! Does this mean that Muslims should sit back until they are devoured by [the unbelievers]? Islam says: Kill them [the non-Muslims], put them to the sword and scatter [their armies]. Does this mean sitting back until [non-Muslims] overcome us? Islam says: Kill in the service of Allah those who may want to kill you! Does this mean that we should surrender [to the enemy]? Islam says: Whatever good there is exists thanks to the sword and in the shadow of the sword! People cannot be made obedient except with the sword!

> The sword is the key to Paradise, which can be opened only for Holy Warriors!
>
> There are hundreds of other psalms [from the Koran] and Hadiths [sayings of Muhammad] urging Muslims to value war and to fight. Does all that mean that Islam is a religion that prevents men from waging war? I spit upon those foolish souls who make such a claim.[5]

This is the language of war, and it has been said that "war is the supremely revolutionary act. No change is more swift or more universal than the change in the mechanism of ordinary lives brought about by war."[6] And war means bloodshed and death! John Wesley, despite being sympathetic to the plight of the Americans, counseled them against war with the British. On the one hand, he warned the British about pushing the Americans too far:

> In spite of my long-rooted prejudice, I cannot avoid thinking, if I think at all, that an *oppressed* people asked for nothing more than their *legal rights*, and that in the most modest and inoffensive manner that the nature of the thing would allow. But waiving all considerations of right and wrong, I ask, is it common sense to use force toward the Americans? These men will not be frightened; and it seems they will not be conquered as easily as was first imagined – they will probably dispute every inch of ground; and if they die, die sword in hand.[7]

On the other hand, Wesley knew the brutal consequences of war, and he gave this vivid depiction of what the clash between armies would entail, counseling the Americans not to go to battle:

> But what are [the opposing armies] going to do? To
> shoot each other through the head or heart, to stab and
> butcher each other. . . . Why so? What harm have they
> done to each other? Why none at all. Most of them are
> entire strangers to each other. But a matter is in dis-
> pute relative to the mode of taxation. So these coun-
> trymen, children of the same parents, are to *murder*
> each other with all possible haste—to *prove* who is in
> the right. What an argument is this! What a method of
> proof! What an amazing way of deciding controver-
> sies![8]

This was the price of the American Revolution: Thousands
shot through the head or heart, stabbed and butchered, killed,
cut down, murdered. Revolutions are costly! Listen again to
these different, militant voices: "You haven't got a revolution
that doesn't involve bloodshed. . . . Blood must flow. . . . People
cannot be made obedient except with the sword!"

Even Mark Twain wrote, "No people in the world ever did
achieve their freedom by goody-goody talk and moral suasion: it
being immutable law that all revolutions that will succeed must
begin in blood, whatever may answer afterward."[9] In the tongue-
in-cheek words of Jerry Rubin, one of the famous Chicago Seven
arrested for sparking riots at the 1968 Democratic convention:
"By the end, everybody had a label—pig, liberal, radical, revolutionary. . . . If you had everything but a gun, you were a radical
but not a revolutionary."[10]

Revolutionaries must be armed! It sounds silly, but it's
true—at least as far as the world is concerned. There can be no
revolution without blood.[11]

The Word of God agrees with this principle too—but in a totally different way. God turns it on its head! Yes, cultural revolution

rarely takes place without the shedding of blood. But in God's economy, when *He* brings a cultural revolution, the blood that is shed is the blood of the Cross. It is the blood of Jesus, the blood of the martyrs, the blood of believers. Our blood! This is the radical twist, the foundation of the Christian revolution, the Jesus-way to change the world.

Our Savior made this perfectly clear, establishing two foundations for battle. The first foundation is, *Take up your cross.* The second foundation is, *Put down your sword.* We tend to get things reversed! We take up our sword, relying on human methods to change the world, and we put down our cross, despising God's method to change the world. God's method runs counter to the flesh. God's method seems weak and foolish. God's method flies in the face of established wisdom. God's method seems doomed to failure and defeat, yet it is the only way to succeed and win. God's method is the Cross!

The Cross? How can it be! This is the scandal of all scandals, the impossible storyline with the utterly absurd climax. It defies all human expectations. The Son of God dying on a tree? The Messiah suffering a criminal's death? The King of kings stripped, mocked, beaten, and tortured to death? To the ancient mind—Jewish, Greek, Roman—this was a total impossibility, a complete contradiction in terms.

> For the message of the cross is foolishness to those who are perishing, but to us who are being saved it is the power of God. . . . Jews demand miraculous signs and Greeks look for wisdom, but we preach Christ crucified: a stumbling block to Jews and foolishness to Gentiles. . . . For to be sure, He was crucified in weakness, yet He lives by God's power (1 Cor. 1:18,22,23; 2 Cor. 13:4).

A stumbling block and foolishness, weakness and dishonor, yet this is the power and wisdom and glory of God. How can this be? God's ways are not man's ways. God's power is revealed in weakness, and His wisdom is revealed in folly. His kingdom advances by humility and service, not by intimidation and fear. The Cross is the ultimate scandal! The flesh cries out: "Jesus, curse Your enemies! Jesus, defend Yourself! Jesus, rally Your disciples to take up their swords! Jesus, call down fire from heaven!" Instead, He *gives Himself up* to be killed:

> "Put your sword back in its place," Jesus said to [Peter], "for all who draw the sword will die by the sword. Do you think I cannot call on my Father, and he will at once put at my disposal more than twelve legions of angels? But how then would the Scriptures be fulfilled that say it must happen in this way?" (Matt 26:53,54).

> Jesus commanded Peter, "Put your sword away! Shall I not drink the cup the Father has given me?" (John 18:11).

> When Jesus' followers saw what was going to happen, they said, "Lord, should we strike with our swords?" And one of them struck the servant of the high priest, cutting off his right ear. But Jesus answered, "No more of this!" And he touched the man's ear and healed him (Luke 22:49-51).

> Pilate then went back inside the palace, summoned Jesus and asked him, "Are you the king of the Jews?" Jesus said, "My kingdom is not of this world. If it were, my servants would fight to prevent my arrest by the Jews. But now my kingdom is from another place" (John 18:33,36).

He willingly went to the Cross! He laid His life down; no one took it from Him (see John 10:11,15,17,18). He *chose* to be despised, mocked, ridiculed, humiliated. Everyone thought He was defeated. Yet this was how the Father was breaking Satan's power; this was how He was liberating prisoners; this was how He was pardoning a rebellious race. The Cross!

From a human point of view, this was not the way to save the world. The Jewish people were not expecting a crucified Messiah. This did not fit into their theology. They could respect a royal warrior, even if he died in battle. They could embrace a victorious ruler, even if he failed to subdue all the enemies of God. They could follow a revered teacher, even if he had neither earthly army nor fighting force. But a crucified King? This was going too far!

To the Greeks and Romans too, it was utterly unthinkable. As Justin Martyr said, "They say that our madness consists in the fact that we put a crucified man in second place after the unchangeable and eternal God, the Creator of the world."[12] Yes, this was insanity in the eyes of man. As Professor Martin Hengel explains:

> To believe that the one pre-existent Son of the one true God, the mediator at creation and the redeemer of the world, had appeared in very recent times in out-of-the-way Galilee as a member of the obscure people of the Jews, and even worse, had died the death of a common criminal on the cross, could only be regarded as a sign of madness.[13]

Most of us fail to realize just how far-fetched, how radical, how truly revolutionary this whole concept really is. It would almost be as jarring as imagining that when Jesus returns in glory, a violent mob will pull Him off His white stallion, rip off His royal robes, beat Him to a blood-spattered pulp, and then blow His brains out. "Never!" you exclaim. "This could never be! This would be contrary to Scripture, a total defeat, an impossible ending to the story." Now you're getting the picture!

This is exactly how Peter felt when Jesus told the disciples that "he must go to Jerusalem and suffer many things at the hands of the elders, chief priests and teachers of the law, and that he must be killed and on the third day be raised to life" (Matt. 16:21). Peter rebuked Him in no uncertain terms: "'Never, Lord!' he said. 'This shall never happen to you!' But Jesus turned and said to Peter, 'Get behind me, Satan! You are a stumbling block to me; you do not have in mind the things of God, but the things of men'" (16:22,23). This was the voice of Satan, not Peter. This was the voice of the flesh, the voice of the world. This was the voice of spiritual and moral blindness, the voice that stands in the way of the Cross. This was a voice from hell!

Without the shedding of blood, redemption could not come. Without the shedding of blood, the doors of heaven would remain closed. What a price Jesus paid to open those doors! It was the price of crucifixion.

This was not just a painful method of execution—it was also the most barbaric, the most degrading, the most horrific, the most humiliating, the most ghastly form of execution known in the ancient world. It was reserved for slaves, for rebels, for traitors, for the worst of criminals. This was the lot of a crucified man: "Punished with limbs outstretched, they see the stake as their fate; they are fastened [and] nailed to the stake in the most bitter torment, evil food for birds of prey and grim picking for dogs."[14] What a grisly death!

First the victim would be severely flogged and then made to carry his cross (i.e., the crossbeam) to the place of execution, where he would be stripped naked and hung up to die a slow, agonizing death. Sometimes he would be nailed to the cross and sometimes he would be tied to the cross, but being nailed to the cross was not the worst part of the punishment, as shocking as this may seem. The worst part of the ordeal was the gradual suffocation the victim would experience as every part of his body strained to get another breath, the muscles in ever-increasing torment, the oxygen escaping drop by drop. And all the while he would hang there naked, unable to cover himself, unable to defend himself against even a fly or a gnat.[15]

On some occasions, a sharp piece of wood would function as a seat, adding to the victim's misery: Every time his body would sag after catching a short, heaving breath, he would fall back onto this cruel torture device. So great was the agony involved that it was an act of mercy to break the victim's legs. This way, unable to push himself up to fill his lungs, he would suffocate in a matter of minutes. What a cruel, demented form of execution! As New Testament scholar Johannes Schneider explained: "The physical and mental sufferings which this slow death involved are unimaginable."[16]

Many ancient writers—eyewitnesses of more crucifixions than they cared to remember—gave vivid descriptions of the horrors involved. It was the "extreme penalty" (Tacitus), "the worst of deaths, a death bound by iron" ("Apollo"), "the most wretched of deaths" (Josephus).[17] The word "cross" (*crux*) was actually "a vulgar taunt among the lower classes . . . found on the lips of slaves and prostitutes . . . an English equivalent might be 'gallows-bird', 'hang-dog'."[18] Yet this was how our Savior died, how the world viewed our Redeemer. This is what the Lord of glory suffered on our behalf!

The ancient Roman author Seneca gives these brutal details:

I see crosses there, not just of one kind but made in many different ways; some have their victims with head down to the ground; some impale their private parts; others stretch out their arms on the gibbet.[19]

Can anyone be found who would prefer wasting away in pain, dying limb by limb, or letting out his life drop by drop, rather than expiring once for all? Can any man be found willing to be fastened to the accursed tree, long sickly, already deformed, swelling with ugly weals on shoulders and chest, and drawing the breath of life amid long-drawn-out agony? He would have many excuses for dying even before mounting the cross.[20]

Jesus mounted the cross willingly, by His own choice, because it was only through His violent, gory death that eternal life could spring forth for the race that was killing Him. Their act of murder would prove to be God's act of mercy! How remarkable all of this is. But this is where the plot thickens, and this is when we will want to run. You see, Jesus calls *each of us* to carry our cross. Otherwise, we cannot be His disciples. There is a crucifixion for each of us too. Jesus is not the only one destined to die!

After rebuking Peter (Satan!), Scripture records that Jesus said to His disciples, "If anyone would come after me, he must deny himself and take up his cross and follow me. For whoever wants to save his life will lose it, but whoever loses his life for me will find it" (Matt. 16:24,25). Yes, "a student is not above his teacher, nor a servant above his master. It is enough for the student to be like his teacher, and the servant like his master. If the head of the house has been called Beelzebub, how much more the members of his household!" (Matt. 10:24,25). He said "how much more," not "how much less." What does this imply for us?

Let's consider what it implied for the men who heard Him that day. The twelve apostles were "first, Simon (who is called Peter) and his brother Andrew; James son of Zebedee, and his brother John; Philip and Bartholomew; Thomas and Matthew the tax collector; James son of Alphaeus, and Thaddaeus; Simon the Zealot and Judas Iscariot, who betrayed him" (Matt. 10:2-4). What was their fate? It seems that at most, only two died natural deaths (John and, probably, Matthew), while according to tradition, the rest were martyred in the following ways:

Peter was crucified upside down.
Andrew, his brother, was crucified on an X-shaped cross.
James, son of Zebedee, was beheaded.
Philip was crucified upside down.
Bartholomew was drowned in a sack.
Thomas was speared to death (or shot with arrows).
James, son of Alphaeus, was stoned to death (or crucified).
Thaddaeus was shot with arrows.
Simon the Zealot was crucified.[21]

And let us not forget that John, the forerunner of Jesus, was beheaded, as was Paul, the greatest of the apostles, while Stephen, one of the first deacons, was stoned. What a violent pedigree! Yet these are the pioneers of the gospel revolution; these are the founding fathers of our faith. And to this day, Jesus says, "Follow Me!"

To this you were called, because Christ suffered for you, leaving you an example, that you should follow in his steps (1 Pet. 2:21).

I tell you the truth, unless a kernel of wheat falls to the ground and dies, it remains only a single seed. But if it dies, it produces many seeds. . . . Whoever serves me must follow me; and where I am, my servant also will be. My Father will honor the one who serves me (John 12:24-26).

We have been called to die, called to glorify Jesus by life or by death, called to suffer before we are entitled to reign. When Paul said, "For me, to live is Christ and to die is gain" (Phil. 1:21), he was simply concluding the thought of the previous verse: "I eagerly expect and hope that I will in no way be ashamed, but will have sufficient courage so that now as always Christ will be exalted in my body, whether by life or by death" (Phil. 1:20).

WE HAVE BEEN CALLED TO DIE, CALLED TO GLORIFY JESUS BY LIFE OR BY DEATH, CALLED TO SUFFER BEFORE WE ARE ENTITLED TO REIGN.

By life or by death! Living consisted in knowing Jesus; death consisted in going to be with Him. Either way was fine. That's why

Jesus could *tell* Peter *by what kind of death* he would glorify Jesus rather than *ask* Peter *if he was willing* to glorify Jesus by death. Peter had already signed up to take up his cross. Peter had already made the commitment to glorify His Master by any means. And so Jesus said to him:

"I tell you the truth, when you were younger you dressed yourself and went where you wanted; but when you are old you will stretch out your hands, and someone else will dress you and lead you where you do not want to go." Jesus said this to indicate the kind of death by which Peter would glorify God. Then he said to him, "Follow me!" (John 21:18,19).

That's why John could write from exile on the island of Patmos: "I, John, your brother and companion in the *suffering* and *kingdom* and *patient endurance* that are *ours in Jesus*, was on the island of Patmos because of the word of God and the testimony of Jesus" (Rev. 1:9). This is our lot! John locates the "kingdom" right between "suffering" and "patient endurance."[22] In fact, when John catches a vision of the Lion of the Tribe of Judah, the Victor, the Conqueror, the Majestic Ruler, the Root of David, the Triumphant One, he sees "a Lamb, looking as if it had been slain" (Rev. 5:5,6). The Lion is a slain Lamb! The Victor is a victim! And this is the key to our victory. This is how we change the world.

As noted by H. S. Vigeveno in his book *Jesus the Revolutionary*:

Our world has witnessed many a revolution, but none as effective as the one that divided history into B.C. and A.D. Every revolution involves the shedding of blood. So did this one. Not as much blood, perhaps, but the quality of the One far outweighs the quantity of others. Revolutionary, indeed, this mission, to begin with a cross and sway the whole world through suffering love. Revolutionary to build a Church on the sacrifice that offers man forgiveness and atonement with God.[23]

Revolutionary indeed! There is a profound spiritual principle here, a radical, counterculture principle, an against-the-grain, opposition-crushing principle. It is an extremely costly principle—for Jesus and for us. Our Savior was rejected and nailed to a tree, and He says to us, "Follow My example!" Our Lord was hung up to die in agony, and He says to us, "Take up *your* cross!" Our Master was scorned and flogged and pierced, and He says to us, "Expect similar treatment!" Jesus made this perfectly clear. The world would treat us the way it treated Him:

> If the world hates you, keep in mind that it hated me first. If you belonged to the world, it would love you as its own. As it is, you do not belong to the world, but I have chosen you out of the world. That is why the world hates you. Remember the words I spoke to you: "No servant is greater than his master." If they persecuted me, they will persecute you also. If they obeyed my teaching, they will obey yours also (John 15:18-20).

This is how we impact a generation. This is how we transform society. This is how we win God's war: By death! Malcolm X was right—in a totally wrong way—when he said, "You haven't got a revolution that doesn't involve bloodshed." Yes, but it will be our own! Blood must flow. Blood will flow. Blood has flowed. That is the key to victory and conquest. We save our lives by losing them. We keep our lives by giving them away. We win by surrendering. We live by dying. This is the Jesus method of revolution. It simply cannot be stopped.

The class that graduated from our School of Ministry on December 17, 1999, presented me with a plaque inscribed with these words:

"For though ye have ten thousand instructors in Christ, yet have ye not many 'fathers'." It is with love and gratitude we take our place in the harvest and by God's grace resolve to serve—by life or by death.

What weapon can be formed against a commitment like this? Dr. Robert Coleman noted that "the cross was but the crowning climax of Jesus' commitment to do the will of God. It forever showed that obedience could not be compromised—it was always a commitment to death."[24] That must be our commitment too. This is the Word of the Lord:

> Blessed are you when people insult you, persecute you and falsely say all kinds of evil against you because of me. Rejoice and be glad, because great is your reward in heaven, for in the same way they persecuted the prophets who were before you (Matt. 5:11,12).

> Do not be afraid of those who kill the body but cannot kill the soul. Rather, be afraid of the One who can destroy both soul and body in hell (Matt. 10:28).

> They called the apostles in and had them flogged. Then they ordered them not to speak in the name of Jesus, and let them go. The apostles left the Sanhedrin, rejoicing because they had been counted worthy of suffering disgrace for the Name (Acts 5:40,41).

> Now if we are children, then we are heirs—heirs of God and co-heirs with Christ, if indeed we share in his sufferings in order that we may also share in his glory (Rom. 8:17).

Are they servants of Christ? (I am out of my mind to talk like this.) I am more. I have worked much harder, been in prison more frequently, been flogged more severely, and been exposed to death again and again. Five times I received from the Jews the forty lashes minus one. Three times I was beaten with rods, once I was stoned. I will not boast about myself, except about my weaknesses (2 Cor. 11:23-25; 12:5).

Finally, let no one cause me trouble, for I bear on my body the marks of Jesus (Gal. 6:17).

For it has been granted to you on behalf of Christ not only to believe on him, but also to suffer for him (Phil. 1:29).

Now I rejoice in what was suffered for you, and I fill up in my flesh what is still lacking in regard to Christ's afflictions, for the sake of his body, which is the church (Col. 1:24).

You became imitators of us and of the Lord; in spite of severe suffering, you welcomed the message with the joy given by the Holy Spirit. And so you became a model to all the believers in Macedonia and Achaia (1 Thess. 1:6,7).

You, however, know all about my teaching, my way of life, my purpose, faith, patience, love, endurance, persecutions, sufferings—what kinds of things happened to me in Antioch, Iconium and Lystra, the persecutions I endured. Yet the Lord rescued me from all of them. In fact, everyone who wants to live a godly life in Christ Jesus will be persecuted (2 Tim. 3:10-12).

This last verse says it all: "Everyone who wants to live a godly life in Christ Jesus will be persecuted." Everyone! That's why Jesus said to the church of Smyrna, one of only two churches the Lord did not rebuke in Revelation 2,3, "Do not be afraid of what you are about to suffer. I tell you, the devil will put some of you in prison to test you, and you will suffer persecution for ten days. Be faithful, even to the point of death, and I will give you the crown of life" (Rev. 2:10). That's why Peter could write, "And the God of all grace, who called you to his eternal glory in Christ, after you have suffered a little while, will himself restore you and make you strong, firm and steadfast" (1 Pet. 5:10). This was actually reason to rejoice! "Dear friends, [Peter exhorted,] do not be surprised at the painful trial you are suffering, as though something strange were happening to you. But rejoice that you participate in the sufferings of Christ, so that you may be overjoyed when his glory is revealed" (1 Pet. 4:12,13).

THE BATTLE FOR THE SOUL OF THIS GENERATION WILL NOT BE WON BY A SHOW OF BRUTE FORCE. TRUE CONVERSION DOES NOT COME BY THE SWORD BUT BY THE CROSS; NOT BY THE TAKING OF LIFE BUT BY THE LAYING DOWN OF LIFE.

It is our privilege, our honor, our high calling, our joy to participate in the sufferings of the Savior. It is the way we change the world! You see, the battle for the soul of this generation, or any generation, will not be won by a show of brute force. True conversion does not come by the sword but by the Cross, not by the taking of life but by the laying down of life. That is the Jesus way to change society. That is the Jesus method of revolution. It is unstoppable; it is unconquerable; it is unbeatable.

> The great dragon was hurled down—that ancient serpent called the devil, or Satan, who leads the whole world astray. He was hurled to the earth, and his angels with him. Then I heard a loud voice in heaven say: "Now have come the salvation and the power and the kingdom of our God, and the authority of his Christ. For the accuser of our brothers, who accuses them before our God day and night, has been hurled down. They overcame him by the blood of the Lamb and by the word of their testimony; they did not love their lives so much as to shrink from death" (Rev. 12:9-11).[25]

What a revolutionary concept! All other concepts claiming to be "revolutionary"—including Communism, Socialism, Fascism, fanatical Islam, among others—are common, tame, even "traditional" in comparison. They are primitive and outmoded. They rely on brute force and numbers, on guns, knives, and explosives, on terrorist tactics and guerrilla warfare, on hatred, anger, and revenge. How barbaric! How fleshly! How impotent!

That is not the Jesus way. We live by dying; we receive by giving; we overcome evil with good, defeating hatred with love. This is how we transform society. This is how we triumph over the world. We have already defeated death; we have already vanquished fear; we have already conquered Satan. He has nothing in his arsenal great enough to defeat us. For us to live is Christ and to die is gain. Death has lost its sting!

There is a supernatural power released when we make the break with the pull of this world, when we become totally free to live or to die, able to consecrate ourselves to a principle at any cost or consequence. That is when the Church always grows. The blood of martyrs is still the seed![26] Eberhard Arnold, the radical German Christian leader (1883-1935), helps put this in perspective:

> The early Christians were revolutionaries of the Spirit, heralds of the last judgment and the coming transformation; they had to be ready for martyrdom at any moment. Their witness meant they had to reckon with being sentenced to death by state and society. Therefore, "martyrs" were those witnesses ready to die for their faith, those who bore this testimony before kings and judges with the steadfastness of soldiers of God. They were martyrs, that is "confessors," even if they did not have to die. To give witness is the essence of martyrdom. Martyrs uphold the truth of their testimony as eyewitnesses of the Lord and his resurrection. They see Christ and become his prophetic spirit-bearers. Through the Spirit, the blood-witness of the martyrs becomes part of the decisive battle waged by Jesus, the battle in which he himself died as champion and leader of the future. By dying, he finally judged and routed the hostile powers of the present age. Put to death by the most devout Jewish people and the Roman state, Christ fettered and disarmed the demons and their darkness through his cross. Since then, each new martyrdom—each new dying with Christ—becomes a celebration of victory over the forces of Satan.[27]

Some of the greatest leaders in the Early Church included men like Ignatius, who was fed to wild beasts; Polycarp, who was burned at the stake; and Justin Martyr, who was beheaded. Some of the greatest reformers of the late Middle Ages included men like John Huss, who was burned at the stake; Girolamo Savonarola, who was tortured, strangled, and burned at the stake; and William Tyndale, who was also strangled and burned at the stake. (Never forget that the English Bible you hold in your hand today cost Tyndale his life!) More recently, missionary martyrs like Jim Elliot, Nate Saint, Roger Youderian, Ed McCully, and Peter Fleming (martyred in 1956), or twenty years before them, John and Betty Stam, left an eternal legacy in just a few short moments of obedience to death. Listen to their stories and you will understand.

John and Betty Stam were graduates of Moody Bible Institute. They sailed for China as missionaries during a difficult time for missionaries. (They were actually married in China, Betty preceding John to the mission field by one year.) They knew the risks involved: The China Inland Mission was specifically recruiting laborers to work in dangerous Communist-infested areas. But both of them had been inspired by a poem written after Southern Presbyterian missionary Jack Vinson was martyred in 1931. Vinson had showed no fear of death to his Chinese captors, telling them, "Kill me, if you wish. I will go straight to God." The calmness he showed inspired his colleague E. H. Hamilton to write this poem:

Afraid? Of What?
To feel the spirit's glad release?
To pass from pain to perfect peace,
The strife and strain of life to cease?
Afraid—of that?

Afraid? Of What?
Afraid to see the Saviour's face,

To hear His welcome, and to trace
The glory gleam from wounds of grace?
Afraid—of that?

Afraid? Of What?
A flash, a crash, a pierced heart;
Darkness, light, O Heaven's art!
A wound of His a counterpart!
Afraid—of that?

Afraid? Of What?
To do by death what life could not—
Baptize with blood a stony plot,
Till souls shall blossom from the spot?
Afraid—of that?

With courage and faith, John had challenged the graduating class at Moody in 1932:

Shall we beat a retreat, and turn back from our high calling in Christ Jesus; or dare we advance at God's command in face of the impossible? Let us remind ourselves that the Great Commission was never qualified by clauses calling for advance only if funds were plentiful and no hardship or self-denial involved. On the contrary, we are told to expect tribulation and even persecution, but with it victory in Christ.[28]

The day of reckoning came for John and Betty Stam. (One recent book, obviously based on John Stam's words to his class at Moody, calls it, "Victory Day for the Stams." What a concept!)[29] They were captured by Communists (their little baby,

Priscilla, was miraculously spared), then painfully bound, stripped down to their underwear, and kept under guard for the night. The next morning, they were paraded down the street while being mocked and ridiculed, after which they were beheaded—baptizing with blood a stony plot, till souls have blossomed from that spot. They were not afraid of that!

As word got out about their martyrdom, the impact was dramatic, both in terms of new missionary volunteers, new student prayer meetings, and large monetary donations to the work in China. A missionary with the China Inland Mission wrote to Betty's parents: "A life which had the longest span of years might not have been able to accomplish one-hundredth of the work for Christ which they have done in a day."[30] That is the power of martyrdom! Jesus said, "I tell you the truth, unless a kernel of wheat falls to the ground and dies, it remains only a single seed. But if it dies, it produces many seeds" (John 12:24). One short act of obedience to death gave many others eternal life!

Consider also the fruit produced by the five martyrs in Ecuador in 1956. Steve Saint, the son of martyred pilot Nate Saint, learned the details of their martyrdom many years after the fact. Steve had frequently worked among the people who killed his father, since all of them had become believers through the widows and relatives of the martyred men. (Yes, the widows of the martyred men led their husbands' murderers to Jesus.) He knew that his father and the other missionaries had guns, but they had made a covenant never to use those guns in self-defense against a human attack. What then actually happened on that fateful day in 1956?

It turns out that the killers—most of whom were teenagers and not experienced killers—were involved in a dispute with their own tribe, and they tried to shift the blame to the missionaries, taking out their anger on them. But the missionaries did not defend themselves or try to flee, a striking fact that the natives noticed, paving the way for their conversion later. After killing their victims, the Indians saw and heard strange sights and sounds: They saw people who looked just like the martyred foreigners (called *cowodi* in the Indian dialect) standing above the trees, singing songs that they later identified with choir music (which, of course, they had never heard before). Others saw the sky filled with lights, moving around and shining. It seems the angels—or heavenly witnesses—were singing! What a sacred moment to God.

Five young men were killed in the line of duty that day, leaving widows and children behind. These men were cut down— actually speared to death—by the most violent of the Huaorani Indians (called Auca, meaning "savage," in their language). Was it worth it? Steve Saint, who was left as a boy without a father, looked back 40 years later and gave the answer:

> God took five common young men of uncommon commitment and used them for his own glory. They never had the privilege they so enthusiastically pursued to tell the Huaorani of the God they loved and served. But for every Huaorani who today follows God's trail in part because of their efforts, there are a thousand *cowodi* [foreigners] who follow God's trail more resolutely because of their example. The success withheld from them in life God multiplied and continues to multiply as a memorial to their obedience and his faithfulness.[31]

This is the Jesus way to win the world, the principle of multiplication by martyrdom. It is the forgotten secret of Church growth, the unstoppable weapon of our revolution. It is the spark that will ignite a whole generation, just as one short sentence—"Yes, I believe!"—spoken by two teenage girls facing death helped spark a youth revival at the end of the twentieth century. This is how we overcome; this is how we change society; this is how we make disciples; this is how God's kingdom grows. We die and we multiply!

Ask Cassie and Rachel. Ask Jim Elliot and Nate Saint. Ask John and Betty Stam. Ask Tyndale and Savonarola and Huss. Ask Ignatius and Polycarp and Justin Martyr. Ask Paul and Stephen and John. Ask Peter and Andrew and James and Philip and Bartholomew and Thomas and the other James and Thaddaeus and Simon. Ask Jesus, our Lord, our Savior, our example. What do all of them say to us? "Follow me!" In unison all of them cry: "Take up your cross and put down your sword. The time for battle is now!"

This is our day, our moment of truth. This is our sacred hour, our time for holy service. Are you still coming along? Will you serve the Lord by life or by death? Then on with the revolution!

Chapter Eleven

To Save Your Life Is to Lose Your Life: The Power of Revolution

Dead to all one's natural earthly plans and hopes, dead to all voices, however dear, which would deafen our ear to His.

AMY CARMICHAEL
EXPLAINING WHAT IT MEANT TO BE DEAD TO SELF AND ALIVE TO GOD

Now I have given up on everything else
I have found it to be the only way
To really know Christ and to experience
The mighty power that brought
Him back to life again, and to find
Out what it means to suffer and to
Die with him. So, whatever it takes
I will be one who lives in the fresh
Newness of life of those who are
Alive from the dead.

CASSIE BERNALL
COLOMBINE MARTYR

I have no more personal friends at school. But you know what? I am not going to apologize for speaking the name of Jesus. I am not going to justify my faith to them, and I am not going to hide the light that God has put into me. If I have to sacrifice everything, I will. I will take it. If my friends have to become my enemies for me to be with my best friend, Jesus, then that's fine with me.

RACHEL SCOTT
COLOMBINE MARTYR

Father, take my life, yes, my blood if Thou wilt, and consume it with Thine enveloping fire. I would not save it, for it is not mine to save. Have it Lord, have it all. Pour out my life as an oblation for the world. Blood is only of value as it flows before Thine altar.

JIM ELLIOT
WRITTEN AT AGE 21

I love life. I enjoy life. I live with exuberance and excitement. Every night I go to sleep looking forward to a brand-new day. I can't wait to get up and start afresh. Life is fulfilling, rewarding, challenging—anything but boring.

Whether it is having a night out with my wife or going on a ministry trip overseas; whether it is spending a day in study and prayer or playing family games during the holidays; whether it is getting the latest computer or purchasing a new set of books; whether it is participating in a worship service with the students or taking a long flight with a colleague—whatever I do, I enjoy. Despite the pain and hardship we all encounter in this world, despite seasons of terrible suffering and real loss, I thoroughly love life. It is normal—and scriptural—to feel like this:

> Whoever of you loves life and desires to see many good days, keep your tongue from evil and your lips from speaking lies. Turn from evil and do good; seek peace and pursue it (Ps. 34:12-14; see also 1 Pet. 3:10-12).

> "Because he loves me," says the LORD, "I will rescue him; I will protect him, for he acknowledges my name. He will call upon me, and I will answer him; I will be with him in trouble, I will deliver him and honor him. With long life will I satisfy him and show him my salvation" (Ps. 91:14-16).

Long, enjoyable life is a gift from God! He is the one "who gives life to everything" and "who richly provides us with everything for our enjoyment" (1 Tim. 6:13,17). Of Him the psalmist wrote, "How priceless is your unfailing love! Both high and low among men find refuge in the shadow of your wings. They feast on the abundance of your house; you give them drink from your river of delights. For with you is the fountain of life; in your light we see light" (Ps. 36:7-9). Yes, in Him is life, and that life is the light of men (see John 1:4).

That's why we who serve the Lord "are filled with an inexpressible and glorious joy" (1 Pet. 1:8). That's why Jesus could say, "Whoever drinks the water I give him will never thirst. Indeed, the water I give him will become in him a spring of water welling up to eternal life" (John 4:14). That's why He could promise, "If anyone is thirsty, let him come to me and drink. Whoever believes in me, as the Scripture has said, streams of living water will flow from within him" (John 7:37-38). Yes, Jesus came that we "may have life, and have it to the full" (John 10:10).

That's why I enjoy life so fully. That's why I savor life so deeply. That's why I *love life*. But I don't love *my own life*. There is quite a difference! As Jesus said, "The man who loves his life will lose it, while the man who hates his life in this world will keep it for eternal life" (John 12:25). You lose your life by loving it; you keep it by renouncing it—renouncing your rights, renouncing your preferences, renouncing your claims.

It boils down to this: We belong to God and to God alone. We live to do His will, period. If His will can be accomplished most fully through our living, so be it. If His will can be accomplished most fully through our dying, so be it. That should be our normal expression of faith.

Paul wrote to Timothy, "Fight the good fight of the faith. *Take hold of the eternal life* to which you were called when you made your good confession in the presence of many witnesses" (1 Tim. 6:12). This is the key to living our lives rightly in the here and now. As C. S. Lewis wrote, "It is since Christians have largely ceased to think of the other world that they have become so ineffective in this one." Without an eternal perspective, we are shortsighted and blind. Our vision is impaired! In the light of eternity, we see clearly. In that light, we can make sensible choices that we will never live to regret—even if we live to be a million years old. (In a very real sense, we will live to be a million years old, endless millions of times!)

You see, we have already received eternal life (see John 5:24; 1 John 5:11,12) and we are already seated with the Messiah in heavenly places (see Eph. 2:1-7; Col. 3:1-3). We live with one foot in this world and one foot in the world to come. What awaits us is the life that is really life (see 1 Tim. 6:17). We live the first frail, shadowy part of our lives here in this age. We live the rest of it in fullness and unveiled glory in the age to come. But it is the same life! The greater, fuller, more wonderful expression of our lives is yet to be. The only question is, How much time do we spend here in this place of service and sacrifice? How many years do we get to labor for the Lord before we go to our reward?

There *is* importance to everyday life in this world, so we cry at weddings, rejoice at the birth of healthy babies, weep at funerals, applaud at graduations, and shout at sporting events. But life here is fragmented and degraded, marred by sin, sickness, pain, and death. It is not the full life that God intended for us. No! Only the heavenly life—how wonderful!—is truly life. That alone is perfect life, unblemished life, incorruptible life, endless life! Only life without death is fully life.

Of course it is here in this world, here in this life, that we have the opportunity to repay our debt of gratitude to Jesus. It is here in this life that we can touch a multitude of lost and dying people. It is here in this life that we can be tested and refined as we walk by faith. It is here in this life that we can fight the battles of the Lord. The reality is that this life is all we have ever known, and if we are going to be here for 60 or 70 or 80 years, then we need a place to live, a way to support ourselves, and a certain amount of education and skills. But all these things are just the externals, just the peripherals. What really matters is our relationship with God.

WHAT IS YET TO COME IS FAR SUPERIOR TO ANYTHING WE COULD EVER EXPERIENCE IN THIS PRESENT WORLD. THIS PERSPECTIVE IS REALITY; THIS PERSPECTIVE IS TRUTH.

In this world, we are like people living under the earth, carefully cultivating the roots of a plant. We know by faith that something beautiful is growing on the other side, although at present it is invisible to us. One day we will live on that other side and enjoy the full beauty of that plant. For now, our perspective is limited as we labor under the ground. But our labors are real! They are producing fruit that will remain.

In this world, we are like babies in the womb—alive and growing, but limited in our consciousness and completely enclosed within our temporary home. One day we will emerge from the womb! But life in the womb is real and essential, and without it we would have no life in the outside world.

This is the perspective we must have:

Though outwardly we are wasting away [all of us, even in the best of health, are destined to grow old and die], yet inwardly we are being renewed day by day. For our light and momentary troubles are achieving for us an eternal glory that far outweighs them all. So we fix our eyes not on what is seen, but on what is unseen. For what is seen is temporary, but what is unseen is eternal (2 Cor. 4:16-18).

I consider that our present sufferings are not worth comparing with the glory that will be revealed in us (Rom. 8:18).

What is yet to come is far superior to anything we could ever experience in this present world. *This* perspective is reality. *This* perspective is truth. If we try to save our lives in this world, then we lose the real meaning of life. If we lose our lives for the gospel, then we really live. Even those without an eternal perspective have taken hold of this principle: They realize that life is not simply a matter of being and having and doing and existing. There is an objective, an aim, a purpose to our lives.

That's why atheistic Communists are willing to die for their cause and even nonreligious soldiers are willing to die for their country. They see the purpose of their lives as being much more than self-preservation and self-improvement. They recognize that the fulfillment of their ideals might require them to lay down their lives—whether those ideals consist of an improved society or national independence or secure borders. They do it out of necessity, for the sake of their children, for the sake of their colleagues, for the sake of the present, for the sake of the future. They do it to choose the higher good.

Dov Gruner was a Jewish freedom fighter captured by the British in 1947 and sentenced to be hung. He wrote this shortly before his execution:

Of course I want to live. Who does not? But if I am sorry that I am about to finish, it is mainly because I did not manage to do enough. I too could have let the future fend for itself, taken the job I was promised, or left the country altogether and lived securely in America. But that would not have given me satisfaction as a Jew and certainly not as a Zionist. . . .

[The way of the Jewish people these days should be] to stand up for what is ours and be ready for battle, even if some instances it leads to the gallows. . . .

I write these lines forty-eight hours before the time fixed by our oppressors to carry out their murder, and at such moments one does not lie. I swear that if I had the choice of starting again I would choose the same road, regardless of the possible consequences for me.[1]

Yes, "if I am sorry that I am about to finish, it is mainly because I did not manage to do enough"; or in the famous words of Nathan Hale before his execution in September 1776, "I only regret that I have but one life to lose for my country." Life is more than just living! Life has meaning and purpose. Life continues from generation to generation and from this world to the world to come. Life should produce something lasting. What is the fruit of our lives? What is our legacy? What do we have to show for our years here on Earth? What road do we choose, the road of least resistance (i.e., the road of saving our lives) or the road of revolution (i.e., the road of losing our lives)?

During the horrors of World War II, Jews in Eastern Europe were rounded up into ghettos before being shipped to concentration camps to be exterminated. The living conditions within these ghettoes were almost unimaginable with terrible suffering—starvation, disease, filth, overcrowding, depression—on every hand. Emmanuel Ringelblum was the historian of the Jewish ghetto in Warsaw, Poland. His chronicles were discovered buried in the ghetto rubble years after his tragic death. Read carefully what he observed:

> The older generation, with half a lifetime behind it, spoke, thought and concerned itself about surviving the war, dreamed about life. The youth—the best, the finest that the Jewish people possessed—spoke and thought only about an honourable death. They did not think about surviving the war. They did not procure Aryan [i.e., forged, non-Jewish identity] papers for themselves [so they could escape]. They had no dwellings on the other side. Their only concern was to discover the most dignified and honourable death, befitting an ancient people with a history stretching back over several thousand years.[2]

So many of us are like that older generation! Our goal is to survive and have a nice life. True revolutionaries see things differently: Their goal is to live and die with honor, to make a difference in this world, to effect a lasting change. The cost is inconsequential. It is the cause that is important. (It was Augustine, followed by Napoleon, who said that, "It is the cause, and not the death, that makes the martyr.")[3]

Less than one year after forming a guerrilla army in Bolivia, Che Guevara's troops had paid a high price:

> By August, Che was sick and exhausted, and so were many of the two dozen men still with him. On August 7, [1967], the nine-month anniversary of the guerrilla army's birth, he noted: "Of the [original] six men, two are dead, one has disappeared, two are wounded, and I with a case of asthma that I am unable to control."[4]

Such is the cost of worldly revolution! And worldly revolutionaries freely pay that price without any hope of life in the world to come. They are motivated only by their goals in this world. How much more readily do *religious revolutionaries* give their lives for their cause?

Consider these testimonies from the fundamentalist world of Islam. Here are the words of the mother of a Hamas terrorist who blew himself up the last Sunday of December 1994, wounding 13 people through his death. "I am very happy that my son has reached paradise," she said. "He has made us very proud and brought dignity to the entire family. I don't feel pain and am not crying. This is like a wedding."[5] A wedding!

From Egypt come these faith-filled, fanatical words: "To give your life for the sake of Islam is the highest calling. We must free the world of the Zionist and American threats. They are the source of all evil."[6] A news report from Cairo gives this chilling perspective:

Two brothers sentenced to death in an attack on German tourists which left 10 civilians dead will not ask for a government pardon. According to a 1 November [1997] newspaper report, the two men were unrepentant and were prepared to die as martyrs for the Islamic cause. "A death sentence would be like a day of feasts," Saber Abu el-Ulla reportedly said before the verdict was handed down.[7]

So, a death sentence would be like a day of feasts while a son's death through a terrorist act is like a wedding. What does this say about the mentality of extremist Islam? What does this say about the mind-set of religious revolutionaries? And what is it that these extremists have in common with all religious martyrs?

Three characteristics are essential: First, a strong hope in an after-life; second, a feeling of disillusionment with this present world; third, an absolute commitment to one's cause. These are the distinguishing traits of religious martyrdom, yet they are found in so few of us!

We speak much about the world to come but live as though this world was everything. Our disillusionment with earthly life is fleeting, easily displaced by the latest pleasure, taste, fad, or game. And our dedication to the cause is questionable. So often we are cowardly and compromised rather than confrontational and committed. Our devotion is dubious! Worldly revolutionaries and religious revolutionaries stand together and rebuke our skin-deep faith.

Mahatma Gandhi, who gained India's independence from England through nonviolent revolution, once said that "a reformer has to sail not with the current. Very often he has to go against it even though it may cost him his life."[8] So be it! Such convictions ultimately cost Gandhi his life. And such convictions also cost Martin Luther King, Jr., his life—although he did more for civil rights through nonviolence than any of his contemporaries did through violence. Both of these men were assassinated. Both of them knew that they could well die violent deaths. Both of them still chose their course!

Christian martyrs may be thought of as those who are assassinated for righteousness. Yet all of us are called to hunger and thirst for righteousness, to seek earnestly God's kingdom and His righteousness (see Matt. 5:6; 6:33). Will we determine to steer a straight, unbending course? Will we put principle over pleasure? Will we esteem the favor of God more highly than the favor of man? Will we stand for righteousness?

Just look at how far-reaching Gandhi's nonviolent principles actually were (for him, they were principles of righteousness).

His code of discipline for volunteers in his 1930 movement included the following:

1. Harbor no anger but suffer the anger of the opponent. Refuse to return the assaults of the opponent.
2. Do not submit to any order given in anger, even though severe punishment is threatened for disobeying.
3. Refrain from insults and swearing.
4. Protect opponents [that's right, opponents!] from insult or attack, even at the risk of life.
5. Do not resist arrest nor the attachment of property, unless holding property as a trustee.
6. Refuse to surrender any property held in trust at the risk of life.
7. If taken prisoner, behave in an exemplary manner.[9]

Why would so many people do such things? Why would they willfully subject themselves to suffering, pain, and even death? Why would they refuse to act violently, even at the cost of their own lives? It is because they were opposing violence, and only through nonviolence could the battle be won. To become violent was to lose! To hold to the principle of nonviolence—even at the cost of life—was to gain life and win the war. It worked!

Do you see the power of living and dying for a principle? Do you see how you can save your life by losing it—especially in terms of the gospel and eternal life? Do you see how loving your own life—clinging

DO YOU SEE HOW YOU CAN SAVE YOUR LIFE BY LOSING IT—ESPECIALLY IN TERMS OF THE GOSPEL AND ETERNAL LIFE?

to it, holding on to it, refusing to let it go—can thwart your spiritual effectiveness? Consider the example of Stephen, the first martyr of the Church. Why didn't he back down when he saw that the Sanhedrin, the governing religious body, was becoming enraged with him? Why didn't he try to pacify them? After all, he was probably a young man with a wife and children. His whole future lay before him. His family was dependent on him. There may have been a toddler waiting to greet him that day when he came home. But he never came home!

And then there was his ministry. He was a powerful preacher, anointed to heal the sick and perform miracles. Think of all the lives he could touch! Think of all the good he could do for the kingdom of God. Why didn't Stephen simply deny the false charges? "Men and brothers, the accusations are not true!" Why didn't he politely dismiss their questions and calm their anger? Why did he continue to stand up and speak out? The answer challenges us all: *He was not seeking to save his life; he was seeking to be a witness.* "For whoever wants to save his life will lose it, but whoever loses his life for me will find it" (Matt. 16:25).

This is the story of the true Church in every nation and in every age: "You did not renounce your faith in me, even in the days of Antipas, *my faithful witness,* who was put to death in your city—where Satan lives" (Rev. 2:13).[10] This is the gospel of martyrdom, the gospel of Jesus. It is the gospel that Paul preached and lived: "I consider my life worth nothing to me, if only I may finish the race and complete the task the Lord Jesus has given me—the task of testifying to the gospel of God's grace" (Acts 20:24). As Leonard Ravenhill observed, Paul didn't mind if the cost of his obedience was prison, "for it were better that he should be 'the prisoner of the Lord' *for a few years* than that his fellow men should be the devil's prisoners in hell *forever.*"[11] This is a biblical perspective!

In 1984, after hearing K. P. Yohannan of Gospel for Asia preach a challenging message, a Christian man named Samuel gave up his good job in South India and moved with his family to the region of Karnataka. There he began preaching to unreached Hindus known for their hostility to the gospel. The Lord blessed the work, and even a Hindu priest was born again.

This was more than the Hindu radicals could take. They burst into a meeting one Sunday and severely beat Samuel with iron rods, breaking his hand, arm, leg, and collarbone. When his seven-year-old son ran up and cried out, "Please don't kill our daddy!" they struck the boy on the spine, breaking his back. Then they left, warning Samuel that if he ever preached there again, they would kill him. The beating was so severe that Samuel and his son were hospitalized for several months.

After his release, Samuel attended a workers' meeting with K. P. Yohannan. The first night, during a time of prayer, his arm was supernaturally healed of paralysis he was suffering as a result of his beating. The next night he testified of the things he had recently experienced for the Lord.

K. P. asked Samuel, "What are you going to do now?" With a peaceful determination, the young man replied: "I am going back. Even if I am killed, my blood will be the foundation for many more churches." And he did return! He continued to preach and baptize many more converts, and his son returned to school. He has also been beaten again. Perhaps his blood *will* be the foundation for many more churches.

Of course, it's easy for us to admire him from a distance, but what if we were in his shoes? Would we have gone back and preached? K. P. Yohannan was honest enough to admit that his own reaction might have been different. First, he would have come up with lots of good Scriptures to justify not going back. And then he would have used his best argument:

> I'm only forty-some years old! God wants me to use my brain for His kingdom. With all the investment He has made in my life since I was sixteen, would it be right for me to be killed by some fanatics next week? Don't be stupid! I am going to leave this place so I will have another forty years of my life to invest in and build God's kingdom.[12]

Samuel thought differently. He was not out to save his life—he was out to save sinners. With such resolve, how could he be defeated? He realized that his life was not his own. In past centuries, missionaries endued with the same spirit sailed off to faraway lands with their belongings packed in *caskets*. They were making a one-way trip![13]

In the late 1980s, a young evangelist moved into an area in Asia famous for its violent resistance to Jesus. The radical religious opposition immediately came to his apartment and made their intentions clear: "We'll kill you if you stay here and preach!" The evangelist only smiled. "I came to die," he replied. Ten years later, his church had 200 members. That is the power of the gospel of martyrdom. That is true success. That is how we save our lives—by losing them for the Lord.

We can learn a lesson from the tragic, yet inspiring, account of the Treblinka concentration camp, burned down and destroyed by its Jewish prisoners in an astonishingly daring revolt. The story unfolds gradually. Over a period of many months, as train-loads of Jews arrived in the camp, they were greeted with a surprisingly peaceful scene. The train station was brightly painted, masking the terror that awaited the hapless victims. There was, of course, one thing that could have caught the attention of the arriving Jews: The large clock on the wall never changed time. It too was painted! But the ruse worked, and most of the Jews did not realize how near death was.

Of course, many of them had some idea of the dangers that awaited them, but still they did not fight or resist. Why? Because they thought to fight or resist was to guarantee immediate death, while if they quietly complied, they hoped that they could somehow save their lives.

They were wrong! To *comply* was to guarantee death—only the gas chambers awaited them—whereas to resist was the only possible way to escape. You see, if all the Jews tried to revolt, most of them would die in the process. But others would survive. It was their only hope. And yet hundreds of thousands of Jews went to their deaths with no resistance at all, paralyzed by the save-your-life mentality.

This mentality was particularly strong among the Sonderkommando, a special group of Jews that had the horrific job of removing the corpses of their fellow Jews from the gas chambers and bringing them to the crematoria. Because they needed to be strong for their grim work, they were fed better than the other prisoners, and because their job was so psychologically draining, they were also allowed special privileges, like playing soccer during their free time.

Yet here we find the irony of it all: Of all the Jews in Treblinka, these men knew *exactly* what fate awaited their people. Yet they refused to ask the obvious question, namely, What happened to the previous group of Sonderkommando workers?

"Perhaps," they reasoned, "if we do our job well we will somehow survive. Perhaps, if we can stay alive, the nightmare will end and we will be liberated. Perhaps . . ." This was exactly what the Nazis wanted. It paralyzed the captive Jews, robbing them of their ability to fight back.

And so the cycle continued, until soon enough a new group of Sonderkommando workers carried the bodies of the last group into the crematoria—that last group who lost their lives by trying to save their lives. And then something happened. One of the prisoners escaped on a train and made his way into a village in another city. But as soon as his Jewish identity was suspected, he had to flee for his life. As he made his way from town to town, he came to a frightful conclusion. His people were doomed! Everywhere he went, Jews were being herded into cattle cars and sent off to their deaths, with the full cooperation of the local people. There was no hope!

So this courageous Jew allowed himself to be recaptured and brought back to Treblinka and certain death, with one message: "Someone must survive and be a witness. Our people are perishing and we are all going to die. But the world must know! If we die, let us die with dignity. If we fight back, at least we have a chance to tell the world our story."

And so the plot to revolt began. But it was next to impossible to do: How could the Jews coordinate their efforts from bunker to bunker and from one part of the camp to the other? How could they obtain the needed weapons when even a stick was hard to find? And with such a short concentration-camp life span—most of them would be exterminated in a matter of weeks or months—how could they hatch a successful plan and then implement it? All these factors made the revolt more a matter of talk than reality until the breaking point finally came. The chilling account needs to be told in full.

There was a Jewish man named Langner whose father owned a shoe store in the town of Czestochowa in Poland. Like hundreds of thousands of other Jews, he had heard the rumors about a mass extermination of his people but hoped against hope that they were not true. Still, he was sufficiently afraid of the potential Nazi danger that he hid whenever there was a raid in his area.

And then one day, like millions of other Jews, he had been flushed out of his hiding place. In the train that took him to Treblinka he had preferred to cling to the promises of the Germans rather than finally accept the truth. There were one hundred in his car, one hundred praying, weeping, discussing *ad infinitum* the exact purpose of their voyage. When one of them had stood up and said, "Let us revolt!" the others had given him the eternal argument: "If we revolt we will all be killed on the spot, whereas if we wait we may be killed too, but maybe not, and maybe not right away." And the discussions had resumed. When there had been no more water in the car, the children had begun licking the sweat on their mothers' faces, and the adults had withdrawn into themselves. Then the man who wanted to revolt had announced, "I'm getting out of here. Who wants to come with me?" As he asked this question, his eye had fallen on Langner, who without thinking replied, "Me!"[14]

These two then managed to tear off the grating that covered the window—although the others tried to stop them—and Langner watched the other man, chosen to go first by drawing straws, jump out the window. He saw him "roll over, get up, and run zigzagging toward a clump of trees."

At this moment shots had rung out and Langner had lost his desire to jump. He had collapsed at the foot of the window, weeping. Several times he had tried to stand up again in order to jump, but his legs, which were trembling, had refused to support him, and fear had descended upon him, sovereign, paralyzing.

When he had arrived at Treblinka he had been saved by an old friend from Czestochowa who had recognized him. The fear had never left him, but another emotion joined it: the sense of having acted like a coward in refusing to jump. He remembered the face of the man who had fled and saw him again, suddenly getting up amid the dying and saying, "Let us revolt!" simply, as if it were a natural thing. He had said, "Let us revolt!" as others would have said, "Let us pray, my brothers." At the time, this idea of revolt had seemed absurd to Langner. What could you do with your bare hands against tanks; what could women and old men do against these strong young soldiers, well trained and armed? It was madness. But now Langner lived in a world of madness [Treblinka!], and the voice of the other man re-echoed in his heart. He still did not know how to revolt, but the idea filled him more each day, and little by little he forgot both his fear and his cowardice.[15]

Unfortunately, he was caught by a guard as he attempted to steal some money, and the Nazis, glad to have a culprit, decided to make a public example of him. After whipping him severely in the morning, they hung him by his feet from a gallows erected in the middle of the yard, continuing to whip him as he helplessly swayed back and forth. A convoy of Jews passed by him, marching slowly to their deaths in the gas chambers. (This was the daily routine.) By the afternoon, as the last of the Jews had been processed and taken to what was called "the road to heaven," the other Jewish prisoners were made to line up in columns in the yard. Langner, in the meantime, continued to moan and cry out, begging the guard to kill him.

The head of the camp (a Nazi named Lalka) then explained to the prisoners that Langner would soon die but not before he suffered a few more hours of agony. His terrible treatment would serve as an example to all other prisoners who tried to escape! Lalka then forced the prisoners to walk by Langner single file, singing the Treblinka anthem as they went, and then he sent them back to work.

> The afternoon lasted an eternity. No one said a word. The silence was so profound that Langner's groans could be heard from every corner of the immense yard. When he called for his mother, every man thought of his own. When he begged to be killed, every man wanted to die. Langner's agony was the agony of all of them, his cries were their cries, his pain their pain. They would have liked to run away so they would no longer hear, to stop their ears, to become deaf, if only they could stop hearing him, if only they could stop seeing the torn body of their brother which still quivered at each blow of the whip. In spite of themselves they looked at him secretly where he hung, bloody, mutilated, shapeless. They saw the blood trickle slowly from his hair as from a flayed animal, they saw large shreds of skin that hung down, revealing raw flesh of a brilliant red. Suddenly he uttered a great cry that chilled the prisoners and the guards, and everyone thought that he was finally going to die. But immediately the prisoners heard him calling them in Yiddish [their native, Jewish tongue]:

"*Yiden! Yiden!* Jews, Jews my brothers!" (A silence, and once again the voice that seemed to come out of nowhere.) "Revolt! Revolt! Don't listen to their promises. You will all be killed. They can't let you leave this place after what you have seen. Even if they wanted to spare your lives they would be forced to kill you, for the world will never forgive them for what they are doing and they know it. Revolt! Avenge your fathers and your brothers, avenge yourselves. Save the honor of Israel! Since you are going to die, die fighting! Long live Israel, long live the Jewish people!"[16]

Although the Nazis did not understand what was being said at first, they began to catch on when Langner called out, "Long live Israel!" And so Lalka ran over to Langner—now jerking violently—and shattered his head with the barrel of a rifle. But it was too late. It was as if a light had suddenly gone on. At last the truth was out. At last the spell was broken.

The Jews finally realized the inevitable: If they tried to save their lives, they would lose them. If they lost their lives for their people and their cause, they would save them—meaning that at least they would save their dignity and their self-worth, and at most they would save their earthly lives and the earthly lives of their children. Their incredibly heroic uprising against all possible odds resulted in the deaths of 40 Nazis, the incinerating of the concentration camp (which never operated again and never gassed or burned another Jew), and the escape of approximately 70 Jews, who preserved their story as a witness for all generations.[17]

Now, what is the point of all this for us? Why share this story now? I believe there are several lessons we can learn—that we must learn. Treblinka's painted train station is like the world. It looks so good, so inviting, so cozy. But the impressions are false! Yet we are so easily deceived. As A. W. Tozer noted many years ago, "That this world is a playground instead of a battleground has now been accepted by the vast majority of fundamentalist Christians."[18] We're in a war—a spiritual war, a cultural war, a moral war—but we often lose sight of it, choosing to play, to simply get on with the business of our lives rather than fight. Life in this world casts its spell on us, and we live and die just like the people of the world live and die. Our values as believers are barely distinguishable from theirs!

Just like the Jews of Treblinka, we are paralyzed by the save-your-life mentality. We dare not risk our lives—our reputations, our careers, our educations, our dreams, our finances, our families, ourselves—for the gospel. After all, we reason, if we can simply position ourselves properly in the society, avoiding reproach, gaining the respect of the unsaved, fitting in well without rocking the boat, then we can live long enough to do something for Jesus.

NOW IS THE TIME—OUR TIME—TO TAKE THE JESUS ROAD, THE ROAD OF MULTIPLICATION BY MARTYRDOM, THE ROAD OF GAINING BY LOSING, OF LIVING BY DYING, OF EXALTATION BY ABASEMENT.

Yet this is the guaranteed road to failure! This is the guaranteed road to *losing* our lives—losing what really matters, losing our opportunity to change this world, losing the purpose for which we have been redeemed, losing our true dignity and value. As William Ralph Inge, English theologian and dean of St Paul's Cathedral, remarked, "We are losing our Christianity because Christianity is a creed for heroes while we are mainly harmless, good-natured people who want everybody to have a good time."[19] How true—but no more!

Now is the time—*our* time—to take the Jesus road, the road of multiplication by martyrdom, the road of gaining by losing, of living by dying, of exaltation by abasement. Now is our time to stand up for what we know is right rather than conform to the standards of the world. Now is our time to swim against the tide and go against the grain, thereby fulfilling God's purposes for us.[20]

This is how we really live: by breaking the power of death—the ultimate fear—over our lives (see Heb. 2:14). This is how we really succeed: by going forth like sheep among wolves, being as shrewd as snakes but as innocent as doves (see Matt. 10:16). We need only fear God! We need not fear people or what they can do to us (see Matt. 10:28; 1 Pet. 3:13-15). The power of this world is broken!

Once we realize that our lives do not consist in the abundance of our possessions or in the greatness of our reputations but rather in our identity in the Lord, then we are free. What have we to fear? What have we to lose? What threat can be brought against us? By "losing our lives" we gain freedom and the ability to truly live, free from fear and the intimidation of Satan.

The sad fact is that for too long, we have played by the devil's rules and, as a result, have been losing the game. While he has mounted a frontal assault on this generation, we have simply gone along, not wanting to endanger our interests, not wanting to hurt our chances of worldly success and comfort, not wanting to risk our lives. Yet all that we have worked for in this world—if it is not for the glory of God and the good of His kingdom—will go up in smoke on judgment day. Then just like the Jews at Treblinka, we will realize too late that the only way to avoid the flames is *not* by taking the path of least resistance but rather by taking the path of obedience. What else can we do?

It is one thing to use wisdom, to flee from persecution when possible, to steer clear of danger when forewarned, to keep up our health and believe for our healing, to do every-thing possible to avoid dying prematurely (see, e.g., Matt. 10:23; Acts 9:23-25; 20:3; 23:12-24). But all this has one pri-mary motivation: We want to avoid premature death so that we can use our lives for the Lord. We want to keep living because it's not our time to go! Our mentality is that of the soldier: We press on in battle, determined not to live for ourselves but to live for others, for the kingdom, for the Lord, for this holy cause and this holy war.

We must determine that without Jesus, life in this sin-filled, suffering-cursed world is not worth living and that only with Him does life have meaning. As David Brainerd said more than 250 years ago, "As long as I see anything to be done for God, life is worth having; but O how vain and unworthy it is to live for any lower end!"[21] In the light of eternity, in the light of the Cross, the only thing that makes sense is for us to give our lives for God's cause—the cause of the gospel, the cause of helping this current generation and giving hope to the coming genera-tion. Once we see the higher purpose for our lives—not what we can get but what we can give, not how we can improve the qual-ity of our own lives but how we can improve the quality of the lives of others—then we can embrace the words of Jesus: "For whoever wants to save his life will lose it, but whoever loses his life for me will save it" (Luke 9:24).

This is a choice we make every day! "If anyone would come after me," Jesus said, "he must deny himself and take up his cross *daily* and follow me" (Luke 9:23). Paul understood this fully: The resurrection to come makes sense of it all!

And as for us, why do we endanger ourselves every hour? *I die every day*—I mean that, brothers—just as surely as I glory over you in Christ Jesus our Lord. If I fought wild beasts in Ephesus for merely human reasons, what have I gained? If the dead are not raised, "Let us eat and drink, for tomorrow we die" (1 Cor. 15:30-32, emphasis added).

But the dead *are* raised! And so we do not merely eat, drink, and have a good time. No! We march on, pushing forward with the message of life, refusing to retreat.

Shortly before his death, C. T. Studd, the great missionary pioneer, received these words from a colleague:

> Let the victors when they come,
> When the forts of folly fall,
> Find thy body near the wall.

So be it! Since we're in a war, let's fight. Since we're in a race, let's run. Since we're following Jesus, let's go for it. What do we gain by holding back, by seeking to save our lives? As James B. Taylor said (in words that I have often used to rally our students to action): "The world may frown—Satan may rage—but go on! Live for God. May I die in the field of battle." Yes, go on!

We have only this life to live, and death comes around but once. We might as well make the most of it! As an Indian brother said at a leaders conference we held in Andhra Pradesh in 1999 (some of his colleagues had been killed, and he had received daily death threats from Hindu militants), "Why die a natural death when I can die a martyr's death? For me to live is

Christ and to die is gain!" And he said this with head held high, shoulders erect, and a big smile on his face. One year later, he was still smiling, still preaching, still dying daily, and still fully alive. One day he might die a martyr's death. For now, he is living a martyr's life—dead to this world, dead to fear, dead to sin, alive only to God. (His wife and children stand with him.)

So on with the revolution! Nothing can stop us now.

Turn Back, Press In, Step Out:
Themes for the Gospel Revolution

My crime is the ancient and familiar one of corrupting the minds of
the youth. This charge is a valid one.

It is true that Jesus never called for a political, revolutionary transformation of Jewish society. Yet the repentance which he demanded
as a consequence of his preaching of the reign of God sought to ignite
within the people of God a movement in comparison to which the normal type of revolution is insignificant.

GERHARD LOHFINK
JESUS AND COMMUNITY

Our expectation of the future must mean certainty that the divine will
conquer the demonic, that love will conquer hate, that the all-embrac-
ing will conquer the isolated. And certainty tolerates no limitation. God
embraces everything. When we trust in him for the future, we trust
for the present. When we have the innermost faith in him, this faith
will prove valid for all areas of life.

EBERHARD ARNOLD
GOD'S REVOLUTION

After C. T. Studd committed his life to Jesus, he came across a tract, written by an atheist, that made a radical impact on his life. The tract read as follows:

Did I firmly believe, as millions say they do, that the knowledge and practice of religion in this life influences destiny in another, religion would mean to me everything. I would cast away earthly enjoyments as dross, earthly cares as follies, and earthly thoughts and feelings as vanity. Religion would be my first waking thought, and my last image before sleep sank me into unconsciousness. I should labour in its cause alone. I would take thought for the morrow of Eternity alone. I would esteem one soul gained for heaven worth a life of suffering. Earthly consequences should never stay my hand, nor seal my lips. Earth, its joys and its griefs, would occupy no moment of my thoughts. I would strive to look upon Eternity alone, and on the Immortal Souls around me, soon to be everlastingly happy or everlastingly miserable. I would go forth to the world and preach to it in season and out of season, and my text would be, WHAT SHALL IT PROFIT A MAN IF HE GAIN THE WHOLE WORLD AND LOSE HIS OWN SOUL?[1]

Studd was convinced that this atheist did, in fact, describe "the truly consistent life," but when he looked at his own life, he saw "how inconsistent it had been." And so he determined that, "from that time forth my life should be consistent, and I set myself to know what was God's will for me."[2] How simple! And yet consistency is a trait we often lack, even though God's will is totally and perfectly consistent: consistent with eternal values, consistent with absolute truth, consistent with the highest reality. By following God's will, we live consistent lives that make sense in the light of eternity. What could be more logical?

But we are so inconsistent, so double-minded, so indecisive. And Satan exploits this to the full! As Amy Carmichael remarked early in her missions career, "Satan is so much more in earnest than we are—he buys up the opportunity while we are wondering how much it will cost."[3] She was not exaggerating! Look at the state of the sinning world, look at state of the Church in the West, and then tell me if you disagree with what Amy wrote.

But she determined that this would not be the case in her own life. She would be more earnest than the devil and his hordes. She would follow the example of her Savior, who was more earnest in His love—a million times over!—than Satan was in his hate. This quote from Francis Coillard, a missionary for many years to the Zambesi, was a constant inspiration in her life. He said, "The evangelization of the world is a desperate struggle with the Prince of Darkness and with everything his rage can stir up in the shape of obstacles, vexations, oppositions, and hatred, whether by circumstances or by the hand of man. It is a serious task. Oh, it should mean a life of consecration."[4] There is no other choice!

Only a fully consecrated, fully committed army will be able to reverse the flood tide of sin in our society. Only a fully equipped, fully armed band of soldiers will be able to drive the enemy back. But drive him back we must, and drive him back we will! There is no way we can let him gain more ground, no way we can let him drag more lives down, no way we can sit back idly while he mauls and rapes and kills. It's time for God's holy army to arise! If we do, Satan will flee. William Gurnall, the famous Puritan author, knew this principle well: "Let the devil choose his way; God is a match for him at every weapon. The devil and his whole council are but fools to God; nay, their wisdom foolishness."[5] Who can withstand the Lord?

Of course, there is much uncertainty at the present time: Will this generation turn back to God? What will happen to our society? Will the Great Commission be fulfilled in our lifetimes? But these questions have more to do with our lack of obedience than with God's lack of willingness. He desires to move! Will we seek His face, get His plan, and attack and overcome the powers of darkness, or will we become a bunch of noisy, righteous windbags, expressing our displeasure with the moral corruption of the world but doing nothing to change it? What will we do?

Jesus outlined a clear and definite plan of action: "When a strong man, fully armed, guards his own house, his possessions are safe. But when someone stronger attacks and overpowers him, he takes away the armor in which the man trusted and divides up the spoils" (Luke 11:21,22). These are words of war! There is no passivity here, no lack of aggression, no retreating, no sitting back and waiting. No! Jesus made it plain: We must be stronger than the enemy, and we must attack and overcome him.[6] Then the victory is sure. Souls will be saved, strongholds will be broken, captives will be set free, and God's kingdom will be advanced. But we must have a strategy. No war is ever won without it. No battle is ever won without it. No general can succeed without it. Strategy is essential!

Satan certainly has his strategy, and it is multifaceted, multi-pronged, and bent on multiplication: One Satan-touched life quickly touches another![7] Just consider the many different ways in which he attacks the human race (and in doing this, attacks the Lord): He inspires counterfeit religions and cults, confusing multitudes about the truth. Where people do know the truth, he brings in legalism and license, discouragement and doubt. He tells one man there is no God while telling another man there are many gods. He pushes one person to total self-denial while pushing another person to total gratification. He lures people into sinful pleasures and then plagues them with guilt and condemnation. He turns neutral things into obsessions and bad things into addictions. He helps some people get rich through exploiting the poor and then urges the poor to fight back against the rich. He pushes a woman to give herself to a stranger, and then when she learns she's pregnant, he provokes her to abort her baby; then he calls her a murderer. He drives one man into homosexuality and then drives another man into beating up gays.

He inspires every kind of sinful emotion and desire—like hatred, lying, violence, lust, greed, rage, and envy. He devises new forms of sinful pleasure—like more potent drugs and wild new highs and pornography via the Internet. He divides families and nations and cities and churches. He uses music and sex and food and sports and money and art and movies and media and war and philosophy and education and books and tapes and technology to accomplish his diabolical purposes. Just look at all the ways he assaults the human race!

And what do we do? We have a poorly attended prayer meeting once a week. We sponsor a sporadic "feed the hungry" program. We hold an occasional outreach to the lost. We launch a superficial plan to keep the church youth happy. And then we add in a little fasting here and a special conference there, and we think we're warriors and giants. Not so! We're like children playing with toy soldiers, conquering wooden blocks rather than city blocks. This must change if we are to wage a successful revolution. We must have a call to arms![8]

One of the secrets of psychological warfare (called psywar by the military) is to try to convince enemy troops that surrender is sweet, that it is better to capitulate than to continue to fight, that defeat is inevitable. During World War I, psywar pamphlets were air-dropped among the German troops. Shortly after the end of the war, Field Marshall Paul von Hindenburg, the chief of staff of the kaiser's army, complained:

> In the shower of pamphlets which was scattered by enemy airmen our adversaries said and wrote that they did not think so badly of us; that we must only be reasonable and perhaps here and there renounce something we had conquered. Then everything would soon be right again and we could live together in peace, perpetual international peace. As regards peace within our own borders, new men and new Governments would see to that. What a blessing peace would be after all the fighting. There was, therefore, no point in continuing the struggle.[9]

And what were the results of this strategy? Military historian Stanley Sandler writes: "As German Army discipline wavered or broke, these leaflets became responsible for defections on a large scale. Not surprisingly, Adolph Hitler termed Allied military psywar 'psychologically efficient.'"[10]

Satan knows this too! He tells us that things really aren't so bad, that we shouldn't get so worked up about sin and the flesh, that compromise is far better than conflict. "Don't listen to those fanatical Bible-thumpers," he says. "Be reasonable. Be balanced. Be normal. Why get so upset about human nature? What's so bad about sex between consenting adults who really love each other, even if they're not married? What's so evil about calming your nerves with a drink? What's wrong with a man being intimate with another man (that's the way he's been since birth!) or a woman being intimate with another woman (really, she has no interest in males at all!)?

"What's the problem with people being people? Why not just enjoy life? Why not be a realist? Kids will be kids; teens will be teens; adults will be adults. That's the way it's always been, and that's the way it will always be. Don't be such an extremist. Just stay away from the really ugly things, like murder or rape or theft, and learn to be tolerant—unless, of course, you really think that you're the only one who's right and that everyone outside of your little group is doomed to hell. Grow up! There is beauty in all religions, not just yours, and there are plenty of deeply spiritual people who do not believe like you. Calm down! The era of religious extremism is over. It's time for peace and understanding. Relax, live in harmony, be at rest."

Soon enough, we're slumbering!

A less radical version of Satan's psychological warfare—and a version more acceptable to believers—goes like this: "Of course your beliefs are true. Jesus really is the only Savior! But you don't want to be fanatical like those crazies who kill abortion doctors or those survivalists who hide in the mountains and wait for the end of the world. Read Church history! There have always been weirdoes—like David Koresh and the Branch Davidians—who think there are demons lurking everywhere and that everyone is out to get them. Don't get wacky! Just lead a good, moral life and take care of your family. There is no higher calling than that! Demonstrate your Christianity without saying much about it, and give your tithes to your local church. And whatever you do, don't let those legalistic killjoys tell you there's anything wrong with spending all your nights watching sports or enjoying a good soap opera during the day or taking in an exciting movie with a little 'spice' in it.[11] And don't get hung up over a little sin here and there. God understands your nature. Rest in Him. Rest . . . just rest."

Soon enough, we're in a deep sleep!

Yes, Satan's psywar, in one form or another, has worked. We must shake it off! The hour *is* urgent; the battle *is* intense; the stakes *are* high; we *are* in the struggle of the ages. Wake up! Be strong! March on! Don't let the enemy mess with your mind. Now is hardly the time to compromise. Now is hardly the time to go into neutral gear. It's time to accelerate!

I find it interesting that Gandhi's nonviolent approach to change was also a no-compromise approach. His method—called Satyagraha—included these fundamental rules: "*Refusal to surrender essentials in negotiation.* Satyagraha excludes all compromise that affects basic principles or essential portions of valid objectives. Care must be exercised not to engage in bargaining or barter. *Insistence upon full agreement* on fundamentals before accepting a settlement."[12] If you're fighting for a cause, don't quit until your goal is realized. Otherwise, your fighting has been in vain—at least in part. Otherwise, you leave an open door for the enemy, and that can be fatal.

Yet some of us are not fighting because we have little hope that change can come, little hope there can really be a spiritual and moral revolution in our society. No wonder we're so defeated! As D. L. Moody said, "What a difference in the men who go into battle intending to conquer *if they can,* and those who go into battle intending to conquer." Or as C. H. Mackintosh expressed it, "A coward heart will not do for the day of battle; a doubting spirit will not stand in conflict."[13] How can we win the war or even the battle with an attitude like this?

Che Guevara felt that the Cuban Revolution, which succeeded in overthrowing the Batista regime, put the lie to "the defeatist attitude of revolutionaries or pseudorevolutionaries who remain inactive and take refuge in the pretext that against a professional army nothing can be done, who sit and wait until in some mechanical way all necessary objective and subjective conditions are given without working to accelerate them."[14]

So many believers are just like this, hoping that things will somehow change for the better or, even more pathetically, waiting aimlessly for the Lord's return, assuming that matters will only get worse.[15] We are called to action! We are called to go and preach, to go and make disciples, to go and set the captives free, to go and make a difference. What are we waiting for? The darkness is dark enough, the needs are great enough, and Satan is active enough. As for the Lord, there is no shortage of power and wisdom with Him. What is it that holds us back? Why are we so feeble when it comes to having a clear, definite plan of action?[16]

We put our trust in the political system, believing time and time again that every politician who says he or she is a practicing Christian really *is* a practicing Christian, believing that this suddenly religious public official, if elected, will really stir things up, believing that this time around it will be different than the last time around. Hardly! We're deceiving ourselves—unless this politician has a no-compromise track record, unless holding to conviction is more important than holding office, unless what is preached in public is lived in private. Otherwise, we're fooling ourselves. (But why rock the boat. After all, ignorance is bliss, right?)[17]

Those of us who don't trust the government often put our trust in the Church, somehow thinking that the latest fad or the newest technique will usher in revival, that some hyped-up, red-hot revelation (one of those never-before-disclosed spiritual secrets) is the key to changing the world, that the most recently crowned Christian superstar can somehow save the hour. When will we learn? It is only when we give ourselves selflessly to the task, when we realize that the battle can only be won by a persevering and holy faith, when we break out of our comfort zone and discard our save-your-life mentality, when we determine to be Great Commission believers—living and dying for the advancement of God's kingdom—*then* we will see results. *Then* we could even see a nation changed!

Stop and think: If Satan can change a generation, Jesus can change a generation. If the flesh can drag a society down, the Spirit can lift a society up. If lies can bring people into captivity, the truth can set them free. Why not? America has been in a mess before, and revival has turned things around. Why not once more?[18]

In the 1960s, John Lennon sang, "You say you want a revolution, well you know, we all want to change the world"—and a cultural revolution came, and the world was changed. We are still feeling the effects of it!

Timothy Leary, the LSD-guru who left Harvard to pursue his psychedelic experiments, counseled young people to "Turn on, tune in, and drop out," and countless young adults heeded his advice.[19] But John Lennon has been dead since 1980 (the victim of a demented fan's bullet), while Timothy Leary died of cancer in 1996. (His last words were "Why not.")[20] Isn't it about time for another revolution? Isn't it about time for young people to get some new marching orders? The old ones have long since gone stale!

We don't have a Vietnam War to protest. We don't have a Civil Rights movement to join. Drugs, hard rock, and free sex have been around for a long time. So what will stir this current generation? How about repulsion with the state of our society? How about pain and grief over the condition of the family? How about eternal values and goals? How about a holy anger that says enough is enough!

Maybe we can start with some new revolutionary lyrics like these, written by two of our ministry students early in 2000:

> In these walls voices cry,
>   Crying out for something more
> In our hearts a fire burns.
>
> You've sent Your fire, You've sent Your rain
>   But our hunger still remains,
> Let Your glory fill this place.
>
> Let the mountains shake, let our hearts be changed,
>   Let us claim this power in Jesus' name
> Let the dead man rise, let the blind man see,
>   Let the lame man walk, set the captives free. . . .
>   A Revolution![21]

Or how about these "enough is enough" words, written by gospel rap artist Kirk Franklin in 1998:

> Do you want a revolution? Do you want a revolution?
> Sick and tired of my brotha Killing each other Sick and
> tired of daddies leaving Babies with their mothers To
> every man that wants to lay around and play around
> Listen potnah, you should be man enough to stay

around Sick and tired of the church talking religion But yet they talk about each other makin decisions No mo racism Two facism No pollution The solution A revolution Do you want a revolution? Do you want a revolution?[22]

And maybe we can alter the meaning of Dr. Leary's words and make them into something relevant: "*Turn on* to Jesus! *Tune in* to the Spirit! *Drop out* of the rat race and get into God's race!" To repeat Leary's last words, "Why not?" Or maybe we could urge this generation to "Turn back, press in, step out"—yes, *turn back* to the Word, *press in* to God, *step out* of your safety zone!

I know this sounds trite, but today's generation is not looking for a lofty philosophical treatise. One good slogan will do. How about "Revolution now!" Why not? And once we are enlisted in God's army, we can advance to "Move on, crush sin, break out." Simply determining that we are determined is half the battle. Simply deciding to get up and go is half the race.

What about you? Are you determined, are you in the battle, are you running your race? The Spirit is saying "NOW!" If we really hate what sin has done to our society, if we really despise the destructive works of the devil, we will act. According to guerrilla-warfare expert Bob Newman,

One of the strongest and most causative of emotions—a deep-seated, festering hatred of whomever the would-be-guerrilla sees as an invader or unworthy and repugnant political entity—is often the single most powerful catalyst to his becoming a guerrilla and his being willing to carry the fight for as long as it takes to realize victory over his oppressor.[23]

Holy hatred can drive us too—but not a hatred for people. No![24] We need a hatred for wickedness and evil. Wisdom says,"To fear the LORD is to hate evil; I hate pride and arrogance, evil behavior and perverse speech" (Prov. 8:13). Paul wrote, "Love must be sincere. Hate what is evil; cling to what is good" (Rom. 12:9). Let us be wholeheartedly pure, wholeheartedly righteous, wholeheartedly committed. If we could unconditionally give ourselves to sin before we knew the Lord, how much more unconditionally should we give ourselves to Him? "Just as you used to offer the parts of your body in slavery to impurity and to ever-increasing wickedness, so now offer them in slavery to righteousness leading to holiness" (Rom. 6:19). All of us must say "Here I am, Lord. Send me! Use me!" And He will!

The world has had enough carnal revolutions. More than 60 years ago, Roger Lloyd made this clear in his book *Revolutionary Religion: Christianity, Fascism and Communism*. He wrote:

> Fascism comes always by force, and the force is generally mingled with fraud. By violence it is born, by violence it comes to power, and by increasing waves of violence it maintains itself. It therefore leads inevitably from crime to atrocity, and from atrocity to war.... War is an essentially revolutionary act, and because Fascism, as by a law of its own being, leads to war, it is in its own nature a profoundly revolutionary force.
>
> Communism is no less revolutionary.... Its tendency is to bring about civil wars within boundaries of single nations, rather than international wars. For that reason, it is deadly and its effects horrifying. War between

nations is bad enough, but civil war within a nation is the nearest approach to hell on earth that history can show.

Thus the two great revolutionary ideas can only work themselves out to the accompaniment of an overwhelming tale of human misery and wretchedness. The triumph of either involves appalling wastes of bloodshed and tears wept in futility.[25]

Not so the gospel! Listen again to Lloyd:

There remains the third form of revolution, the Christian religion. Of all ideas which have taken hold of the imagination of mankind, this contains the fullest content of explosive force. It has always been so from the days when Jesus was crucified, and overcame death. The supply of men and women of the best type, in whom the divine fire issues in profoundly revolutionary action, has not ceased, or even abated. . . . The whole purpose of the Christian life is to produce precisely that profound interruption in life which is the very essence of the revolutionary idea. The main thing which the Christian religion always and everywhere seeks to do with people is to convert them, that is, to turn them inside out, to spin them round, so that their will and desires face another way from that which has hitherto been normal with them. It intends wholly to change the values they put upon life, to bring them into touch with the very Majesty of the Universe, the Possessor of all imaginable power, so that having themselves been passed through the fires of the most profound revolution of all, they all become magazines [i.e., arsenals] stored with the explosive energy of God.[26]

What revolutionary concepts! What revolutionary language! What revolutionary inspiration! What revolutionary religion, impelled by "the explosive energy of God." I say, "Revolution now!"

In Ephesians 6, Paul exhorted the Ephesians to "be strong in the Lord and in his mighty power." He urged them to "put on the full armor of God so that you can take your stand against the devil's schemes. For our struggle is not against flesh and blood, but against the rulers, against the authorities, against the powers of this dark world and against the spiritual forces of evil in the heavenly realms" (Eph. 6:10-12). It's clear that Satan is serious and organized. Are we?

THE BATTLE IS OFTEN HAND-TO-HAND COMBAT—ONE LIFE AT A TIME, ONE QUALITY DECISION AT A TIME, ONE PRAYER AT A TIME, ONE ACT OF OBEDIENCE AT A TIME, ONE DEATH AT A TIME.

Our battle is not with people. Our battle is with the devil himself, with his skilled demonic army, with his schemes and plots and strategies and plans. And this battle is fought with prayer, consecration, sacrifice, service, faith, outreach—with the power of God. It is fought in the corridors of our minds, in the chambers of our homes, in the battlefields of our schools, in the combat zones of our workplaces. It is waged in the cities and in the suburbs, in the streets and in the churches, in the halls of Congress and in the studios of Hollywood.

It is often hand-to-hand combat—one life at a time, one quality decision at a time, one prayer at a time, one act of obedience at a time, one death at a time. But if we refuse to quit, if we refuse to buckle, if we refuse to cave in, give in, back up, back down, we will see the triumph of the Lord. Of course, we will not see every soul saved or every city transformed or the whole nation reformed. But we can be sure that just as the hell-inspired counterculture revolution dragged us down, the heaven-fired gospel revolution will bring us up. And millions *will* be saved, and many cities *will* be transformed, and much of the nation *will* be reformed. I have a dream! I have a vision! Do you?

The worst thing we could do is take out our frustration and aggression against people. Certainly, there is a place for Spirit-led prophetic rebuke, for loving confrontation, for calling leaders to account, both publicly and privately. And we have failed here, being too soft, too wimpy, too nice. But the reason America is in such a mess today is not so much because of corrupt politicians and sinful movie stars. No. The primary problem is the backslidden, compromised Church. The reason there is so much darkness is because the light within the land—the house of God!—has been dark. That's just one of the reasons why we must categorically reject the call coming from some Christian quarters for believers to consider taking up arms against the government. As I wrote in my journal while ministering in Finland in 1995:

> The whole problem with the "Christian" call to take up arms is that if we were to be honest, we would have to admit that "we have seen the enemy, and it is us." America is aborting babies and exporting smut around the world because the "light that is within us is darkness." To be consistent, the call to violent activism would have to sound like this: "Kill the compromised clergy! Slaughter the sleeping saints! Shoot the sinning shepherds! Nuke the noncommitted! Blow up the bank-

rupt believers! Wipe out the worldly watchmen!" Would
you like to lead the attack? Who among us can throw the
first stone—or shoot the first bullet?[27]

The inference is clear: It is not time to pick up arms and
guns; it's time to put on the armor of God. That is the key to our
success. That is how we win. The warfare begins with us, God's
people. And when we are changed, we can change the world. No
other system or method or plan can effect a lasting change. Only
the message of the gospel delivered in the power of the Spirit can
bring a nation to God and establish true morality.

Of course, we must recognize the important role that God-
fearing politicians and judges and professors and businesspeople
can play. And we must do our best to make an impact on every area
of society, infiltrating and influencing on all possible levels. But we
must never forget that our revolution is not a revolution of bullets
and bombs, nor is it a revolution of partisan politics and Wall
Street economics. It is a revolution of Holy Spirit fire, a supernatural revolution. It is the only revolution worthy of the name.

In 1971, seminary professor Vernon C. Grounds published a
masterly book, *Revolution and the Christian Faith*, analyzing in
great detail the claim of some modern theologians that the message of Jesus can be used to justify violent revolutionary movements.[28] Grounds came to two important conclusions: First,
there was no New Testament support for violent revolutionary
movements (past or present). Second, the ultimate revolutionary
movement was Christianity itself. He hit the nail on the head!

Taking into consideration the writings of other Christian
thinkers, he stated:

When a person undergoes a revolutionary encounter with Jesus Christ in the dimension of the spirit, he becomes a catalyst of revolution; for "there can be no renewal of heart and mind without concern for social reform. Conversely, there can be no healthy and effective attempt to reform conditions without constant conversion of mind and attitudes" [quoting Bernard Häring]. Hence [Jacques] Ellul does not put the case too strongly: If a person "really lives by the power of Christ, if, by hope, he makes the coming of the kingdom actual, 'that person, regardless of any appearance to the contrary,' is a true revolutionary."

The Christian revolution, therefore, moves in a deeper dimension and a different dimension, too. The Christian revolution eschews a self-defeating resort to violence; it is a spiritual revolution, a revolution not by the sword but by the cross. . . . This new revolution, this different revolution which takes the cross as its sign, is a revolution of love—a love [James W.] Douglas reminds us, which sees and suffers and shares and serves and sacrifices, a love which acts, remembering that God, because He loved the world, did His own God-sized act in Jesus Christ.[29]

Therefore, in the words of Douglas, "Revolution begins in the revolutionary himself by his response to the present world, creating through the crisis of vision and shared agony the kind of power which rises anew to meet a torn world with the word of love and the act of transformation."[30] Yes, as impossible as it seems in the eyes of the world, our revolution is a revolution of love—of selfless, sacrificial, supernatural love.[31] When our enemies curse us, we bless them. When they do evil to us, we do good to them. When they persecute us, we pray for them. When they hate us, we love them. This is how we overcome![32] Even when they mow us down, we multiply. And when they kill us, we live. Talk about being radical! What could be more radical than this?

Wallace Henley, a former White House staff member and then pastor, said it well:

> The militant church is always in danger of becoming, in philosophy and strategy, exactly like the structures she wars against. Her passion turns to hatred, she becomes increasingly aggressive, and out of that uses ever stronger tactics, until at last she is making bombs.
>
> How [then] does the church get in society's face without succumbing to the mentality of anger-driven militancy? The key is to start with the character of God, revealed in Jesus. . . . Prior to the cross, during His incarnate life, Jesus secured [the right to get into society's face] by going into society as a servant. . . . When the church understands this and acts in it, her militancy becomes redemptive and healing. . . . The church, then, wins the right to speak head-on to its culture by being a servant, not a mean-spirited crusader.
>
> As repugnant as it may sound, if the church wants to get in the face of homosexuals, it must first wash the feet of homosexuals. The church *should* be in the face of the monstrous practice of abortion on demand. She wins the right to do this when she cares for unwed mothers and their babies, when she helps heal those who have had abortion, and bear the spiritual and emotional scars.[33]

Henley calls this "militant love," clarifying this concept with a series of contrasts:

Assault Christianity is one institution besieging other institutions, one arsenal of ideas seeking to outgun other arsenals of ideas. Militant love is life attacking death, light coming against darkness, truth colliding with lies. . . . Militant Islam, for example, may call for the death of the "infidel," and may issue death warrants against its enemies, but Jesus of Nazareth will not allow His followers to call down the fire [see Luke 9:55,56]. Militant institutional Christianity may hurl its bombs in Belfast, Beirut, or Sarajevo, but Jesus and His militant love will minister healing, deliverance and hope.

Jesus shows that militant love does not inflict suffering on others, but is willing to receive it on itself for the sake of others. Militant love does not nail its enemies to the cross, but goes to the cross on behalf of the enemy. . . . Militant love does aggressive acts of kindness toward those who cause it hurt. It washes the feet of those who would betray it.[34]

Militant love wins! Just look at how Paul waged his war:

As servants of God we commend ourselves in every way: in great endurance; in troubles, hardships and distresses; in beatings, imprisonments and riots; in hard work, sleepless nights and hunger; in purity, understanding, patience and kindness; in the Holy Spirit and in sincere love; in truthful speech and in the power of God; with weapons of righteousness in the right hand and in the left; through glory and dishonor, bad report and good report; genuine, yet regarded as impostors; known, yet regarded as unknown; dying, and yet we live on; beaten, and yet not killed; sorrowful, yet always rejoicing; poor,

yet making many rich; having nothing, and yet possess-
ing everything (2 Cor. 6:4-10).

What a flesh-defying, world-conquering method. It worked
in Paul's day, and it has continued to work until this very day.
Let us then turn on the intensity, tune in to the "now" purposes
of God, and drop out of our self-pitying, self-excusing mode. If
this is not the hour, the hour will never come. So what will it be?
On with the revolution?

Can anyone say no?

Chapter Thirteen

The Great Commission Battle Plan: God's Strategy for Successful Revolution

We have given too much attention to methods and to machinery
and to resources, and too little to the Source of Power, the
filling with the Holy Ghost.

J. HUDSON TAYLOR
FOUNDER OF THE CHINA INLAND MISSION

But while you strive to deliver [the outcasts and the poor] from their
temporal distress, and endeavour to rescue them for the causes that
have led to their unfortunate condition, you must seek, above all, to
turn their miseries to good account by making them help the salvation
of their souls and their deliverance from the wrath to come. It will be
a very small reward for all your toils if, after bringing them into condition of well-being here, they perish hereafter. . . . To change the
nature of the individual, to get at the heart, to save his soul is the
only real, lasting method of doing him any good.

WILLIAM BOOTH
FOUNDER OF THE SALVATION ARMY

Revolutions, like trees, are recognized by the fruit they bear.

IGNAZIO SILONE
ITALIAN NOVELIST AND JOURNALIST (1900-1978)

We socialists would have nothing to do if you Christians had continued
the revolution begun by Jesus.

SPOKEN IN THE 1920S BY A LEADING SOCIALIST

Come, my friends. 'Tis not too late to seek a newer world.

ALFRED, LORD TENNYSON
FROM HIS POEM "ULYSSES"

Have you ever looked at a map of the missionary journeys of Paul? They follow a distinct pattern and order. Why? Because Paul had a strategy. He was a visionary, a master builder, an apostolic leader. He had a plan! But how could it be otherwise? How could anyone—especially a Spirit-led servant of God—build without a plan? And yet so many of us have no plan. We have words, we have excitement, and we may even have vision. But we have no plan!

Businesses are expected to have a statement of mission along with a statement of vision. How will they achieve their goals? How will they realize their aims? How will they get from point A to point B? The same is true in the world of sports. Without a plan of attack, the team will lose. Even a team lacking in talent can defeat a superior (but unprepared) team, as long as the underdog works hard, is in good condition, and has a successful strategy.

The same applies in the academic world: Counselors sit down with students and discuss which program is best for them, telling them the classes they need to take to fulfill the requirements of their major. Even when it comes to writing a research paper, many teachers will require their pupils to submit an outline, introduction, and bibliography before the paper will be approved. Why? They want to be sure the student has a plan that will work! How then can we who have been entrusted with the most sacred task of all—the task of fulfilling the Great Commission—be so lethargic and listless when it comes to having a plan of action?

Of course, some might claim the only thing we need is the leading of the Spirit. Still we must ask: Has the Spirit no plan? Does He simply rely on random and haphazard acts to carry out His purposes? Perish the thought! It is impossible to read the Gospels and Acts without seeing a divine strategy. The fact that

God often takes us by surprise and that His methods are often contrary to the ways of the flesh does *not* mean He doesn't know where He's going or is ignorant of how He will get there.

The book of Proverbs says to "make plans by seeking advice; if you wage war, obtain guidance"; and "for waging war you need guidance, and for victory many advisers" (Prov. 20:18; 24:6). Surely, God has given us guidance through His Word; surely, He promises to lead us by His Spirit; surely, He has placed wise advisers in the Body. Let us, then, avail ourselves of His wisdom and get on with His work.

Military writer Bob Newman praised Mao Zedong for his carefully thought-out, seven-fold strategy for guerrilla war: (1) arouse and organize the people; (2) achieve internal unification politically; (3) establish bases; (4) equip forces; (5) recover national strength; (6) destroy the enemy's national strength; (7) regain lost territories.

GOD IS THE ULTIMATE STRATEGIST, AND HE WILL SHARE HIS STRATEGY WITH US IF WE WILL GIVE CONSIDERABLE THOUGHT AND PRAYER AND STUDY TO THE EFFORT.

"Mao," Newman writes, "did not fashion these seven steps helter-skelter. He gave considerable thought to what order they must be taken in—and in doing so showed an astute understanding of the foundation that must be laid for a guerrilla force to at least have a chance of success."[1] Yet God is the ultimate strategist, and He will share His strategy with us if we will give considerable thought and prayer and study to the effort.

Naturally, I am aware that some leaders are totally overwhelmed with the needs that surround them, working desperately just to keep their heads above water and to keep their flocks somewhat healthy. Still, I believe all of us can make time to seek God if we so desire. And if we seek Him, we will find Him. And in finding Him, we find all that we need.

King Josiah sought God for four years before he began his reform, and then he went to work, turning a nation back to God (see 2 Chron. 34:1-3).[2] Is there a lesson here for us? Let us seek, let us learn, and let us act.

Here are some keys to winning the war for this generation. We dare not lose a moment.

First, we must keep our goals clearly in view, identifying the purpose of our spiritual battle and focusing on the enemies we must combat. This is a fundamental principle of revolution, as Roger Lloyd notes: "You cannot have a revolution until you have some enemies to destroy."[3] Don't just fight to fight. Don't get worked up just to get worked up. Live with purpose. Lay out the Master's agenda: What is His will for the Church in this hour? How does He want to change our society?

We must have some clearly defined goals. Otherwise, we can easily become ineffective. Newman stated this plainly when speaking of guerrilla warfare which, despite its bloody, violent nature, is intended to be warfare against perceived injustice, oppressive forces, and the status quo:

> The guerrilla army must be united politically and have a single, clear, attainable goal in mind when it initiates hostilities. Guerrillas and potential guerrillas who are waffling or who are unclear as to why a certain political

goal is needed must be convinced through education and sound leadership that the political goal of the guerrillas is one of noble purpose, that everyone is going to benefit from the actions taken by the guerrillas, and that it is their duty to work toward that end.[4]

Do we believe that things are not the way the Lord wants them to be right now? Do we believe the gospel is His solution for the problems of the hour? Do we believe that the people of God can make an impact on this generation? Do we believe there is still hope for our nation? Do we believe the blood of Jesus can undo the damage that sin has done?

It is true: We *are* in a conflict and we *do* have serious opposition, but we *can* triumph. Let us therefore march out and make disciples for the Master, pulling down strongholds, breaking shackles, and liberating prisoners as we go. We must believe that things can change!

Jesus had this in mind when He taught us to pray "your kingdom come" (Matt. 6:10). This is not just a petition for the future. New Testament scholars agree that to some extent, the coming of that kingdom is to occur here, in this age. And while we know that the final and complete coming of the kingdom will be in the age to come, His kingdom broke into this world 2,000 years ago and it will continue to grow and expand until the Lord returns.

As Professor D. A. Carson noted, whoever reads these words in Matthew's Gospel "perceives that the kingdom has already broken in and prays for its extension as well as for its unqualified manifestation."[5] That is what we pray for—the "extension" and the "unqualified manifestation" of God's kingdom on Earth.[6] So be it, Father! And let us mix our prayers with action.

Second, we must establish bases. This was part of the highly successful (and murderous) strategy of the Muslim leader Hassan al-Sabah, as Amir Taheri explains:

> Almost a modern revolutionary, Hassan understood the four phases of a successful politico-religious movement: study, propagate, organize, and attack. He also knew that a genuine revolutionary movement needs at least one 'liberated zone' from which to launch its bid for the conquest of the world.[7]

There must be "liberated zones"—spiritual beachheads or model operations—from which we equip the troops, sharpen our strategy, and launch our attack. If there is not a strong home front, it will be difficult to succeed in the thick of enemy territory. We need prayer bases, training bases, worship bases, sending bases. On the smallest level, this can happen in a home filled with the life and power of God. At the next level, it can occur in a truly biblical, radical congregation. Next is the level of the revived community (which is a much greater challenge), and at the highest, the level of the transformed region (this is rare but quite possible).[8] Such bases also serve as havens of refuge for the battle-worn and weary.

Newman spoke of the role of bases in guerrilla warfare:

> The guerrillas must constantly demonstrate to the populace the evil ways of the enemy, and then the civilians must be shown how the guerrillas are capable and worthy of protecting and serving them. To do this, the guer-

rillas must establish bases that facilitate the conduct of offensive operations.[9]

Just substitute the word "believers" for the word "guerrillas" and we have a formula that works. Christian campuses can be bases; youth organizations can be bases; cell groups can be bases. But we must remember that the base exists for training and sending, for equipping and commissioning, for imparting and releasing, for strategizing and thrusting out. The base must never become a resort!

Third, we must propagate the message. We do this through the spoken and written word, through books, pamphlets, tracts, tapes, videos, CDs, TV, radio, and Internet. Jesus told His disciples that that they were to make and baptize disciples, "teaching them to obey everything I have commanded you" (Matt. 28:20). We must get the Word out, and we must get the Word in—out before the public and into hungry hearts. History is filled with examples of one book or one document or one speech bringing large-scale upheaval or reconciliation.

Just think of the impact of Luther's 95 Theses on Christian history. (And how interesting it is to realize that he simply posted his theses for public debate, little realizing this would spark the Reformation!) Or consider the impact of Harriet Beecher Stowe's *Uncle Tom's Cabin*. When Abraham Lincoln met her, he said, "So you're the little woman who wrote the book that made this great war!"[10]

In the late 1970s, Khomeini overthrew the Shah of Iran by means of taped messages that were smuggled into Iran and reproduced there, making their way into the sermons of the local Muslim preachers.[11] The war was won through mass-produced messages more than through military might!

Let us listen to Newman once again:

> Education is key. The enemy will have a propaganda machine up and running full tilt [how true!], a machine designed to lace a few truths with misinformation, half truths, and outright lies meant to confuse, scare, and otherwise weaken the resolve of the individual guerrilla and the civilian populace who are or might be leaning toward assisting the guerrillas. Fighting this propaganda will be a major concern of the guerrillas for as long as the war goes on. Education of the masses and of the individual guerrilla must be undertaken from the very beginning and carried out until victory is achieved, and it must be given on all levels, from one-on-one discussions between a leader and his charge to village town classes and information dissemination.[12]

This was also part of the strategy of Hassan, 900 years ago:

> [He] divided his fraternity into three categories. First were the *murshids*, who devoted themselves to study and to the preparation of propaganda material. Then there were the *da'is* or propagators, who were sent on proselytizing missions throughout the Muslim world. These *da'is* were often men of great learning who, instead of instructing only a few pupils, toured the countryside to take the message to everyone, including the humble and the poor. . . . Finally came the *fedayeen*—those prepared to sacrifice their lives, as well as to kill, for Allah.[13]

We too need such divisions of workers (although with some obvious changes!): We need those who will give themselves to developing and mastering the message; we need those who will skillfully and effectively carry the message; and we need those who will live and die for the message. And what a message we have! How the Word of God can wreak havoc on demonic domains! How the Word of God can rebuild broken societies! How the Word of God can confront and convert, bless and build, transform and reform. It is a lamp, a light, a tree of life, a burning fire, a powerful hammer, a piercing sword, a healing balm.[14] We must set ourselves to the task of getting this message out!

Would that all of us saw ourselves as missionaries to a dying world. Would that all of us had the perspective urged many years ago by A. H. Strong: "What are churches for, but to make missionaries? What is education for, but to train them? What is commerce for, but to carry them? What is money for, but to support them? What is life itself for, but to fulfill the purpose of missions—the enthroning of Jesus Christ in the hearts of men?"[15] Do you think the Father differs with this?

Fourth, we must be filled with the power and knowledge of God. This is not a battle we can fight through human strength, and human thinking will not do.[16] We need both the indwelling Word and the life-giving Spirit, both the enlightening and the empowering. Jesus opened the minds of the disciples so they could understand the Word, and then He instructed them to wait for power from on high (see Luke 24:44-49). Both are essential! We serve a God who speaks and acts. He is not mute, neither is He weak.

Our strength flows out of our intimacy with God. We need

to recover the secret place, the all-night prayer watch, the hours of intercessory wrestling. We need to pray like Jacob, who in holy desperation said to the angel, "I won't let you go until you bless me." He would not let go because to let go was to die. He would not let go because he could not let go.[17] It is no less urgent for us.

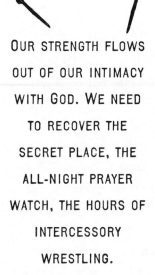

OUR STRENGTH FLOWS OUT OF OUR INTIMACY WITH GOD. WE NEED TO RECOVER THE SECRET PLACE, THE ALL-NIGHT PRAYER WATCH, THE HOURS OF INTERCESSORY WRESTLING.

E. M. Bounds wrote more than one century ago, "What the church needs today is not more machinery or better, not new organizations or more novel methods—but men whom the Holy Spirit can use—men of prayer, men of mighty prayer"—and every honest servant of the Lord would have to say "Amen" to this.[18] That's why Gordon Lindsay could say with confidence, "Determined prayer by faithful prayer warriors can make possible the successful gospel invasion of the foreign fields." This holds true for the gospel invasion of any field. Through determined prayer, we can receive definite empowerment through which we can defeat the foe.

But we must not "fight like a man beating the air" (1 Cor. 9:26). We need to be people of the Word! We need to know what we are doing and how we are to do it. Ignorance of the Word will defeat our efforts before we even start. And we have no excuse for ignorance. The Bible is really not that big a book, especially when you consider that we have a lifetime to learn it. (Without question, the New Testament is not a big book at all.) We simply need to apply ourselves more diligently.

When I was 18 years old, I got so hungry for the Word that I memorized 20 verses every day for 6 months straight. One New Testament scholar told me that when he was a still a teenager, he read the New Testament from cover to cover once a week and tried to read the Bible through once a month.[19] The Word is our military manual! By feeding on it, we grow strong and victorious.

Maybe you could never memorize thousands of Scriptures or read the Bible through 12 times in a year, but did you realize that in just 30 minutes a day at average reading speed, you could read the entire Bible out loud in just four months? Muslim children learn large portions of the Koran by heart, while Orthodox Jewish boys commit lengthy sections of the Hebrew Scriptures to memory. Could it be that at least *some of us* are suffering from mental sloth or a lack of training and discipline? Could it be that we have failed to apply ourselves fully?

God gave this battle strategy to Joshua before he led the armies of Israel into the promised land: "Do not let this Book of the Law depart from your mouth; meditate on it day and night, so that you may be careful to do everything written in it. Then you will be prosperous and successful" (Josh. 1:8). We wage war by the Word!

Proverbs also urges us to give careful attention to the Word: "My son, pay attention to what I say; listen closely to my words. Do not let them out of your sight, keep them within your heart; for they are life to those who find them and health to a man's whole body" (Prov. 4:20-22). This is repeated in Paul's letter to the Colossians: "Let the word of Christ dwell in you richly as you teach and admonish one another with all wisdom, and as you sing psalms, hymns and spiritual songs with gratitude in your hearts to God" (Col. 3:16). The Word is our ammunition, our supply, our life, our strength. Jesus defeated Satan in the wilderness using three verses from Deuteronomy!

We must get into the Word and get the Word into us. Then we can move mountains by faith. Then we can believe for the impossible. Then we can wield an unstoppable weapon—the sword of the Spirit. We outduel the devil with the Word!

Let's shut off the TV and VCR, turn off the computer and video games, put down the newspapers and novels, and make time for the Word and prayer. It is through prayer that the power of the Word is so mightily released. As E. M. Bounds wrote, "Holy men have, in the past, changed the whole force of affairs; they have revolutionized character and country by prayer. And such achievements are still possible for us. The power is only waiting to be used."[20] It is therefore with good reason that John "Praying" Hyde, one of the Church's greatest men of prayer, asked early last century, "The disciples were then [i.e., at Pentecost] shut up to prayer, and can anyone say what would happen now if God's Church should give herself up to this same resource?"[21] What *would* happen? Let's not leave this Earth without finding out!

Fifth, we must go on the attack, refusing to quit until the day we see Jesus face-to-face. The one guaranteed way to lose the battle is to retreat. That's why so many of us are defeated: We live in the retreat mode. We retreat from conflict, from confrontation, from rejection, from revolution. That is not the gospel way! Cowards and unbelievers have their place in the lake of fire whereas heaven will be populated by conquerors and believers. Which group best describes you and me?

Paul said in Romans 8:37 that "in all these things [namely, "trouble or hardship or persecution or famine or nakedness or danger or sword"—see v. 35] we are more than conquerors through Him who loved us." Nothing can stop us—not even death itself—if we keep our eyes fixed on Jesus, "the author and perfecter of our faith, who for the joy set before Him endured the cross, scorning its shame, and sat down at the right hand of the throne of God" (Heb. 12:2). He is our example, and He is anything but a coward. The words "coward" and "Jesus" are no more related than the words "God" and "sin"!

One dictionary of New Testament Greek noted, "In some languages a 'coward' [as in Rev. 21:8] is 'one who always runs' or 'one who runs away at nothing'," defining the Greek word for "cowardice" [deilia] as "a state of fear because of lack of courage or moral strength."[22] That should not apply to any of us! Rather, we should be like those who, in Paul's description (see Rom. 8:37), are "completely and overwhelmingly victorious."[23] Through Jesus, that is who we really are. And so we follow the guaranteed way to victory: Attack!

We have the enemy totally outmanned and outgunned. Retreat spells defeat. Defiance spells triumph. What will we do? The Great Commission is a commission to go, to speak, to act. As Brother Andrew observed, "Our Lord said go. He said nothing about coming back. [Yes!] There are no closed doors to the gospel, provided that, once you go through the door, you don't care whether or not you come back out."[24] Will we take the challenge?

Other missions leaders have urged us on, reminding us that "the Church that does not evangelize will fossilize," and "the supreme task of the Church is the evangelization of the world" (Oswald Smith). But, as Carl F. H. Henry said, "The gospel is good news only if it arrives in time." What are we waiting for?

One of the great reformers in Church history was the British political leader William Wilberforce (1759-1833). Converted at the age of 25, he and his group, called the Clapham Sect, "sought to do for the upper classes what Wesley had done for the lower. They used their wealth and influence in Christian outreach. He supported missions, fought to improve the condition of the poor and prisoners, and in 1804 helped to form the British and Foreign Bible Society."[25] His most famous act was to abolish the British slave trade, and eventually slavery itself, in Great Britain and her colonies.[26] Charles Spurgeon had this to say about the efforts of Wilberforce:

> A healthy church kills error, and tears in pieces evil. Not so very long ago our nation tolerated slavery in our colonies. Philanthropists endeavored to destroy slavery; but when was it utterly abolished?
>
> It was when Wilberforce roused the church of God, and when the church of God addressed herself to the conflict, then she tore the evil thing to pieces. I have been amused with what Wilberforce said the day after they passed the Act of Emancipation. He merrily said to a friend when it was all done: "Is there not something else we can abolish?" That was said playfully, but it shows the spirit of the church of God. She lives in conflict and victory; her mission is to destroy everything that is bad in the land.[27]

What revolutionary truths! The Church "lives in conflict and victory; her mission is to destroy everything that is bad in the land," and when the Church addresses herself to the conflict, then she "kills error, and tears in pieces evil." Yes! By attacking, we overcome. By holy aggression, we drive the enemy back. By obeying to the full—whether by life or by death—we effect a change. As Vernon Grounds proclaimed, "Such a radicalized church, taking its discipleship with a joyful seriousness, will be a revolutionary catalyst in society. Imagine the power of a fellowship composed of [such] revolutionaries."[28] Imagine!

There is no reason to put the battle off, no reason to wait for another day, no reason to leave the task to the next generation. Right now, this very hour, is the perfect time to wage war. The enemy of our souls is on red alert, sensing the coming onslaught. The world is waiting and wondering, staggering in sin, and yet restless and unsure. And heaven's troops stand at attention, awaiting the command of the Lord. At any moment the divine word could be spoken, and soon, a nation could be shaken and a society transformed. Soon our dreams could come true!

Even now, something is at the door. Something is stirring at this moment. A word is being released, even as I write and as you read. The Spirit is speaking and God's people are hearing. The message is simple and clear, radical and timely. It is a call to arms, a call to action, a call to rise up, a call to *revolution now*.

I say, "On with the revolution!" How about you?

Endnotes

Preface

1. David G. Myers, "Wanting More in an Age of Plenty," *Christianity Today* (April 24, 2000), p. 95, adapted from David G. Myers, *The American Paradox: Spiritual Hunger in an Age of Plenty* (New Haven, CT: Yale, 2000).

2. David Aikman, "The New Counterculture," *Charisma* (May 2000), p. 112, with specific reference for this concept to Os Guinness, *Time for Truth: Living Free in a World of Lies, Hype and Spin* (Grand Rapids, MI: Baker Books, 2000).

3. From the song, *Revolution Now!* words and music by Charles Ciepiel (©Meantime Music, 2000), additional lyrics by M. John Cava. Used by permission. For another revolution song written by students of the school of ministry, see chapter 12 of this book. I have no doubt that God will use anointed music as a great tool of the revolution; for more on this, see chapter 7 of this book. Relevant to this is a quote supplied to me by Louis Vigo, also a graduate of the school, from Kent McClard, owner of Ebullition Records, an underground producer of vinyl records: "Music as product, as entertainment, as diversion, or music as a weapon, as protest, as outcry, as expression . . . music as ebullition. This is war on entertainment, war on the industry of music. Music that burns the emotion, that burns the mind, that burns the system, that inspires the war. . . . Music is more than notes and chords. Music is a tool in the hands of the artist of the terrorist or the revolutionary." (The quote, a favorite of Louis's before he was a believer, was taken from an unattributed record insert; for the background of Ebullition Records, see http://www.ebullition.com.)

4. *Spiritual Awakenings in North America: Christian History*, Issue 23, 1997, Christian History Interactive CD-ROM (emphasis in the original).

5. See, for example, Otto Scott, *The Great Christian Revolution: How Christianity Transformed the World* (Windsor, NY: The Reformer, 1995); Steven Ozment, *Protestants: The Birth of a Revolution* (New York: Doubleday, 1992); note also that one edition of Gene Edwards' nontechnical historical study was called *Revolution: The Story of the Early Church* (Beaumont, TX: The Seed Sowers, 1974).

6. Interestingly, Raymond Lajoie notes that the writings of William Tyndale, penned in exile, "had to be launched surreptitiously, like catch-as-catch-can guerilla attacks against a much larger and more impressively arrayed army. Yet it was these 'guerilla attacks' which effectively won the day, firmly paving the way for the English Reformation. . . . Probably few at the time recognized them as the first shots of a revolution." See *William Tyndale: Christian History*, Issue 16, 1997, Christian History Interactive CD-ROM. On the importance of the printed page for Tyndale (and, I might add, for revolutionary movements in general), the comments of Lajoie are of interest: "As much as English-speaking and reading Christians should consider themselves indebted to Tyndale, they should consider themselves equally indebted to Johannes Gutenberg—without him, Tyndale's 'revolution' might well have been almost inconsequential" (ibid.).

7. John Trott, a founding member of Jesus People USA, eloquently describes the spiritual search of many hippies: "We were the flotsam and jetsam of a generation which had set out to prove man's innocence when freed from Western culture, but which instead had proved man's evil is an intrinsic part of him. And then came Jesus: someone to live for, someone to be loved by without conditions, someone to love in return. And someone to answer the aching questions: Who am I? Why am I here? What is my significance? As a result, just as we had given our all to drugs, sex, and various ideologies, we now knew following Jesus was no halfway thing" ("Life's Lessons: A History of Jesus People USA," *Cornerstone Magazine*, vol. 22, Issue 102/103 [1994], p. 11. Will Croney, yet another BRSM graduate, provided me with this article.)

Chapter One

1. For those unfamiliar with Jewish customs, the Bar Mitzvah is a rite of passage in which a 13-year-old becomes fully responsible to keep all the commandments of the Law. In Orthodox Jewish circles, it is taken very seriously; in less religious Jewish circles, it is more of an extravagant social affair, highlighted by a large, expensive party.

2. The second chapter of Bernard Häring's book *A Theology of Protest* (New York: Farrar, Straus, and Giroux, 1970) is entitled "Protesting the Status Quo." The type of protest he advocates is totally nonviolent, based on the spirit of the Sermon on the Mount. See also John R. W. Stott, *The Message of the Sermon on the Mount (Matthew 5-7): Christian Counterculture* (Downers Grove, IL: InterVarsity Press, 1988).

3. In the late 1960s and early 1970s, some of the rock stars who became mercenary in their approach, challenging our idealistic attitudes, were accused of selling out.

4. According to Stott, young people seeking for truth and reality in the 1960s and 1970s were often disappointed with what they found in the church: "For too often what they see in the church is not counter-culture but conformism, not a new society which embodies their ideals but another version of the old society which they have renounced, not life but death. They would readily endorse today what Jesus said of a church in the first century [Rev 3:1]: 'You have the name of being alive, and you are dead'" (Stott, *Sermon on the Mount*, p. 16).

5. *The End of the American Gospel Enterprise*, 2nd ed. (Shippensburg, PA: Destiny Image, 1993), pp. 85-86.

6. This was the title given to the expanded edition (Shippensburg, PA: Destiny Image, 1996).

Chapter Two

1. It's interesting to note that in 1949, Billy Graham's Los Angeles message entitled "Christ in the Crisis" dealt with "the worldwide crisis of fear, of atomic warfare, of economic, social and political problems. And of moral degeneration in this country" (Richard Reynolds, *Los Angeles Daily News*, September 30, 1949). Think of it! Moral degeneration in 1949. Where does that put us in the year 2000?

2. See Michael L. Brown, *The End of the American Gospel Enterprise*, pp. 81-96; idem, *How*

Saved Are We? (Shippensburg, PA: Destiny Image, 1990), pp. 113-123; idem, *Let No One Deceive You: Confronting the Critics of Revival* (Shippensburg, PA: Destiny Image, 1997), pp. 201-216.

3. William J. Bennett, *The Index of Leading Cultural Indicators: American Society at the End of the Twentieth Century*, 2nd ed. (Colorado Springs: Random House/WaterBrook Press, 1999), pp. 2-3.

4. Ibid., p. 61. Bennett also notes that "in 1999, out of 102 prime-time shows on ABC, NBC, CBS, Fox, and Warner Bros. networks, only 15 included fathers as regular central characters" (ibid., p. 163).

5. Ibid., p. 58. As Bennett observes, "Children who grow up with only one of their biological parents, when compared to children who grow up with both biological parents, are three times more likely to have a child out of wedlock, 2.5 times more likely to become teenage mothers, twice as likely to drop out of high school, and 1.4 times more likely to be out of school and not working" (ibid., p. 62).

6. Cf. ibid., pp. 173-174.

7. Ibid., p. 175.

8. Irwin and Debbie Unger, eds., *the times were a changin': the sixties reader* (New York: Three Rivers, 1998), p. 2.

9. Ibid., p. 7.

10. Stonewall was the name given to the 1969 riot in New York City's Greenwich Village when homosexuals decided to fight back when police raided their gay bar.

11. Bennett, *Index*, pp. 15-16.

12. Ibid., p. 27. Adding in local jails to federal and state prisons, the total number of all inmates in 1998 swelled to 1.8 million. Sadly, it is estimated that 28.5 percent of all black males and 16 percent of all Hispanic males will serve at least some time in a federal or state prison during their lives, as compared with 4 percent of white males.

13. According to a *Time* magazine report, June 15, 1998, vol. 151, no. 23, "With so much talk of sex in the air, the extinction of the hapless, sexually naive kid seems an inevitability. Indeed, kids today as young as seven to 10 are picking up the first details of sex even in Saturday-morning cartoons. Brett, a 14-year-old in Denver, says it doesn't matter to him whether his parents chat with him about sex or not because he gets so much from TV. Whenever he's curious about something sexual, he channel-surfs his way to certainty. 'If you watch TV, they've got everything you want to know,' he says. 'That's how I learned to kiss, when I was eight. And the girl told me, "Oh, you sure know how to do it"'" (Ron Stodghill II, "When Sex Is Kid Stuff," *Time*, June 15, 1998. http://www.time.com/time/magazine/1998/dom/980615/cover1.html).

14. "Between January 1997 and November 1998—a period during which a television-ratings system was adopted—sexual content, foul language, and violent content rose by more than 30 percent on network television" (Bennett, *Index*, p. 163). According to a report from the Parents Television Council, analyzing the content of programming on major network TV, "in terms of sexual content, coarse language, and violent material combined, the per-hour figure almost tripled from 1989 to 1999; on a per-hour basis, sexual material was more than three times as frequent; the level of violence on television has remained about the same" ("What a Difference a Decade Makes: A Comparison of Prime Time Sex, Language, and Violence in 1989 and 1999," *Parents Television Council*, March 30, 2000. http://www. parentstv.org).

15. See above, chapter 2, n. 13.

16. Thom Mount, president of the Producers Guild of America, cited in the *Calgary Herald*, November 21, 1999, sec. A, p. 12.

17. These statistics come from a crime report released in 1995 and forwarded to me without citing the original source. However, the statistics are in harmony with other reports I have seen relative to handgun murders.

18. Sylvio Izquierda-Leyva, the suspect in the Tampa shootings at the year's end, was arrested within 20 minutes of the incident. Police Chief Bennie Holder gave this amazing description of the arrest: "When I arrived on the scene, it was just like someone having been stopped for a traffic violation. He was not upset; he was very calm. He's upstairs sleeping; he's obviously not too concerned about it" (December 30, 1999, http://www.msnbc.com). And this man had just murdered five people! The Columbine killers, as is well known, laughed as they viciously gunned down their peers.

19. "The remarkable—and in ways lamentable—product of youthful promiscuity and higher sexual IQ is the degree to which kids learn to navigate the complex hyper-sexual world that reaches out seductively to them at every turn. One of the most positive results: the incidence of sexually transmitted diseases and of teenage pregnancy is declining. Over the past few years, kids have managed to chip away at the teenage birthrate, which in 1991 peaked at 62.1 births per 1,000 females. Since then the birthrate has dropped 12 percent, to 54.7. Surveys suggest that as many as two-thirds of teenagers now use condoms, a proportion that is three times as high as reported in the 1970s" (Ron Stodghill II, "When Sex Is Kid Stuff").

20. Here are excerpts from Mark Englehart's review of the movie *South Park: Bigger, Longer & Uncut*: "OK, let's get all the disclaimers out of the way first. Despite its colorful (if crude) animation, *South Park: Bigger, Longer & Uncut* is in no way meant for kids. It is chock full of profanity that might even make Quentin Tarantino blanch and has blasphemous references to God, Satan, Saddam Hussein (who's sleeping with Satan, literally), and Canada. It's rife with scato-logical [i.e., toilet-language] humor, suggestive sexual situations, political incorrectness, and gleeful, rampant vulgarity. And it's probably one of the most brilliant satires ever made. . . . And in advocating free speech and satirizing well-meaning but misguided parental censorship groups (with a special nod to the MPAA), *Bigger, Longer & Uncut* hits home against adult paranoia and hypocrisy with a vengeance. And the jokes, while indeed vulgar and gross, are hysterical; we can't repeat them here, especially the lyrics to Terrance and Philip's hit song, but you'll be rolling on the floor. Don't worry, though—to paraphrase Cartman, this movie won't warp your fragile little mind. Unless you have some-thing against the First Amendment" (Englehart, "Editorial Reviews," http://www.amazon.com/exec/obidos/ASIN/6305627347/qid=955987973/sr-1-2/104-5724946-0430058).

21. Already in 1985, Susan Baker, the wife of former Senator Howard Baker, testified before Congress on behalf of the PMRC (Parents Music Resource Center), calling on the music industry to place "warning labels on all albums if the lyrics 'portray explicit sex and violence and glorify the use of drugs and alcohol.'" She argued in part that "while a few outrageous recordings have always existed in the past, the

proliferation of songs glorifying rape, sadomasochism, incest, the occult, and suicide by a growing number of bands illustrates this escalating trend that is alarming.... There certainly are many causes for these ills in our society, but it is our contention that the pervasive messages aimed at children which promote and glorify suicide, rape, sadomasochism, and so on, have to be numbered among the contributing factors" (Senator Robert Torricelli and Andrew Carroll, eds., *In Our Words: Extraordinary Speeches of the American Century* [New York: Kodansha International, 1999], pp. 360-361). In rebuttal, rock musician Frank Zappa said (in part), "Bad facts make bad law, and people who write bad laws are in my opinion more dangerous than songwriters who celebrate sexuality. Freedom of speech, freedom of religious thought, and the right to due process for composers, performers, and retailers are imperiled if the PMRC and the major labels consummate this nasty bargain" (ibid., p. 363).

22. *The Capitol Hill Prayer Alert,* November 11, 1999, newsletter (e-mailed). Also included in the e-mail alert was this announcement: "House Passes 'Baby Parts Harvesting' Resolution: When Will Action to Stop the Harvest Take Place?" See http://www.prayeralert.org.

23. Examples of such books include the following: Jennie Brand Miller, et al., *The Glucose Revolution: The Authoritative Guide to the Glycemic Index-The Groundbreaking Medical Discovery* (New York: Marlowe & Co., 1999); Robert Arnot, *Dr. Bob Arnot's Revolutionary Weight Control Program* (New York: Little, Brown & Co., 1998); Robert C. Atkins, *Dr. Atkins New Diet Revolution* (New York: HarperCollins Publishers, 1997); Robert E. Kowalski, *The Revolutionary Cholesterol Breakthrough: How to Eat Everything You Want and Have Your Heart to Thank for It* (Kansas City, MO: Andrews McMeel Publishing, 1996); Jeffrey S. Bland, *The 20-Day Rejuvenation Diet Program: With the Revolutionary Phytonutrient Diet* (New Canaan, CT: Keats Publishing, 1996). One book title contains both the words "renewal" and "revolution"—but not in a spiritual context; see Timothy J. Smith, M.D., *Renewal: The Anti-Aging Revolution* (New York: St. Martin's Press, 1999).

24. According to a report on MSNBC news, 30 percent of our cats and dogs are overweight. In fact, pet obesity is considered to be the leading health problem by veterinarians. The report notes that "sedentary people tend to have sedentary pets, and owners who enjoy high-calorie diets tend to pamper their pets with high-calorie treats." According to Evan Kirk of the Brewer Animal Hospital in Springfield, Illinois, "Our dogs and cats are eating themselves to death"; and Julie Churchill, who operates a weight-loss clinic [that's right!] at the University of Minnesota's College of Veterinary Medicine, states, "The average American dog these days is a couch potato" (*MSNBC*, February 16, 2000. http://www.msnbc.com). So while humans forage for food in other nations, America is filled with fat cats and couch-potato canines.

25. Bennett, *Index*, p. 3.

26. Ibid., p. 175. According to a 1999 George Barna report, the figures are even higher: "39% of Americans describe themselves as 'committed born-again Christians.' Nearly two-thirds of Americans (64%) say they have made a personal commitment to Jesus Christ that is still important in their life today." These statistics are even more troubling, making us wonder: *Where are these people, and where is their*

commitment? ("Faith Commitment," *Barna Research Online*, April 5, 2000. http://www.barna.org/cgi-bin/PageCategory.asp?CategoryID-19).

27. Ibid., pp. 217-218.
28. Ibid., pp. 219-220.
29. Ibid., pp. 221-222.
30. Ibid., pp. 223-224.
31. Ibid., pp. 227-228.
32. Ibid., p. 229. The exact figure is 21.3%; next highest was Spain, with 17.5%, and then Canada, with 14.9%. Finland, Denmark, France, Sweden, and Germany ranged downward from 6.1% to 4.4%.
33. Even more amazing is the fact that "fewer than one-quarter of American parents think their child watches too much television" (ibid., p. 162).
34. Ibid., p. 47.
35. Ibid., p. 48.
36. Ibid., pp. 175-176.
37. Ibid., pp. 48-49.
38. Ibid., p. 53, note.
39. Ibid., 50, his emphasis.
40. Ibid., p. 138.
41. Ibid.
42. Ibid., p. 139.
43. Ibid., p. 132.
44. Ibid., pp. 132-133.
45. Ibid., p. 178.

Chapter Three

1. Jon Lee Anderson, introduction to *Che Guevara: A Revolutionary Life* (New York: Grove Press, 1997). Anderson asks (ibid.), "Who was this man who, at the age of thirty-six, had left his wife and five children, as well as given up his honorary citizenship, ministerial position, and commander's rank in revolutionary Cuba, in hopes of sparking a 'continental revolution'? What had compelled this son of an aristocratic Argentine family, a medical school graduate, to try to change the world?" It was the prominent historian Robert Conquest who commented that in his book reviewing the twentieth century, he had "not given enough attention to . . . the persistence to this day of an adolescent revolutionary romanticism, as one of the unfortunate afflictions to which the human mind was and is prone. This is now being demonstrated yet again with (hardly credible though it may be) a revival of the cult of the totalitarian terrorist Che Guevara" (Conquest, *Reflections on a Ravaged Century* [New York: W. W. Norton, 2000], p. 295).

2. William English Walling described the price paid by the Russian workingmen in the 1905 Revolution: They were "shot down, executed by hundreds in Moscow, Riga and Odessa, imprisoned by thousands in every Russian jail, and exiled to the deserts and the arctic regions" (Walling, *Russia's Message: The True World Import of the Revolution* [New York: Doubleday, 1908] cited in John Reed, introduction to *Ten Days That Shook the World* [1935, reprint with an introduction by John Howard

Lawson, New York: International Publishers, 1989], n. p.).

3. Unger and Unger, *the times were a changin'*, p. 187. Describing this same time period, John Stott wrote, "Others today are repudiating the greedy affluence of the West which seems to grow ever fatter either by the spoliation of the natural environment or by the exploitation of developing nations or by both at once; and they register the completeness of their rejection by living simply, dressing casually, going barefoot and avoiding waste. Instead of the shams of bourgeois socializing they hunger for the authentic relationships of love. They despise the superficiality of both irreligious materialism and religion's conformism, for they sense that there is an awesome 'reality' far bigger than these trivialities, and they seek this elusive 'transcendental' dimension through meditation, drugs or sex. They abominate the very concept of the rat race, and consider it more honorourable to drop out than to participate. All this is symptomatic of the inability of the younger generation to accommodate themselves to the status quo or acclimatize themselves to the prevailing culture. They are not at home. They are alienated" (Stott, *Sermon on the Mount*, pp. 15-16). Stott perceptively noted that "in a way Christians find this search for a cultural alternative one of the most hopeful, even exciting, signs of the times. For we recognize in it the activity of that Spirit who before he is the comforter is the disturber, and we know to whom their quest will lead them if it is ever to find fulfillment" (ibid., p. 16).

4. Vinita Hampton and Carol Plueddeman, comp. *World Shapers: A Treasury of Quotes from Great Missionaries* (Wheaton, IL.: Harold Shaw Publishers, 1991), p. 10.

5. Jim Elliot, from a journal entry in 1948. See Elisabeth Elliot, *Shadow of the Almighty: The Life and Testament of Jim Elliot* (San Francisco: HarperSanFrancisco, 1989), p. 247.

6. J. Wesley Bready, *This Freedom—Whence?* (Winona Lake, IN.: Light and Life Press, 1950), pp. 95-97.

7. W. E. DuBois, "The Battle for Humanity," delivered August 1906, cited in Torricelli and Carroll, *In Our Own Words*, p. 18.

8. Bill Bright, *Come Help Change the World* (Orlando, FL: New Life, 1999).

9. In the words of evangelist Billy Sunday, "Hell is the highest reward that the devil can offer you for being a servant of his."

10. Niu-Niu, *No Tears for Mao: Growing Up in the Cultural Revolution*, trans. Enne and Peter Amman (Chicago: Academy Chicago Publisher, 1995), p. 20.

11. Ibid., pp. 22-23.

12. See *The Barna Report*, 1997 (http://www.barna.org).

13. Brown, *The End of the American Gospel Enterprise*, p. 39.

14. The practice of widow burning was quite common. When a married man died, it was customary to burn his widow along with him in the funeral pyre. This horrible custom was carried out by the Hindus for social and religious reasons: It would not leave the widow destitute and without means of financial support, and it was believed to help her in the next (reincarnated) life. Carey fought against this for years before making any progress.

15. See e.g., D. James Kennedy and Jerry Newcombe, *What If Jesus had Never been Born? The Positive Impact of Christianity in History* (Nashville: Thomas Nelson, 1994); see also *Christianity Today* (December 6, 1999), devoted to the theme "Where Would Civilization Be Without Christianity."

16. Source unknown.

Chapter Four

1. Note, for example, the response of some Athenians listening to Paul on Mars Hill: "'He seems to be advocating foreign gods.' They said this because Paul was preaching the good news about Jesus and the resurrection" (Acts 17:18).

2. Pastor Castellanos was shot six times but, miraculously, no vital organs were hit. He made the doctors leave one bullet in his body as a testimony to unbelievers he meets.

3. F. F. Bruce, *The Book of the Acts* , New International Commentary on the New Testament, rev. ed., (Grand Rapids, MI: Wm. B. Eerdmans Publishing Co., 1988), p. 167.

4. See Acts 9:23,24,29; 21:31; 23:15,27; 25:3; 26:21; 27:42.

5. F. F. Bruce, *The Book of the Acts,* pp. 324-325. According to Professor James D. G. Dunn, "The problem of a possible conflict between the authority of God and that of Caesar must have been a very real one for the early Christians and is specifically tackled in . . . Mark 12:13-17. . . . The question whether it was lawful or permitted to pay the tax to Caesar or not was therefore well chosen to trap Jesus on the horns of a dilemma: either deny the authority of Caesar (rebellion) or deny the full authority of God (treason and blasphemy). Jesus' reply makes it clear that in his view the antithesis was false: political and divine authority need not necessarily conflict. Man can live with human relationships of authority and obligation and still 'pay to God what is due to God' [see Matt. 22:21]. There is however the possibility of real conflict between obligation to Caesar and obligation to God. Loyalty to Caesar can become an excuse for evading higher obligation to the truth (see John 18:38; 19:12-16). Whoever limits his motives and aims to friendship with Caesar shuts himself off from an answer to the question, What is truth? Whoever affirms loyalty only to Caesar is thereby self-condemned (cf. John 16:8-11)." See his article, "Caesar, Consul, Governor," in Colin Brown, ed., *The New International Dictionary of New Testament Theology,* vol. 1 (Grand Rapids, MI: Zondervan Publishing House, 1986), p. 270.

6. See Adolph Deissmann, *Light from the Ancient East* (reprint, Peabody, MA: Hendrickson Publishers, 1995), p. 84; Johannes P. Louw and Eugene A. Nida, eds., *Greek-English Lexicon of the New Testament Based on Semantic Domains,* vol. 1 (New York: United Bible Societies, 1988), p. 498, #39.41. Richard N. Longenecker, "Acts," *Expositor's Bible Commentary,* vol. 9, ed. Frank E. Gaebelein (Grand Rapids, MI: Zondervan Publishing House, 1981), p. 469, notes, "Certainly the assembly of citizens and the politarchs at Thessalonica would have known of the troubles within the Jewish community at Rome in connection with Christianity and of Claudius's edict of A.D. 49-50 for all Jews to leave that city (see Suetonius Vita Claudius 25.4, who speaks of 'constant riots at the instigation of Chrestus' and tells of the emperor's order of expulsion; see also 18:2). Probably the Jewish opponents of the missionaries played upon the fear that such a situation might be duplicated at Thessalonica, unless Paul and Silas were expelled. In addition, from their charge that the missionaries proclaimed 'another king' (v. 7), it may be inferred that they tried to use Paul's mention of 'the kingdom of God' (cf. 14:22; 19:8; 20:25; 28:23, 31) to arouse suspicion that he was involved in anti-imperial sedition. Indeed, it may be for this reason that Paul avoided the use of 'kingdom' and 'king' in his let-

ters to his converts, lest Gentile imperial authorities misconstrue them to connote opposition to the empire and emperor."

7. Adam Clarke, *Commentary on the Acts of the Apostles,* John Calvin Collection (Albany, OR: Ages Digital Library, 1998), CD-ROM.

8. He wrote: "This is precisely the same way that persecution against the truth and followers of Christ is still carried on. Some wicked man in the parish gets a wicked attorney and a constable to head a mob, which they themselves have raised; and, having committed a number of outrages, abusing men and women, haul the minister of Christ to some magistrate who knows as little of his office as he cares for the Gospel; they there charge the outrages which themselves have committed on the preacher and his peaceable hearers; and the peacemaker, appointed by a good king, according to the wise and excellent regulations of a sound constitution, forgetting whose minister he is, neither administers justice nor maintains truth; but, espousing the part of the mob, assumes, ex officio, the character of a persecutor. The preacher is imprisoned, his hearers fined for listening to that Gospel which has not only made them wise unto salvation, but also peaceable and orderly citizens, and which would have had the same effect on the unprincipled magistrate, the parish squire, and the mob, had they heard it with the same reverence and respect" Adam Clarke, *Commentary to Acts 17,* Sage Digital Library (Albany, OR: Sage Software, 1996), CD-ROM.

9. Note that Jesus was crucified on charges of sedition; cf. Luke 23:2, 14. Notice also that He was *charged* with being "King of the Jews" (Matt. 27:11). What a crime!

10. Note the accusation made against Paul by Jewish leaders who brought him before Gallio: "This man," they charged, "is persuading the people to worship God in ways contrary to the law" (Acts 18:13).

11. Joseph A. Fitzmyer, S.J., *The Acts of the Apostles,* Anchor Bible (New York: Doubleday, 1998), p. 587, to Acts 16:21.

12. Archibald T. Robertson,*Word Pictures in the New Testament,* vol. 3 (Nashville, TN: Broadman & Holman Publishers, 1982; reprint, Grand Rapids, MI: Baker Books, 1991), p. 273, to Acts 17:6.

13. W. C. H. Frend, *The Rise of Christianity* (Philadelphia: Fortress, 1984), p. 103.

14. Note that the fine New Testament scholar, N. T. (Tom) Wright, subtitled his illustrated book *The Original Jesus* with *The Life and Vision of a Revolutionary* (Grand Rapids, MI: Wm. B. Eerdmans Publishing Co., 1997). Even Friedrich Nietzsche believed that Jesus was a true revolutionary. See Robert C. Solomon and Kathleen C. Higgins, *What Nietzsche Really Said* (New York: Schocken, 2000), p.143. (According to Nietzsche, Jesus was the first and "only" Christian!)

15. Juan Carlos Ortiz, *Disciple: A Handbook for New Believers* (Orlando: Creation House, 1975), p. 12.

16. James D. G. Dunn, "Caesar, Consul, Governor," *New International Dictionary of New Testament Theology,* vol. 1, p. 269. Dunn describes the Thessalonian Jewish response to Paul's preaching.

17. Acts 21:38; remember that this verse also uses the same Greek verb found in Acts 17:6.

18. According to Eberhard Arnold, *The Early Christians in Their Own Words* (Farmington, PA: Plough, 1997), p. 59, "The witness of the early church was forged in the fires of false accusation, torture, and death. With a unified state religion and a govern-

318 Endnotes for Chapter 4

mental structure that kept every citizen under its iron grip, the Roman Empire tolerated no authority other than its own and regarded anything that resisted or opposed it as an extremely dangerous threat. Jesus warned his first disciples, 'On my account you will be brought before governors and kings. . . . All people will hate you because of me' (Matt. 10:18, 22). And so it happened and continues to happen for all who uncompromisingly follow him."

19. See, e.g., Matt. 5:10-12; 10:24; Phil. 1:29.

20. H. N. Bilalik and Y. H. Ravnitzky, eds., *The Book of Legends: Sefer Ha-Aggadah,* trans. W. G. Braude (New York: Schocken, 1992), p. 238, #177 (b. Berakhot 61b with Eyn Yaakov).

21. I heartily affirm the language of Teen Mania's "Teenage Bill of Rights" (which is a revolutionary document for today's young people [see www.teenmania.org/tbor.html]) in which young people commit to the following: "We will Respect the authorities God has placed in our lives, even though some may have character that we do not admire. We realize that all authority comes from God. We refuse to subvert our parents or other authority figures." However, when, e.g., a Muslim father tells his son, "You cannot follow Jesus!" the son must say, "I have no choice. I must follow Jesus!" This, then, would be considered subversive, even though that Christian son is committed to respectful submission in all possible cases.

22. Danyun, *Lilies Amongst Thorns: Chinese Christians Tell Their Story Through Blood and Tears* (Ventura, CA: Gospel Light, Renew Books, 1993), p. 167.

23. Niu-Niu, *No Tears for Mao,* p. 35.

24. In a statement released October 14, 1917 by the moderate Socialists in Russia, "The drama of Revolution has two acts; the destruction of the old régime and the creation of the new one" (cited in Reed, *Ten Days That Shook the World,* p. 2).

25. Niu-Niu, *No Tears for Mao,* p. 96.

26. Fitzmyer, *The Acts of the Apostles,* p. 596, to Acts 17:7.

27. Law from the Twelve Tables, 450 B.C. Cicero, *On the Laws,* vol. II, p. 19, cited in Arnold, *The Early Christians,* p. 61.

28. Legal decree according to the second-century pagan jurist Julius Paulus. Paulus, *Collected Sentences,* vol. 21, cited in Arnold, ibid.

29. The decree spoken against Justin Martyr and his fellow-believers, roughly A.D. 165. Cited in Arnold, ibid., p. 78.

30. Roughly A.D. 177. Athenagoras, *A Plea Regarding Christians* 7, cited in Arnold, ibid.

31. Tertullian, *To the Heathen; Apology;* and other writings, cited in Arnold, ibid., pp. 61-62. Both Jews and Christians in the Roman empire were accused of being "atheists" because they refused to acknowledge Caesar as lord. When they were being led to execution, it was common for the crowds to cry out, "Away with the atheists!" It is written that Polycarp, one of the most famous early Christian martyrs, waved his hand at the crowd before his execution and exclaimed *to them,* "Away with the atheists!" (The famous account is found in *The Martyrdom of Polycarp.*)

32. Cited in Amir Taheri, *Holy Terror: Inside the World of Islamic Terrorism* (Bethesda, MD: Adler & Adler, 1987), p. 34.

33. Ibid., p. 28.

34. Muslim law in Pakistan decrees death for anyone who "by an imputation, innuendo or insinuation, directly or indirectly, defiles the sacred name of the Holy Prophet

Muhammad." Susan Bergman, ed., *Martyrs: Contemporary Writers on Modern Lives of Faith* (San Francisco: Harper Collins Publishers, 1996), p. 5. Under this law, Muslims who convert to Christianity are often charged with blasphemy by those who (falsely) claim that the Christians blasphemed Muhammad.

35. On the special hatred that the killers had for Jesus, Christianity, and committed Christians, see Steve Rabey, "Videos of Hate," *Christianity Today* (February 7, 2000), p. 21. In the videos, the killers mock the "What Would Jesus Do" concept, ridicule those who say they love Jesus, and cheer on the Romans for crucifying Jesus. According to Darryl Scott, Rachel Scott's father, his daughter "attended class with Dylan Klebold and Eric Harris, she witnessed to them, and she confronted them about the violent videos they were making at the school." She was singled out for scorn by Klebold in one of the videos.

Chapter Five

1. Cited in Taheri, *Holy Terror*, p. 21.
2. Jack Kelley, *USA Today* (December 3, 1997), p. 16A.
3. From a survey conducted by George Barna and published December 21, 1999. For further details, see http://www.barna.org.
4. Taheri, *Holy Terror*, p. 20.
5. Cited in Emanuel Sivan, *Radical Islam: Medieval Theology and Modern Politics* (New Haven: Yale University Press, 1985), p. 17. The writer belonged to the Muslim Brotherhood.
6. Perhaps the most extreme form of Islam in the world today is found among the Taliban in Afghanistan. Their practices include "beatings or floggings for violations of dress codes for men or women or of prescribed beard lengths or shapes for men; amputations of hands and feet for theft; stoning to death for adultery; burial alive for sodomy—punishments carried out in public. The cruelest punishment of all, for women and the society as a whole . . . was exclusion of women from education and the work place" (John K. Cooley, *Unholy Wars: Afghanistan, America and International Terrorism* [London: Pluto, 1999], p. 3). See also Ahmed Rashid, *Taliban* (New Haven, CT: Yale University Press, 2000); Peter Marsden, *The Taliban: War, Religion and the New World Order in Afghanistan* (London: Zed, 1998); William Maley, ed., *Fundamentalism Reborn? Afghanistan and the Taliban* (Washington Square, NY: New York University Press, 1998). For a broader, nonalarmist perspective, see John L. Esposito, *The Islamic Threat: Myth or Reality*, 3rd ed. (New York: Oxford, 1999). For the background of Jihad, see Reuven Firestone, *Jihad: The Origin of Holy War in Islam* (New York: Oxford, 1999); Paul Fregosi, *Jihad in the West: Muslim Conquests from the 7th to the 21st Centuries* (New York: Prometheus, 1998). It should be noted that Islam, in general, has not banned all music, as the Taliban have in Afghanistan.
7. As expressed concisely by Taheri, "Under Islam it is not religion that is a part of life, but life a part of religion" (Taheri, *Holy Terror*, p. 22).
8. For a comprehensive critique of the Christian theology of revolution, see Vernon C. Grounds, *Revolution and the Christian Faith* (Philadelphia: J. B. Lippincott, 1971); see also Os Guinness, *The Dust of Death: The Sixties Counterculture and How It Changed America Forever*, 2nd ed. (Wheaton, IL: Crossway, 1994). For an introduction to lib-

eration theology, some of which is highly questionably from a New Testament perspective despite its noble intentions, see the classic study of Gustavo Gutiérrez, *A Theology of Liberation*, trans. and ed. Sister Caridad Inda and John Eagleson, rev. ed. (Maryknoll, NY: Orbis, 1998); see also Christopher Rowland, ed., *The Cambridge Companion to Liberation Theology* (Cambridge, England: Cambridge, 1999); Curt Cadorette, Marie Gibbin, Marilyn J. Legge, and Mary H. Snyder, eds., *Liberation Theology: An Introductory Reader* (Maryknoll, NY: Orbis, 1992); Leonard Boff and Clodovis Boff, *Introducing Liberation Theology*, trans. Paul Burns (Maryknoll, NY: Orbis, 1987).

9. For a discussion of some of the more radical sayings of Jesus, see Michael L. Brown, *Answering Jewish Objections to Jesus*, vol. 3, *Messianic Prophecy, New Testament, and Traditional Jewish Objections* (forthcoming, Grand Rapids, MI: Baker Book House, 2001); Walter C. Kaiser, Jr., Peter H. Davids, F. F. Bruce, and Manfred Brauch, *Hard Sayings of the Bible* (Downers Grove, IL: InterVarsity Press, 1996).

10. According to Professor Nahum Sarna, "This command . . . warns against violating the covenant by recognizing in any manner or form what other peoples accept as deities. Israel's God demands uncompromising and exclusive loyalty" *Exodus*, Jewish Publication Society Torah Commentary (Philadelphia: JPS, 1991), p. 109.

11. See, e.g., Gen. 35:1-4; 2 Chron. 15:8; 2 Kings 23:4-7.

12. Tony Campolo, introduction to *Wake Up America! Answering God's Radical Call While Living in the Real World* (San Francisco: HarperSanFrancisco, 1991).

13. Ibid.

14. My statement here should not be construed in any way as an expression of endorsement or admiration for Islam or Marxism. To the contrary, the fact that these systems, one primarily religious and the other primarily social, find such fault with Western Christianity is all the more an indictment of the shallow nature of our brand of Christianity, since true life is found only in the gospel, not in any other religious or social system.

15. *The Gates of Zion*, newsletter (September 1993), p. 1.

16. William J. Bennett, ed., *Our Sacred Honor: Words of Advice from the Founders in Stories, Letters, Poems, and Speeches* (New York: Simon & Schuster, 1997), pp. 88-89. Rush actually wished that he could remove his name from the Declaration of Independence, a sentiment for which Adams quickly took him to task (ibid.). Interestingly, revival historians point to America's moral and spiritual decline in the decades following the American Revolution—perhaps our freedom brought complacency?—noting that revival (in particular, the Second Great Awakening) turned things around again.

17. If you would like to get involved with helping these worthy laborers on the mission field, contact Brownsville International, 8594 Hwy. 98 W., Pensacola, FL 32506.

18. A. W. Tozer, *The Best of A. W. Tozer* (Grand Rapids, MI.: Baker Book House, 1978), p. 179.

19. Brown, *How Saved Are We?* pp. 61-63 (I have rearranged and edited afresh some of the material cited).

Chapter Six

1. David Van Biema, "A Surge of Teen Spirit: A Christian girl, martyred at Columbine

High, sparks a revival among many evangelical teens," *TIME*, May 31, 1999. http://www.time.com/time/magazine/articles/0,32566,25681,00.html.

2. Wendy Murray Zoba, *Generation 2K: What Parents & Others Need to Know About the Millennials* (Downers Grove, IL: InterVarsity Press, 1999).

3. Bennett notes that "between 1973 and 1998, [music unit] sales [including CDs, CD singles, cassettes, cassette singles, LPs/EPs, vinyl singles, and music videos] have increased more than 80 percent. . . . Americans devote almost five times as much time to watching television and videotapes as they do to reading. . . . In 1993, 3 million people were connected to the Internet, compared to roughly 80 million in 1999. . . . The average child plays . . . video games seven hours a week" (Bennett, *Index*, pp. 168, 170-171).

4. Bennett states that, "The total number of violent crimes on television (excluding news and other nonfiction programming) increased by 74 percent in three years—from 1,002 in 1992 to 1,738 in 1995—and reached an average of almost ten incidents of violence per channel during the 1995-1996 television season. Violence is most concentrated in cable movies and cartoon shows. . . . A sexual act or reference occurs every four minutes on average during prime-time television" (ibid., pp. 162-163).

5. According to Bennett, ibid., p. 166, in 1998, "NC-17 and R movies made up 66 percent of all rated movies, while PG-13 made up 17 percent and PG and G movies combined made up 17 percent. Between 1988 and 1997, 4 times more R-rated films were produced than G-rated films. At the same time, the average G-rated film produced a 78 percent greater rate of return than the average R-rated film." This shows that Hollywood is not just driven by greed; it is often driven by godlessness as well.

6. This happened in Colombia after the World Cup in soccer in 1994. Andres Escobar accidentally kicked the ball into his own team's net in a 2-1 upset loss to the United States. Shortly after that, he was shot to death in a bar.

7. In the ancient Christian world, it was generally forbidden for believers to engage in the organized, public athletic games, many of which were conducted in the nude and some of which were extremely violent, sadistic, or fatal. Regarding baptismal candidates, note the teaching of the respected Church leader Hipollytus (160-236): "A charioteer, an athlete, a gladiator, a trainer of gladiators, or one who fights wild beasts or hunts them or holds public office at the circus games shall give it up or be rejected" (Hipollytus, *Church Order,* cited in Arnold, *Early Christians*, p. 113). For a perspective from modern, fundamentalist Islam, see Sivan, *Radical Islam*, p. 4 (Sivan notes that, in the eyes of some Muslims, professional sports "brings the idolatry of pagan-inspired body worship to a peak").

8. " 'God does not give a rip about who wins or loses. God is engaged in the world, but not in things like athletic contests. That is too frivolous,' says Emory University theologian James Freeman, an expert on sports and religion. 'I think God could care less who wins or loses,' says James Mitchell, former Tennessee Titans chaplain and national director of outreach for Pro Athletes Outreach. God may intervene at times when it truly matters—when Hitler threatens to conquer the world—but He doesn't concern Himself with boys' games. Other evangelicals, including the FCA and AIA, hold that God may care who wins the game and may even intervene, but that it's

foolish of players to presume to read His mind. 'Does God care? I would say yes, but we don't know who He wants to win. God has plans for you however the game comes out,' says Petersburg. AIA spokesman Greg Stoughton says that while God may answer a player's prayer for a win, 'victory to God may look a whole lot different than it does to the player. . . . Even if you lose, God is about building character.' The 'genie in a bottle' theory, they note, is incoherent about defeat. If God wants you to win because you are faithful, does that mean He wants your opponents—who profess equal devotion—to lose? If your opponents lose, does that mean they didn't have enough faith? If you lose, does that mean you don't have enough faith? The genie has no answer. Most evangelicals turn the 'genie in a bottle' theology on its head. That theology views God as the instrument. God proves Himself to you by making the catch or causing the fumble. But most evangelicals see the *player* as the instrument: The player glorifies God by playing his best. Petersburg says that his Browns players never pray for victory. They pray 'that they play with honor, that that they play to their best ability, that they honor God in the way they play, that they play injury-free.' It's not about who wins and who loses. It's about how they play the game." (David Plotz, "The God of the Gridiron: Does He Care Who Wins the Super Bowl?"*Slate*, February 3, 2000 (http://slate.msn.com/Assessment/00-02-04/Assessment.asp). For a recent study on sports and evangelical Christianity, see Tony Ladd and James A. Mathisen, *Muscular Christianity: Evangelical Protestants and the Development of American Sport* (Grand Rapids, MI: Baker Book House, 1999).

9. Studd came from a wealthy aristocratic family and was one of the top cricket players in the nation while attending Cambridge. For his story, see Norman Grubb, *C. T. Studd: Cricketeer and Pioneer* (1933; reprint, Fort Washington, PA: Christian Literature Crusade, 1988).

10. This is not hyperbole; it has been said and done, and I have read the exact quote in question with my own eyes. I trust, however, that no one will fault me for choosing not to reveal the athlete's name.

11. Two principles suggested to me by a friend are (1) we should dress so as to draw attention to the face, and (2) the object of our clothes is what we are trying to cover, not what we're trying to reveal.

12. Richard Wurmbrand, *The Overcomers* (Tunbridge Wells, England: Monarch, 1993), p. 82.

13. Bennett, *Index*, p. 171.

14. Ibid., pp. 166-167.

15. Ibid., p. 172.

16. "The Spread of the Obesity Epidemic in the United States, 1991-1998," *Journal for the American Medical Association*, vol. 282 (October 27, 1999), n.p. For an abstract of the report on Internet, see http://jama.ama-assn.org/issues/v282n16/abs/joc91119.html; for the full text, see http://jama.ama-assn.org/issues/ v282n16/full/joc91119.html. Obesity is defined differently by medical authorities, although a commonly accepted rule of thumb categorizes obesity as weighing 20% more than your proper body weight. This would mean that if your proper body weight is 150 pounds, you are obese if you weigh 180 pounds or more.

17. This is based on the fact that phone surveys were done asking for the height and weight of those responding, and it is recognized that people tend to understate

their weight and overestimate their height! Also, other surveys recently conducted put the obesity rate at over 21 percent of the population.

18. Bob Newman, *Guerrillas in the Mist: A Battlefield Guide to Clandestine Warfare* (Boulder, CO: Paladin, 1997), p. 95. Two hundred years ago, the Hasidic Jewish leader Rabbi Nahman of Bratslav said, "More people die from overeating than from undernourishment."

19. R. A. Torrey, in E. E. Shelhamer, *Heart Searching Talks to Ministers* (Louisville, KY: Pentecostal Publishing Co., 1914), pp. 124-127, cited in Wesley L. Duewel, *Ablaze for God* (Grand Rapids, MI: Zondervan Publishing House, 1989), p. 88.

20. Interestingly, the Ungers note that "by the later Sixties, the postwar baby boom had created a youth population larger in proportion to the proportion as a whole than any since the previous century. Activated by the new prosperity, by new federal aid, and by the growing sense that a college degree was indispensable for success in the modern 'knowledge society,' young people poured into the colleges. In 1960, there were fewer than 3 million college undergraduates; by 1970, there were more than 6.3 million" (Unger and Unger, *the times were a changin'*, p. 8). For a broad-ranging discussion of the failures of contemporary American education, see Thomas Sowell, *Inside American Education: The Decline, the Deception, the Dogmas* (New York: The Free Press, a div. of Simon and Schuster, 1993); see also the watershed study of Alan Bloom, *The Closing of the American Mind* (New York: Simon and Schuster, 1987).

21. This stands in stark contrast with the responses given by graduates of Christian colleges, the vast majority of whom say that their college experience did, in fact, help them move toward fulfilling God's purposes for their lives.

22. Here are excerpts from an e-mail received by a student in our School of Ministry from her mother, who professes to be a Christian: "When you are brainwashed by these so-called professors of the ministry, you obviously give your life over to them and become their puppets. This school has done that to you. ACCREDITED SCHOOLS do not teach in this manner. . . . I pray each night to God that you will see the light and finally understand our fears about what you have gotten yourself into. You were a prime target—they like innocent, young people who are easily brainwashed and led down their primrose path. Wake up . . . and realize you should be enjoying life like everyone your age. Mom."

23. For another related critique, see David F. Wells, "The D-Min-ization of the Ministry," *No God But God: Breaking with the Idols of Our Age*, eds. Os Guinness and John Seel (Chicago: Moody, 1992), pp. 175-188; for a fuller discussion, see David F. Wells, *No Place for Truth* (Grand Rapids, MI: Wm. B. Eerdmans Publishing Co., 1992). For an even sharper critique, see Eta Linnemann, *Historical Criticism of the Bible: Methodology or Ideology?* trans. Robert W. Yarbrough (Grand Rapids, MI: Baker Book House, 1990). No doubt, there is an important place in Christian college and seminary curriculum for apologetics, if only for the sake of the students, who may have been bombarded with unbiblical concepts and perspectives for years. Still, there is often the subtle, underlying feeling that we as Christian professors and academicians must prove our intellectual integrity over and over again, spending more time refuting error than learning truth.

24. How do you think it feels to contribute an article to a scholarly compendium and

to have my academic affiliation listed as "Brownsville Revival School of Ministry" while the other contributing scholars lecture at Harvard and Princeton and Johns Hopkins and Yale? Yet such is my call—and I embrace it. Most recently, this happened with two of my articles published in 1999, namely, "*Kipper* and Atonement in the Book of Isaiah," in R. Chazan, W. W. Hallo, and L. H. Schiffman, eds., *Kî Barukh Hû': Ancient Near Eastern, Biblical, and Judaic Studies for Baruch A. Levine* (Winona Lake, IN: Eisenbrauns, 1999), pp. 189-202; and "Was There a West Semitic Asklepios?" in *Ugarit Forschungen*, vol. 30 (1998), pp. 133-154.

25. For many more contemporary idols that need to be smashed, see Herbert Schlossberg, *Idols for Destruction: The Conflict of Christian Faith and American Culture* (Wheaton, IL: Crossway Books, 1990).

Chapter Seven

1. Unger and Unger, *the times they were a changin'*, p. 7. Just think: Some of the early FM music (in particular rock and folk) was underground (meaning, pirated!).

2. Originally published by InterVarsity Press in 1973, it was reprinted in 1994 by Crossway Books with a new foreword and afterword by the author.

3. This is similar to the observations made by British Prime Ministers George and Baldwin concerning nineteenth-century England and (early) twentieth-century America: Neither could be understood without understanding the impact of John Wesley! (See above, chapter three.) So also—but with basically opposite results—late twentieth-century to early twenty-first-century America cannot be understood without understanding the impact of rock music.

4. Lisa Law, *Flashing on the Sixties* (San Francisco: Chronicle Books, 1987), p. 13.

5. Os Guinness, *Dust of Death*, p. 119.

6. Baba Ram Dass, foreword to *Flashing on the Sixties*.

7. Unger and Unger, *the times they were a changin'*, pp. 1, 6-7.

8. It is worth pointing out that Talmudic study, which can be extremely taxing, is done to a sing-song style called in Hebrew "niggun" (meaning, "sung; played"). This greatly facilitates the process of memorization.

9. To give just one example, Charles Kaiser, in comparing Eric Clapton's famous 1970 ballad "Layla" to other major rock hits of that era (specifically, "Somebody to Love," "Satisfaction," "Piece of My Heart," "Help!" and "Like a Rolling Stone") describes it as "a seven minute expiation of agony that remains one of rock's most spectacular feats," calling it "a crucial song with a unique emotional resonance for nearly every member of the Vietnam generation." See his important study *1968 in America: Music, Politics, Chaos, Counterculture, and the Shaping of a Generation* (New York: Grove Press, 1988), p. 209; according to Kaiser, Clapton managed to produce "Layla" despite a "heavy dependence on heroin" at that time.

10. Jim Morrison, Elektra Records biography, 1967, cited in "The Life and Death of Jim Morrison," *The Doors Official Website*. http://www.the doors.com/gamma/frame_sets/Jim_home.html.

11. *The Observer*, cited in Guinness, *Dust of Death*, p. 120.

12. Ibid. Two of those three stars were Jimi Hendrix and Janis Joplin.

13. I am very grateful to God, however, for those few contemporary Christian artists

who have put substance before sales and truth before popularity. They should be commended! For a very fair critique of the failure of contemporary Christian music to respond to Amy Grant's recent divorce—without any biblical foundation—and remarriage, see Wendy Murray Zoba, "Take a Little Time Out," *Christianity Today* (February 7, 2000), p. 86.

14. Like many other ministers, I have chosen for years to receive no royalties for any book or tape sales through any means, but I see nothing wrong with Christian authors, speakers, or recording artists receiving royalties from their materials, nor do I judge them in the least. May God bless them a hundredfold! However, in my case, I never wanted to have personal financial gain be the motivation for writing, nor did I want there to be a temptation to believe God for His blessing on the sale of my books—which are written out of passion and conviction—so as to personally make money. That is not why I write!

15. This term is found 56 times in the Old Testament (e.g., Pss. 4:1; 5:1; 6:1; Hab. 3:19), and it is translated as "the director of music" in the *NIV* and as "the choir master" in the *NLT* (cf. the *NRSV* to Hab. 3:19). "Chief musician" is the rendering of the *KJV* and the *NKJV*.

16. A number of psalms apparently begin with instructions for singing; see the *NIV's* rendering of the superscription of Psalms 9, 22, 46, 56-60, 69, 75, 80 ("To the tune of . . ."). Other psalms give other types of musical direction, such as "with stringed instruments" (e.g., Pss. 4, 6, 54-55) or "for flutes" (Ps. 5). See also Willem VanGemeren, "The Psalms," *Expositors Bible Commentary*, vol. 5, pp. 36-37.

17. To some extent, alcohol did this too, since drunkenness can bring out all kinds of outrageous and often antisocial behavior, quickly lowering standards and removing convictions along the way. How many women have woken up the morning after a drinking binge, only to find themselves in bed with a stranger? The difference between the effect of alcohol and that of drugs is that those using drugs are conscious of their acts, even when very high (while drinking can cause blackouts), and those using drugs—especially hallucinogenics—can have their very worldview shaped by those chemicals they ingest.

18. Taheri, *Holy Terror*, pp. 41-42. There is some dispute among scholars as to how much—if at all—hashish was used by the fedayeen. The tradition, however, as to how the term hashasheen caught on, is certain.

19. The most famous hymnist of the era was Charles Wesley, who for a time prepared a new hymn each week to complement the message to be preached by his brother John. (It is worth nothing that while we don't preach the sermons of John Wesley from our pulpits, we do sing the hymns of Charles Wesley in our churches!) Other major hymnists of that day were Isaac Watts, John Newton, William Cowper, and Augustus Toplady. In the nineteenth century, the most famous duo was D. L. Moody and Ira Sankey; for some of the objections brought against Sankey's music, see Brown, *Holy Fire*, p. 52.

Chapter Eight

1. Karl Marx and Friedrich Engels, *The Communist Manifesto: A Modern Edition* (New

York: Verso, 1998), pp. 33-34.

2. Ibid. For the various editions and translations of the work, see Eric Hobsbawm, introduction to *The Communist Manifesto,* pp. 6-11.

3. Ibid., p. 77. For the closing line, I have used the more common "WORKERS" for the translator's "WORKING MEN."

4. Mao Zedong, *Quotations from Chairman Mao Tse-tung* (Peking: Foreign Languages Press, 1972), n. p.

5. Ibid., p. 182. The quotes are taken, respectively, from "On Coalition Government," *Selected Works,* vol. 3 (April 24, 1945), p. 318, and, "The Foolish Old Man Who Removed the Mountains," *Selected Works,* vol. 3 (June 11, 1945), p. 321.

6. For massive documentation of the destructive effects of Communism, see Stéphane Courtois et al., *The Black Book of Communism: Crimes, Terror, Repression,* trans., Jonathan Murphy and Mark Kramer (Cambridge, MA: Harvard, 1999). The information in this book is so damning that Tony Judt, in his *New York Times* review stated, "No one will any longer be able to claim ignorance or uncertainty about the criminal nature of Communism, and those who had begun to forget will be forced to remember." For the crimes of Joseph Stalin in particular, see Robert Conquest, *The Great Terror: A Reassessment* (1968; reprint, New York: Oxford University Press, 1991).

7. Friends of mine who lead a strongly evangelistic church in the Tübingen-Stuttgart area of Germany have been under scrutiny from the government because of their beliefs (which, of course, are being misrepresented and misunderstood). A letter from tax authorities in Tübingen, dated December 1, 1998, states that "it is also of importance to consider to what extent a nonprofit organization moves within the framework of the constitutional laws.... To my understanding, not only the armed struggle against this framework is to be considered an offence, but it is also essential to observe the elementary basic rights such as permissiveness, the right to be heard as guaranteed by the state under the rule of law, the right of assembly and the right to form associations and societies. Part of these rights must be the freedom—like it is with the right to vote—to leave such organizations without further complications. *In the case of religious communities that lay claim to the only true faith this might lead to problems, once the member who wants to leave the association or church is led to believe that he or she will forfeit eternal life upon leaving the community*" (my emphasis; the document was carefully translated before being sent to me). The church has been brought before the court to prove its legal status as a nonprofit organization.

8. Mao Zedong, *Quotations from Chairman Mao Tse-tung,* p. 258.

9. Robert E. Coleman, *The Master Plan of Evangelism* (1964; reprint, Grand Rapids, MI: Fleming H. Revell, 1993), p. 122, n. 13.

10. For important perspectives on the church's call to be a counterculture rather than a subculture, see John Bevere, *A Heart Ablaze: Igniting a Passion for God* (Nashville: Thomas Nelson, 1999), especially pp. 81-93. He notes, "The lines of conservative America have shifted, and the church's lines have moved with them. What would have shocked unbelievers in America in the 1940s is considered normal by most believers in the church today" (ibid., pp. 85-86).

11. Leonard Ravenhill, *Why Revival Tarries* (Minneapolis, MN: Bethany, 1962), p. 98.

12. Mao Zedong, *Quotations from Mao Tse-tung,* pp. 256-257.

13. Danyun, *Lilies Amongst Thorns,* p. 167.

14. For further thoughts on this, see Michael L. Brown, *Go and Sin No More: A Call to Holiness* (Ventura, CA: Regal, 1999).

15. Ibid., pp. 147-162.

16. *Compass* (Autumn 1999), p. 31.

17. Interestingly, there are Jewish leaders today who believe that Jewish assimilation—meaning intermarriage with Gentiles and/or becoming part of the secular culture or joining another religion—is a far greater threat to world Jewry than was the Holocaust.

18. See, for example, the articles by Peter T. Chattaway and Steven Lansingh written for *Christianity Today*, respectively, "My Favorite Films of 1999" and "Ten Films That Made My Year," ChristianityToday.com, 2000. Chattaway article—http://www.christianityonline.com/ct/current/0118/0118b.html. Lansingh article—http://www.christianityonline.com/ct/current/0118/0118a.html. One of the films picked by Mr. Lansingh was *Fight Club*, an *extremely* violent, R-rated movie, while *six* of Mr. Chattaway's ten favorites were rated R, including some with graphic sexual content.

19. "Jude," *Expositor's Bible Commentary*, vol. 12, p. 395, emphasis added.

20. Note that the Hebrew word often translated "blessed" in the Old Testament (e.g., Pss. 1:1; 33:12; 65:4; 84:4) really means "truly happy." See my article on *'ašrê*, in Willem VanGemeren, ed., *The New International Dictionary of Old Testament Theology and Exegesis*, vol. 1 (Grand Rapids, MI: Zondervan Publishing House, 1997), pp. 570-572. The same probably holds true for Greek *makarios*, found, for example, in the beatitudes (i.e., "Truly happy are the poor in spirit," etc.).

21. Marx and Engles, *Communist Manifesto*, p. 77.

22. Winkie Pratney, *Revival* (Springdale, PA: Whitaker, 1983), p. 337, emphasis his. As indicated by the brackets, the words "and revolution" are mine, although they are in complete harmony with Winkie Pratney's current perspective as well.

Chapter Nine

1. These words, written in all caps in red, are on the all-black front cover of the new edition of *The Communist Manifesto* that I own.

2. Frederick Engels, preface to the 1888 English edition of *The Communist Manifesto*, cited in Marx and Engels, *The Communist Manifesto*, p. 86. The relevant portion of his text reads: "that the history of these class struggles forms a series of evolutions in which, nowadays, a stage has been reached where the exploited and oppressed class—the proletariat—cannot attain its emancipation from the sway of the exploiting and ruling class—the bourgeoisie—without, at the same time, and once and for all, emancipating society at large from all exploitation, oppression, class distinctions and class struggles."

3. For the failure of non-Christian worldviews in the twentieth century, see Charles Colson and Nancy Pearcey, *How Now Shall We Live?* (Wheaton, IL: Tyndale, 1999), with reference to earlier relevant literature.

4. See Dale Van Kley, ed., *The French Idea of Freedom: The Old Regime and the Declaration of Rights of 1789* (Stanford, CA: Stanford University Press, 1994), n. p.

5. The quote continues, "How was it carried out? Bloodshed. Number one, it was based

on land, the basis of independence. And the only way they could get it was bloodshed." His whole point was that "you haven't got a revolution that doesn't involve bloodshed." See his speech "There's No Such Thing As a Non-Violent Revolution," delivered November 10, 1963 (several months after the famous Washington, DC speech of Martin Luther King, Jr.), cited in Torricelli and Carroll, *In Our Own Words*, pp. 240-241. For more on the subject of "no revolution without blood," see this book, chapter 10, "Take Up Your Cross, Put Down Your Sword: The Jesus Way to Revolution."

6. Bill Bright and John N. Damoose, *Red Sky in the Morning* (Orlando, FL: New Life, 1998), p. 17. Note that of the signers of the Declaration of Independence, "five of the fifty-six were captured by the British and tortured. Twelve had their homes ransacked, looted, confiscated by the enemy, or burned to the ground. Seventeen lost their fortunes. Two lost their sons in the army; another had two sons captured. Nine of the fifty-six lost their lives in the war, from wounds or hardships inflicted by the enemy." This reference was supplied to me by my friend and colleague Larry Tomczak.

7. Nelson Mandela, "I Am Prepared to Die," African National Congress. http://www.anc.org.za/ancdocs/history/rivonia.html.

8. The first statement was spoken in November 1962, and the second in June 1964, thus sandwiching the 1963 speech of Martin Luther King, Jr. "Malcolm X Quotes," *Elke's Homepage*, April 28, 1998. http://www.unix-ag.uni-kl.de/~moritz/xquotes.html.

9. Anthony Lloyd, "People Willing to Die for Freedom," *GQ* magazine. http://www.chechnya.net/article/wil_fre.shtml.

10. In terms of being freedom fighters, believers in Jesus are freedom fighters in the truest sense of the word, fighting the most real, lasting battle of all for the most real, lasting freedom of all.

11. For passionate statements deploring slavery as a fundamental contradiction of the ideals of the American Revolution, see Bernard Bailyn, *The Ideological Origins of the American Revolution*, enlarged ed. (Cambridge, MA: Belknap Press of Harvard University Press, 1992), especially pp. 232-246. In short, since men like John Adams had said that Americans under the British were "the most abject of slaves" (ibid., p. 233), how could these very same men tolerate a far more harsh, inhumane form of slavery in their midst? In 1774, Richard Wells of Philadelphia asked, "[How can we] reconcile the exercise of SLAVERY with our *professions of freedom*" (ibid., p. 239), while John Allen, a Baptist preacher and pamphleteer, wrote, "Blush ye pretended votaries for freedom! Ye trifling patriots! . . . for while you are fasting, praying, non-importing, nonexporting, remonstrating, resolving, and pleading for a restoration of your charter rights, you at the same time are continuing this lawless, cruel, inhuman, and abominable practice of enslaving your fellow creatures" (ibid., p. 240). As Bailyn explains, "As the [revolutionary] crisis deepened and Americans elaborated their love of liberty and their hatred of slavery, the problem posed by the bondage tolerated in their midst became more and more difficult to evade. What were they to say to the Englishmen who told them flatly to 'put away the accursed thing (that horrid oppression) from among them, before they presumed to implore the interposition of divine justice; for, whilst they retain their brethren . . . in the most shameful involuntary servitude, it is profane in them to look up to the merciful Lord of all, and call Him father!'" (ibid., p. 241).

12. George Grant, *The Patriot's Handbook* (Nashville, TN: Cumberland House, 1996), p. 278.
13. Interestingly, there was correspondence about the title of this paper between Anthony and Elizabeth Cady Stanton (both outspoken feminists), in which the latter assured the former that the name was not too extreme; see, conveniently, Andrew Carroll, ed., *Letters of a Nation: A Collection of Extraordinary American Letters* (New York: Kodansha, 1997), pp. 181-183. Stanton wrote, "A journal called the *Rosebud* might answer for those who come with kid gloves and perfumes to lay immortal wreaths on the monuments which in sweat and tears others have hewn and built; but for us and for that great blacksmith of ours who forges such red-hot thunderbolts for Pharisees, hypocrites, and sinners, there is no name like the *Revolution*" (ibid., p. 182). The name, however, was eventually changed.
14. Grant, *Patriot's Handbook*, p. 278. For more on Garrison, see James Brewer Stewart in Ernest R. Sandeen, ed., *The Bible and Social Reform* (Chico, CA: Fortress/Scholars Press, 1982), pp. 32-49.
15. Grant, *Patriot's Handbook*, p. 278.
16. Abraham Lincoln, from a speech delivered June 16, 1858, cited in the *Oxford Dictionary of Quotations*, 3rd ed. (New York: Oxford University Press, 1980), p. 314, #14.
17. Ibid., p. 314, #22.
18. His views can be contrasted with the totally nonviolent views of Booker T. Washington; for the success of Washington's approach, see Booker T. Washington, *Up from Slavery*, unabridged ed. (New York: Dover Publications, 1995).
19. W. E. DuBois, "The Battle for Humanity," delivered August 1906, cited in Torricelli and Carroll, *In Our Own Words*, p. 19. For an insightful critique of John Brown, see Otto Scott, *The Secret Six: John Brown and the Abolitionist Movement*, 3rd ed. (Seattle, WA: Uncommon Books, 1993).
20. Charles Turner, cited by George Grant, foreword to *Give Me Liberty: The Uncompromising Statesmanship of Patrick Henry*, by David J. Vaughan (Elkton, MD: Highland, 1997), n.p. For important background on the role of Christianity in the birthing of America, see James H. Hutson, ed., *Religion and the New Republic: Faith in the Founding of America* (Lanham, MD: Rowman & Littlefield, 2000); for well-illustrated documentation, see idem, *Religion and the Founding of the American Republic* (Hanover, NH: University Press of New England, 1998).
21. According to J. Blunck, "Strangely enough to modern man, political freedom plays quite a subordinate role in the NT. Jesus unambiguously swept aside all misunderstanding here. He and his kingdom do not live by this external freedom. Otherwise, it would not have been so readily abandoned (Jn. [18]:36). Even in those places where Jesus stressed his earthly authority (Matt. 28:18), no conclusions were drawn about claims for political freedom. He disappointed all the late Jewish expectation of a political messiah. His teaching had quite a different aim. The kind of freedom he preached was that which comes through returning to the Father—not freedom with regard to men (Matt. 4:17; Lk. 24:47; Jn. 8:34 ff. and often)." Blunck, "Freedom," *The New International Dictionary of New Testament Theology*, vol. 1, p. 720 (the entire article is found vol. 1, pp. 715-721).
22. This theme is found throughout Deuteronomy: When you come into the land of promise and enjoy its bounty, "be careful that you do not forget the LORD, who

brought you out of Egypt, out of the land of slavery" (Deut. 6:12; see also 8:11-14). When your son asks you, "What is the meaning of the stipulations, decrees and laws the LORD our God has commanded you?" tell him, "We were slaves of Pharaoh in Egypt, but the LORD brought us out of Egypt with a mighty hand. Before our eyes the LORD sent miraculous signs and wonders—great and terrible—upon Egypt and Pharaoh and his whole household. But he brought us out from there to bring us in and give us the land that he promised on oath to our forefathers" (Deut. 6:20-23). When a false prophet tries to lead Israel into idolatry, put him to death "because he preached rebellion against the LORD your God, who brought you out of Egypt and redeemed you from the land of slavery. . . . Stone him to death, because he tried to turn you away from the LORD your God, who brought you out of Egypt, out of the land of slavery" (Deut. 13:5, 10). The Lord said, "Remember that you were slaves in Egypt and the LORD your God redeemed you. That is why I give you this command today" (Deut. 15:15). He said, "Remember, that you were slaves in Egypt, and follow carefully these decrees" (Deut. 16:12; see also 24:18,22). Remember!

23. For the royal/priestly significance of all the Israelites wearing a blue/purple fringe, see Jacob Milgrom, *Numbers*, The JPS Torah Commentary (Philadelphia: Jewish Publication Society, 1990), pp. 127-128.

24. See Brown, *Go and Sin No More*, pp. 19-89 (listing twenty reasons not to sin).

25. Many scholars believe that in Jesus' day, the weekly synagogue readings from the prophetic books had not yet been fixed. For references and discussion, see I. Howard Marshall, *The Gospel of Luke*, New International Greek Testament Commentary (Grand Rapids, MI: Wm. B. Eerdmans Publishing Co., 1978), pp. 181-182.

26. For relevant literature, see C. H. H. Wright, "Jubilee, Year of," *Anchor Bible Dictionary*, vol. 3, p. 1028; reference is made to the "Nazareth manifesto" (cf. U. Busse, *Das Nazareth-Manifest: Eine Einführung in das lukanische Jesubild nach Lk. 4:16-30* [Stuttgart: Katholisches Bibelwerk, 1978]); see also John Nolland, *Luke 1-9:20* Word Biblical Commentary (Waco, TX: Word, 1989), p. 195; it is noted that "Luke 4:16-30 is widely regarded as a programmatic text for Luke's whole enterprise." See also John G. Lake, the early twentieth-century missionary and healing apostle, "The Platform of Jesus," in Roberts Liardon, *The Complete Collection of His Life Teachings*, ed. John G. Lake (Tulsa, OK: Albury, 1999), pp. 168-177. For further discussion of the ministry of Jesus and the jubilee theme, see Michael L. Brown, *Israel's Divine Healer: Studies in Old Testament Biblical Theology* (Grand Rapid, MI: Zondervan Publishing House, 1995), pp. 217-218, with extensive references. For practical challenges for the contemporary church, see Donald Kraybill, *The Upside-Down Kingdom* (Scottdale, PA: Herald Press, 1994).

27. According to Fidel Castro, "The [Cuban] revolution . . . is a dictatorship of the exploited against the exploiters." http://www.quoteland.com/quotes/author/84.html.

28. *Oxford Dictionary of Quotations*, p. 310, #19; the friend was Duc de la Rochefoucauld-Liancourt.

29. For further background, see Kaiser, *1968 in America*, pp. 37-45.

30. Unger and Unger, *the times are a changin'*, p. 1.

31. Thomas Jefferson, cited in John Sorelli, *The Family* (Tulsa, OK: King's Signet Books, 1997), p. 56, cited in Governor Mike Huckabee, with Dr. George Grant, *Kids Who Kill: Confronting our Culture of Violence* (Nashville, TN: Broadman & Holman, 1998), p. 85.

32. Patrick Henry, cited in *Kids Who Kill,* p. 103. Chapter 6 of Huckabee's book (pp. 85-104, "Families Under Siege") is especially relevant.
33. *Time* (December 20, 1999), p. 42.
34. S. C. Gywnne, "An Act of God?" *Time* (December 20, 1999), p. 58
35. Rutherford L. Decker, introduction to Bready, *This Freedom—Whence?*

Chapter Ten

1. King once said, "The limitation of riots, moral questions aside, is that they cannot win and their participants know it. Hence, rioting is not revolutionary but reactionary because it invites defeat. It involves an emotional catharsis, but it must be followed by a sense of futility."
2. Malcolm X, "There's No Such Thing As a Non-Violent Revolution," cited in Torricelli and Carroll, *In Our Own Words,* pp. 240-241. Interestingly, John Adams wrote to Thomas Jefferson in 1815, "What do we mean by the Revolution? The war? That was no part of the Revolution; it was only an effect and consequence of it. The Revolution was in the minds of the people, and this was effected, from 1760-1775, in the course of fifteen years before a drop of blood was shed in Lexington" (cited in Baylin, *Ideological Origins,* p. 1). In 1787, Benjamin Rush had written, "The American war is over; but this is far from being the case with the American revolution. On the contrary, nothing but the first act of the great drama is closed. It remains yet to establish and perfect our new forms of government, and to prepare the principles, morals, and manners of our citizens for these forms of government after they are established and brought to perfection" (cited in ibid., p. 230). So there was revolution before the war, and there was revolution after the war!
3. Ayatollah Fasl-Allah Mahalati, cited in Taheri, *Holy Terror,* p. 17.
4. Cited in a B'nai Brith report dated May 1995. For further information on Hamas and its goals, see http://www.hamas.org.
5. Ayatollah Ruhollah Khomeini, *Key to the Secrets* (1942; reprint, Qom, Iran: 1986), cited in Taheri, *Holy Terror,* pp. 242-243.
6. Roger Lloyd, *Revolutionary Religion: Christianity, Fascism and Communism* (London: SCM Press, 1938), p. 14. I am indebted to my friend and colleague Pastor Bob Phillips for introducing this book to me.
7. John Wesley, cited in Bready, *This Freedom—Whence?,* pp. 146-147.
8. Ibid., p. 147.
9. Mark Twain, *A Connecticut Yankee in King Arthur's Court* (NY: Harper & Bros., 1917), n.p. According to Mao Zedong, "Political power grows out of the barrel of a gun." http://apachego.com/rights/quotes.htm.
10. Jerry Rubin. http://www.quoteland.com/quotes/author/398.html.
11. Grounds distinguishes between "revolution*aries*," which he defines as "advocates of radical change," and "revolution*ists*," defined as "advocates of radical change by violence." Ironically, followers of Jesus are "advocates of radical change by violence"— the violence of the Cross! (Grounds, *Revolution and the Christian Faith,* p. 13).
12. Justin Martyr, *Apology* I, 13.4, cited in Hengel, *Crucifixion,* p. 1.
13. Ibid., pp. 6-7.
14. Pseudo-Manetho (3rd century, C.E.), *Apotelesmatica* 4.198-200, cited in Hengel,

Crucifixion, p. 9.

15. Most scholars believe that Jesus was crucified naked, in keeping with Roman cus-tom; see the references in Michael L. Brown, *Answering Jewish Objections to Jesus,* vol. 1, *General and Historical Objections* (Grand Rapids, MI: Baker Book House, 1999), p. 249, n. 258.

16. Johannes Schneider, cited in Gerhard Friedrich, ed., *Theological Dictionary of the New Testament,* trans. Geoffrey W. Bromiley, vol. 7 (Grand Rapids, MI: Wm. B. Eerdmans Publishing Co., 1971), pp. 573-574.

17. See Hengel, *Crucifixion,* pp. 2, 4, 8.

18. Ibid., pp. 9-10.

19. Ibid., p. 25.

20. Ibid., pp. 30-31.

21. For discussion of the various traditions, see the standard Bible encyclopedias and dictionaries; in more popular form, see William Steuart McBirnie, *The Search for the Twelve Apostles* (Wheaton, IL: Tyndale House Publishers, 1979).

22. Commenting on this verse (especially the words "patient endurance"), Alan Johnson notes, "John sees the present hidden rule of Christ and his followers man-ifested through their 'patient endurance.' As they look beyond their immediate dis-tresses and put their full confidence in Christ, they share now in his royal dignity and power. Whether those distresses were imprisonment, ostracism, slander, pover-ty, economic discrimination, hostility (both violent and nonviolent by synagogue, marketplace, and police), disruption of the churches by false prophets, and the con-stant threat of death from mob violence or judicial action, believers are to realize their present kingship with Christ in their faithful endurance" ("Revelation," *Expositors Bible Commentary,* vol. 12, p. 424).

23. H. S. Vegeveno, *Jesus the Revolutionary* (Glendale, CA: Gospel Light, 1966), p. 11.

24. Coleman, *The Master Plan of Evangelism,* p. 57.

25. I wrote these words while ministering in India in 1996: "There's one last secret to overcoming the devil that most American believers don't want to learn: Rev. 12:11 ('they did not love their lives so much as to shrink from death'). It's the key to vic-tory and freedom. It breaks the devil's back! He has nothing with which to threat-en you, nothing to take from you. His power is the fear of death. Give yourself to God, even to the point of death, and you break his power."

26. The famous quote is from Tertullian: "As often as we are mown down by you, the more we grow in numbers. The blood of Christians is the seed" (Tertullian, *Apologeticus* 50, 13).

27. Eberhard Arnold, *The Early Christians,* p. 20. Tom Wright points out that the concept of the Messiah's own resurrection was a surprising concept for the Jewish people of the day, stating that "the rule . . . seems clear. If you follow a messiah and he gets killed, you obviously backed the wrong horse. You should either give up, or get yourself another leader from the same family. So why did the followers of Jesus of Nazareth do neither of these things? After Jesus was executed, his followers didn't give up the revolution; nor did they choose another leader from the same would-be royal family. Why not?" (Wright, *The Original Jesus,* p. 70).

28. See James C. and Marti Hefley, *By Their Blood: Christian Martyrs of the Twentieth Century,* 2nd ed. (Grand Rapids, MI: Baker Book House, 1996), pp. 57-58.

29. Ibid., p. 57.

30. Ibid., p. 60. May I confess to you that as I write these words, I find myself in tears, my thoughts going immediately to the young couples who have graduated from our school and who are now laboring in China and other dangerous parts of the world? They too have said, "Afraid—of that?"

31. Steve Saint, "A Cloud of Witness," cited in Bergman, *Martyrs*, p. 154 (the entire chapter runs from pp. 142-154). For the account of five missionaries martyred in 1943 while working with the New Tribes Mission in Bolivia, see Ruth A. Tucker, *From Jerusalem to Irian Jaya: A Biographical History of Christian Missions* (Grand Rapids, MI: Zondervan Publishing House, 1983), pp. 307-312.

Chapter Eleven

1. Dov Gruner, cited in Chaim Herzog, *Heroes of Israel* (Bnei-Brak, Israel: Steimatzky, 1989), pp. 198-199. Dov Gruner was hung by the British for his subversive, pro-Israel activities, May 16, 1947.

2. Emmanuel Ringelblum, *Warsaw Ghetto Diary* (n.p., n.d.), cited in Herzog, *Heroes of Israel*, p. 136.

3. Augustine's exact quote is "The cause, not the suffering, makes genuine martyrs" (Augustine, *Epistles*, 89:2).

4. Anderson, *Che Guevara*, p. 720. According to Marc Becker, "Che's life represents a selfless dedication to the concerns of the underclass, a struggle to encourage people to place the needs of the broader society above their own narrow personal wishes and desires, and a willingness to make extensive personal sacrifices to achieve a more just and equable social order. Che made the ultimate sacrifice for his beliefs. With his death in October 1967 at the hands of the military in Bolivia he became a martyr and a prophet for leftist causes and beliefs" (Becker, introduction to *Guerrilla Warfare*, by Che Guevara [Lincoln,NE: University of Nebraska Press, 1998]).

5. *Jewish Voice Prophetic Magazine* (February 1995), p. 2.

6. Sheik Ahmed Abdul Salim, cited in *USA Today* (December 3, 1997), sec. A, p. 15.

7. AP Cairo, November 1, 1997. Sheik Salim is a spiritual leader of Al Gama'a, the Egyptian-based terrorist oganization.

8. Thomas Merton, ed., *Gandhi on Non-Violence* (New York: New Directions, 1964), p. 57.

9. Joan V. Bondurant, *Conquest of Violence: The Gandhian Philosophy of Conflict*, rev. ed. (Princeton: Princeton University Press, 1988), p. 39. See also the relevant sections in the useful collection edited by Louis Fischer, *The Essential Gandhi: An Anthology of His Writings on Life, Work and Ideas* (New York: Vintage, 1983). More broadly, see A. L Herman, *Community, Violence, and Peace: Aldo Leopold, Mohandas K. Gandhi, Martin Luther King, Jr., and Gautama the Buddha in the Twenty-First Century* (Albany: State University of New York, 1999).

10. As is well known, we get the English word "martyr" from the Greek word for "witness" (*martus; marturos*). See the quote of Arnold cited in the previous chapter, n. 27.

11. Ravenhill, *Why Revival Tarries*, p. 118, emphasis added.

12. K. P. Yohannan, *Living in the Light of Eternity: Your Life Can Make a Difference* (Grand Rapids, MI: Chosen Books, 1995), pp. 159-160.

13. According to one nineteenth-century Swedish missionary manual, missionaries

going to the Congo were required to have enough wood to make their own casket—along with a tool to make the casket!—before leaving for the field.

14. Jean-Francois Steiner, *Treblinka*, trans. Helen Weaver (1967, reprint; New York: Meridian, 1994), pp. 182-183.

15. Ibid., p. 183.

16. Ibid., pp. 185-186.

17. *The Nizkor Project.* http://www.nizkor.org (accessed April 2000). (*Nizkor* is a Hebrew word that means "we will remember.") Of the approximately 850 prisoners who were in the camp at the time of the uprising, almost half were killed in the fighting; 300 more were killed trying to escape into a nearby forest. One hundred prisoners survived to destroy the crematoria but were later killed. Only 40 German soldiers were killed. According to various estimates, about 60 to 70 of the Treblinka escapees were still alive at the end of the war.

18. C. S. Lewis, *This World: Playground or Battleground?* (Camp Hill, PA: Christian Publications, 1989), pp. 5-6.

19. Source unknown.

20. The subtitle to August Kinnear's biography of Watchman Nee (*The Story of Watchman Nee* [Camp Hill, PA: Tyndale House Publishers/Christian Literature Crusade, 1978]) is *Against the Tide*, reflecting the uphill struggle experienced by many Christian leaders in every generation.

21. *World Shapers*, p. 5. David Brainerd (1718-1747), whose life was cut short by tuberculosis, sacrificially served as a missionary to the American Indians. His diary, often reprinted, has been one of the most influential Christian books of its kind; for a glimpse at the trail of lives the book effected, see Ravenhill, *Why Revival Tarries*, pp. 83-86; he writes "Let's line them up: [Edward] Payson, [Robert Murray] M'Cheyne, [William] Carey, [Jonathan] Edwards, [John] Wesley—men of renown, yet all kindled by one flame, and all debtors to the sickly but supplicating Brainerd" (p. 86).

Chapter Twelve

1. Grubb, *C. T. Studd*, pp. 35-36.

2. Ibid., p. 36. Of course, all of us might find the atheist's sentiments slightly exaggerated, in particular, in terms of his claim that, "Earth, its joys and its griefs, would occupy no moment of my thoughts." (See the previous chapter for thoughts on this.) The simple truth, however, is that the message and mind-set of this tract is very consistent with eternal values and a sharp rebuke to most Western believers.

3. Amy Carmichael, cited in Elizabeth Elliot, *A Chance to Die: The Life and Legacy of Amy Carmichael* (Old Tappan, NJ: Fleming H. Revell, 1987), p. 85.

4. Ibid., p. 117.

5. William Gurnall, *The Christian in Complete Armour* (reprint, Carlisle, PA: Banner of Truth, 1964), n.p. William Gurnall was a seventeenth-century English Puritan preacher (1616-1679).

6. It is not my intent here to discuss the question of spiritual warfare over a city and pulling down strongholds through prayer. Rather, I am using these verses in Luke in terms of the clear principles they teach. For sober discussion on spiritual warfare, see, for example, Gregory A. Boyd, *God at War: The Bible and Spiritual Conflict*

(Downers Grove, IL: InterVarsity Press, 1997); Ed Murphy, *Handbook for Spiritual Warfare*, rev. ed. (Nashville, TN: Thomas Nelson, 1997).

7. With regard to homosexuality, it has been noted that homosexuals cannot increase by reproduction but only by seduction. Thus, many gays are not merely content with having the right to live the way they want to live without "discrimination"; rather, they want to encourage others to join them in their lifestyle.

8. I know I'm overstating things a little here: The Church does use many of the same avenues as does the enemy: music, media, technology, education, etc. Still, we tend to use them far less aggressively—and, generally speaking, far less effectively—than does our adversary.

9. *USAF Special Operations School: Psychological Operations* (Macdill AFB, FL: United States Special Operations Command, n.d.), p. 6-1. My appreciation to Capt. Rudy Atallah for making this military source available to me.

10. Ibid.

11. By "a little 'spice'," our adversary really means some foul language, a little nudity, some suggestive sexual themes, and a bit of gratuitous violence thrown in for good measure.

12. Bondurant, *Conquest of Violence*, p. 39, emphasis his.

13. Source unknown.

14. Guevara, *Guerrilla Warfare*, pp. 7-8.

15. Brown, *Let No On Deceive You*, pp. 201-216 ("Is Good News Bad News for the Gloomers and Doomers: Exposing the Laodicean Lie").

16. The most famous saying of Edmund Burke (1729-1797) is probably "The only thing necessary for the triumph of evil is for good men to do nothing." He also had this to say: "The true danger is when liberty is nibbled away, for expedience, and by parts" (written in a letter dated April 3, 1777). Or consider these other warnings from his pen: "Nobody made a greater mistake than he who did nothing because he could only do a little." And, "When bad men combine, the good must associate else they will fall one by one, an unpitied sacrifice in a contemptible struggle."

17. For an eye-opening documentary providing stark contrasts between Islamic fundamentalism and American Christian fundamentalism, I strongly recommend "God Fights Back: The Rise of Religious Fundamentalism," *The People's Century*, Public Broadcasting System, 1999. See also Susan Harding, *The Book of Jerry Falwell: Fundamentalist Language and Politics* (Princeton, NJ: Princeton University, 2000).

18. According to Francis Schaeffer, "the old revivals in Great Britain, in Scandinavia, and so on, and the old revivals in this country [America] did call, without any question and with tremendous clarity, for personal salvation. But they also called for a resulting social action" (Schaeffer, *A Christian Manifesto* [reprint, *The Complete Works of Francis Schaeffer*, vol. 5, Westchester, IL: Crossway Books, 1982], p. 451; this quote is in a part of the important chapter "Revival, Revolution, and Reform," pp. 451-456). For historical studies on the impact of revival on America, see, for example, William G. McLoughlin, *Revivals, Awakenings, and Reform: An Essay on Religion and Social Change in America, 1607-1977*, Chicago History of American Religion (Chicago: University of Chicago: 1978), with suggestions for further reading; J. Edwin Orr, *The Event of the Century: The 1857-1858 Awakening* (Wheaton, IL: International Awakening Press, 1989); Timothy L. Smith, *Revivalism and Social Reform: American*

Protestantism on the Eve of the Civil War, 2nd ed. (Baltimore: Johns Hopkins, 1980); Paul E. Johnson, *A Shopkeeper's Millennium: Society and Revival sin Rochester, New York, 1815-1837* (New York: Hill and Wang, 1978). On a more popular level, see Malcolm McDow and Alvin L. Reid, *Firefall: How God Has Shaped History Through Revivals* (Nashville, TN: Broadman & Holman, 1987). For practical thoughts, see Bill Hull, *Revival That Reforms: Making It Last* (Grand Rapids, MI: Fleming H. Revell, 1998).

19. For his basic philosophy (in his own words), see Unger and Unger, *the times were a changin'*, pp. 177-183.

20. "At one point in his final delerium [sic], [Leary] spoke the words 'Why not.' He uttered the phrase repeatedly, in different intonations: as a question, as a statement, softly, loudly, thoughtfully, ruefully, and confidently. He died soon after, and that was the last thing he said out loud" ("Timothy Leary's Last Trip," *Timothy Leary*, February 18, 1999. http://www.leary.com/LastTrip/index.html). After his death on May 31, 1996, he was cremated, and his ashes were divided among loved ones, while a portion of the ashes was shot into space.

21. Words and music by Ronnie Gorton and J. Brandon Chase. (These are the first two stanzas and the chorus.)

22. Kirk Franklin, "Revolution," *Nu Nation Project*. For those unfamiliar with rap lyrical freedom, I'll give the interpretation of a few of the words: brotha = brother (that one was easy!); potnah = partner (a little harder?); two facism = being two-faced (facism was not a typo for Fascism!).

23. Newman, *Guerrillas in the Mist*, pp. 7-8.

24. For a reasoned response to what is perceived to be highly judgmental and mean-spirited Christian activism and rhetoric, see Francis Frangipane, *America at the Threshold of Destiny* (Cedar Rapids, IA: Arrow, 1999).

25. Lloyd, *Revolutionary Religion*, pp. 14-15.

26. Ibid., pp. 15-16.

27. I am fully aware of the logic behind the "Christian" call to arms, especially in light of the history of our nation. Abraham Lincoln has often been quoted in this regard: "This country, with its institutions, belongs to the people who inhabit it. Whenever they shall grow weary of the existing government, they can exercise their constitutional right of amending it, or exercise their revolutionary right to overthrow it" (*Oxford Dictionary of Quotations*, 3rd ed., p. 314, #19). Note also Francis Schaeffer's famous remarks in the chapter "The Use of Force" in his *Christian Manifesto* (*Complete Works*, vol. 5, pp. 483-491).

28. Grounds, *Revolution and the Christian Faith*, 1971. For the "revolutionary" impact of Christianity, see Otto Scott, *The Great Christian Revolution*.

29. Ibid., pp. 220-221. The citations are from Bernard Häring, *A Theology of Protest* (NY: Farrar, Straus, Giroux, 1970), n.p., and Jacques Ellul, *The Presence of the Kingdom* (Philadelphia: Westminster, 1951), p. 51; see also James W. Douglass, *The Non-Violent Cross: A Theology of Revolution and Peace* (New York: Macmillan, 1968), p. 187. I am aware, of course, that the concept of "the sign of the cross" is repugnant to many Jews, evoking memories of the Crusades, in which the sign of the cross meant death by the sword for thousands of Jews. For the viewpoint of a Jewish believer in Jesus, see Michael L. Brown, *Answering Jewish Objections to Jesus*, vol. 1, pp. 101-177; see also idem, *Our Hands Are Stained with Blood* (Shippensburg, PA: Destiny Image, 1992).

30. *The Non-Violent Cross*, p. 8, cited in Grounds, *Revolution and the Christian Faith*, p. 221. Note also the first chapter of Häring's study, *A Theology of Protest*, "Nonviolence: The Gospel Means Revolution" (pp. 3-20).

31. As Grounds notes, "To a secular revolutionist, the Christian revolution seems the nadir [absolute low] of impotent idealism. And throughout much of the Church's history it has been little more than that—an impotent idealism. So we must clarify the significance of that insufferably abused word 'love'" (ibid., p. 22).

32. See Matt. 5:43-48; Luke 6:30-36; Rom 12:17-21; 1 Pet. 2:19-21; 3:9.

33. Wallace Henley, *Confronting the New World Disorder: The Emerging Church for the 21st Century* (Houston: Encourager Media, 1995), pp. 249-250.

34. Ibid., pp. 252-253.

Chapter Thirteen

1. Newman, *Guerrillas in the Mist*, p. 81.
2. Of course, one reason for the protracted time spent seeking the Lord may have been Josiah's youthfulness—but that too can apply to us!
3. Lloyd, *Revolutionary Religion*, p. 7.
4. Newman, *Guerrillas in the Mist*, p. 83.
5. Here are the relevant comments in more expanded form, along with the comments of other top New Testament scholars. First, D. A. Carson: "That kingdom is breaking in under Christ's ministry, but it is not consummated till the end of the age (28:20). To pray 'your kingdom come' is therefore simultaneously to ask that God's saving, royal rule be extended now as people bow in submission to him and already taste the eschatological blessing of salvation and to cry for the consummation of the kingdom (cf. 1 Cor. 16:22; Rev. 11:17; 22:20). Godly Jews were waiting for the kingdom (Mark 15:43), 'the consolation of Israel' (Luke 2:25). . . . But the Jew looked forward to the kingdom, whereas the reader of Matthew's Gospel, while looking forward to its consummation, perceives that the kingdom has already broken in and prays for its extension as well as for its unqualified manifestation" ("Matthew," *Expositors Bible Commentary*, vol. 8, p. 170). According to Donald A. Hagner, "The gospel is itself, above all, the announcement that God's promised rule has now begun in and through the work of Jesus the Messiah (see [Matt.] 3:2; 4:17, 23), so the disciples are thus encouraged to pray that what has begun in the ministry of Jesus, what they have now begun to participate in, may be experienced in all fullness." (*Matthew 1-13*, Word Biblical Commentary [Dallas: Word Publishing, 1993], p. 148). According to Craig S. Keener, "If the kingdom were wholly future, one might despair of accomplishing any justice now; if one supposed that it were wholly present, the realities of this age would quickly terminate disciples' illusive utopianism. But because the Gospels affirm that in Jesus the kingdom is present in a hidden way, believers in him can begin to make a difference in their world now, contending for the reality to be consummated at Christ's return." (*A Commentary on the Gospel of Matthew* [Grand Rapids, MI: Wm. B. Eerdmans Publishing Co., 1999], p. 200, n. 172).

6. I do not hold to the view known as postmillennialism, which expects the kingdom of God to come fully on Earth before the earthly return of Jesus, although I am aware of the fact that many Christian leaders (such as Jonathan Edwards and Charles Finney) held to such a view and that this view helped fuel their faith for the transforming power of the gospel. My views would best be described as classic pre-millennialism. For comparison and discussion, cf. Robert G. Clouse, ed., *The Meaning of the Millennium: Four Views* (Downers Grove, IL: InterVarsity Press, 1977); Millard J. Erickson, *A Basic Guide to Eschatology: Making Sense of the Millennium*, rev. ed. (Grand Rapids, MI: Baker Book House, 1999).

7. Taheri, *Holy Terror*, p. 38.

8. Some have defined revival as a "community saturated with God." Sadly, where such revivals have taken place in the past, the communities in question generally failed to maximize the moment, failed to train and export, failed to conceive a battle plan that would produce lasting fruit well into the coming generation. The "Four E's" that have been operative for me since being involved with the revival in Pensacola are: Entrench (go deeper); Expand (more workers; larger facilities); Equip (prepare God's people for action); Export (send out laborers to the ends of the earth). For further thoughts, see Michael L. Brown, *How to Mess Up a Move of God: Twenty Surefire Ways to Kill Revival in Your Church* (Shippensburg, PA: Destiny Image, forthcoming); see also David Ravenhill, *They Drank from the River and Died in the Wilderness* (Shippensburg, PA: Destiny Image, 2000).

9. Newman, *Guerrillas in the Mist*, ibid. For his guerrilla base strategy (which is totally militaristic and does not really apply to our topic), see ibid., pp. 84-85.

10. Abraham Lincoln, cited in the *Oxford Dictionary of Quotations*, p. 315, #6. According to David Remnick, editor of the *New Yorker*, "to some extent, you have to credit the literary works of Alexandr Solzhenitsyn with helping to bring down the last empire [namely, the Soviet empire] on earth" (cited in *Christian History* 65, "The Ten Most Influential Christians of the Twentieth Century" [Vol. XIX], p. 33). What power there is in the printed page!

11. This is also part of our twofold strategy for dissemination of truth: (1) get it out directly in the largest possible numbers, and (2) get it into the hands—and hearts and minds—of leaders in the Body; then it can become part of their own burden and message.

12. Newman, *Guerrillas in the Mist*, p. 83.

13. Taheri, *Holy Terror*, p. 38.

14. See, e.g., Ps. 119:105; Prov. 3:18; 4:20-22; Jer. 5:14; 23:29; Heb. 4:12.

15. Source unknown.

16. This concept was important for the Salvation Army; see *God As Strategist*, with articlces by Samuel L. Brengle and other Salvation Army leaders (reprint, New York: Salvation Army, 1978).

17. See Michael L. Brown, "Revival's Holy Desperation," *Ministries Today* (July-August 1999), pp. 42-44, based on a videotaped message entitled "Holy Desperation" (preached February 10, 1999 at the Brownsville Revival).

18. Listen to the wisdom of O. Hallesby in his classic book on prayer, "Finally, we should on bended knee pray for the evangelists who go about and preach the Word of God. . . . In this connection, permit me to mention what an ordinary country

girl, Bolette Hinderli, was able to accomplish for the great preacher of God, Lars Olsen Skresfrud. In a vision she saw a prisoner in a prison cell. She saw plainly his face and his whole form. And a voice said to her, 'This man will share the same fate as other criminals if no-one takes up the work of praying for him. Pray for him, and I will send him out to proclaim My praises among the heathen.'

"She was obedient unto the heavenly vision; she suffered and prayed and fought for this prisoner, although she did not know him. She waited longingly, too, to hear of a convict who had become converted and called to missionary work. Finally, during a visit to Stavanger, Norway, she heard that an ex-convict who had been converted was to preach in the town that evening. When Skrefsrud stepped up to the speaker's stand she recognized him immediately as the one she had seen in her vision. This woman had learned the meaning of Jesus' words about praying forth the gifts of grace.

"As far as I am able to understand the Word of God, and as far as I can learn, from the history of the kingdom of God, no prayer-task is more important than this. If the right man gets into the right place, there is almost no end to what he can do" (Hallesby, *Prayer* [Downers Grove, IL: InterVarsity Press, 1961], pp. 59-60).

19. The scholar is Craig Keener, Professor of New Testament Studies at Eastern Baptist Theological Seminary in Pennsylvania.

20. Edward McKendree Bounds, *E. M. Bounds on Prayer* (reprint, Springdale, PA: Whitaker, 1997), p. 37.

21. See Captain E. G. Carré, et al, *Praying Hyde* (South Plainfield, NJ: Bridge, 1982), p. 180.

22. Louw-Nida, *Dictionary*, vol. 1, p. 318, #25.268; vol. 1, p. 317, #25.266.

23. Ibid., vol. 1, p. 501, #3958, to *hupernikrao* (see Rom. 8:37).

24. Source unknown.

25. J. D. Douglas and Philip W. Comfort, eds., *Who's Who in Christian History* (Wheaton, IL: Tyndale, n.d.), cited in Quick Verse 6.0 (Hiawatha, IA: Parsons Technology, 1999), CD-ROM.

26. For Wesley's letter to him, see Michael L. Brown, *It's Time to Rock the Boat* (Shippensburg, PA: Destiny Image, 1992), pp. 182-183.

27. J. B. McClure, ed., *Pearls from Many Seas* (Albany, OR: Ages Software CD, 1996), p. 105.

28. Grounds, *Revolution and the Christian Faith*, p. 230, with reference to Ernst Käsemann's eloquent description of the overcoming believers in the book of Revelation: "They fight not to achieve power, but because they have to become like their Lord. Their wish is not to conquer the world but to defend their Lord's claim to the earth, and they die in doing so . . . Christians who accept the call to resistance are . . . representatives of a misused creation, the spokesmen of all who are oppressed, the people of the desert who remind everyone that Egypt must be finally abandoned, and that salvation is to be found only in the exodus" (Käsemann, *Jesus Means Freedom: A Polemical Survey of the New Testament* [London: SCM, 1969], p. 130).

Other Books by
Michael L. Brown

Answering Jewish Objections to Jesus, vol. 1,
General and Historical Objections

Answering Jewish Objections to Jesus, vol. 2,
Theological Objections

Go and Sin No More:
A Call to Holiness

From Holy Laughter to Holy Fire:
America on the Edge of Revival

Israel's Divine Healer

It's Time to Rock the Boat:
A Call to God's People to Rise Up
and Preach a Confrontational Gospel

Our Hands Are Stained with Blood:
The Tragic Story of the "Church" and the Jewish People

Whatever Happened to the Power of God?
Is the Charismatic Church Slain in the Spirit
or Down for the Count?

How Saved Are We?

The End of the American Gospel Enterprise

BROWNSVILLE REVIVAL
BRSM
SCHOOL OF MINISTRY

HANDS-ON TRAINING FOR
THE COMING REVOLUTION!

———∞∞∞———

Our mission is to impact this entire generation with the fire of revival by raising up an army of radical, Spirit-baptized laborers committed to taking the gospel of Jesus to the ends of the earth–by life or by death.

To enlist in the Brownsville Revival School of Ministry you must be:
- *At least 18 with a high school diploma or the equivalent.*
- *Completely dedicated to Jesus.*
- *Committed to living a holy life.*
- *Feeling that God is calling you to the ministry.*

———∞∞∞———

For more information,
or to request a free informational
video, contact us at:

(850) 458-6787 Fax: (850) 458-1828
email: info@brsm.org
For the most current information, including a special
section of student testimonies, check out our website at:
www.brsm.org
BRSM / 8594 Hwy 98 W / Pensacola, FL 32506

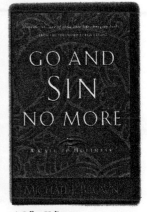
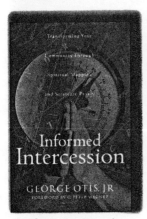
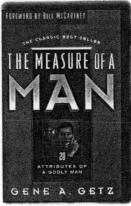
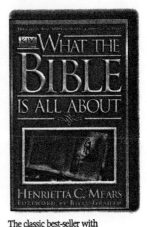